the BINGE WATCHER'S guide

AN UNOFFICIAL COMPANION

To the Harry Potter Films

Cecilia Tan

For more information contact:
Riverdale Avenue Books
5676 Riverdale Avenue
Riverdale, NY 10471.

www.riverdaleavebooks.com
Design by www.formatting4U.com
Cover by Scott Carpenter

Digital ISBN: : 9781626015555
Trade Paperback ISBN: 9781626015562
Hardcover ISBN: 9781626015579

First Edition, June 2020

Table of Contents

Acknowledgments

Thanks to all who shared their tips about watching with kids, throwing Potter-themed parties, and diabolical drinking games, who included these magical individuals: Aida, Alex, Alyse Leung, Amanda, Amy Hallock, B. Cynic, Barbara Martinez, Becky Thomson, Brian Cherry, Claudia Mastroianni, Elfflame, Ellid, Etakyma, Jamesa "Meka" Larimer, Jenny Reed, Jonathon Rosenthal, Kristin, Maureen, Niamh Augurey, Paula, Purity Control, Robin Lynn, saladbats, Shirene B., Shirley Dulcey, Tara, Todd Kissick, tzinnamon, and Vickie McManus.

Thanks to Alyse for bringing the Chinese pastries! Also Jaz, Nicole, Claudia, Kristina, David, and all my binge-watch party guests for letting me pick your brains and feed you experimental pumpkin pasties. My beta readers, Claudia, Rikibeth, and Charlie, thanks for play-testing parts of this guided tour of the cinematic Potterverse. Any errors are purely mine.

And to all the backers on Kickstarter who helped bring this magic to life.

Introductory Chapters

Introduction

When a book club edition of *Harry Potter and the Sorcerer's Stone* landed in my mailbox, I had no idea I was about to start a love affair with the "wizarding world" that is still going on to this day. The year was 1998, the same year I had my first major book published by a big New York publishing house. I just realized that means J.K Rowling and I launched our careers at the same time.

Little did I know then that her books would soon become almost as important to me as my own.

I have always loved science fiction and fantasy—or at least since reading *The Hobbit* when I was 10 years old—but in any given year there are so many books to choose from, why did I pick up *Sorcerer's Stone?* At the time it was getting a lot of buzz within the publishing industry, so I thought *what the hey, let's take a look.* Not because I thought it was similar to what I wrote—on the contrary, my book from Harper was erotic and very definitely *not* for kids!—but because as an author and editor I thought it might be important to keep up on new trends in the genre. Besides, it looked like fun.

As it turned out, *fun* didn't even begin to describe the experience of reading the book. I had forgotten all about boring notions like *the industry* and *trends* by the time I hit page two. I was absolutely hooked by orphan Harry's predicament and the oddly comforting tone of the book, which felt both fresh and familiar at the same time. When my partner got home that night I insisted on reading him Chapter One as a bedtime story. We ended up reading the whole book to each other, night by night, chapter by chapter—a tradition we kept up through all seven books of the series.

But that wasn't all.

It wasn't long before I found a striped tie at Goodwill and donned my old grad school commencement robes to attend a local bookstore's midnight launch party. There we communed with maybe a hundred or so other fanatics eagerly awaiting the next installment. Potter bookstore release parties became a regular thing. That led to cosplaying on opening nights at the movies, too, where here in the Boston area entire megaplexes were sold out—the movie playing on literally every screen—bringing together a thousand or more fans in a single building.

But that still wasn't all. In the mid-2000s my writing career hit a slump. To "stay in shape" I started writing Harry Potter fanfic and essays. Next thing you know I was moderating a tarot-themed fan art and fic community online. I got sucked into an online Harry Potter role-playing game. (I played Draco.) And I started going to Harry Potter conventions where thousands of fans gathered to celebrate their love of all things wizarding. Traveling to these fan enclaves has taken me everywhere from Las Vegas, Nevada, to Canterbury, England.

In the process, Harry Potter fandom became like church for me. Here's what I mean by that: It became a shared community formed around shared beliefs. Those beliefs, embodied in the Harry Potter books and films, are that creativity and goodness and friendship can defeat evil. Harry Potter fandom is where I know the songs that are sung and where we read and discuss and debate the same stories. Where we laugh and cry and grow together. Each new book or movie release was like Christmas or Easter, and each convention was like going off to Bible camp (yes, I went to Bible camp), only even more fun.

I saw the premiere of the sixth film, *Harry Potter and the Half-Blood Prince,* in San Francisco, in an exclusive showing just for the attendees of Azkatraz, an HPEF fan convention. I went all the way to the UK for the eighth and final film, which I saw in a theater full of attendees of Dia-con Alley, that they took us to in red double-decker buses.

Those were once-in-a-lifetime experiences, but I get to re-experience the magic of these films anytime I pop the DVD into the player, and I'm looking forward to being your magical tour guide on this unofficial romp through the Potter movies. As Professor Snape might say, potions can ensnare the senses... but so can movies, which surround us with stunning visuals, incredible music, and captivating performances that bring the wizarding world to life. We've got 10 years of moviemaking, from 2001 through 2011, to cover in this book. That's 10 years of squee and angst and *oh-my-goodness look how they've grown!*

There's never been a book quite like this one. Most of the books about the Potter movies are official coffee-table photo books, presented by the filmmakers, and of course I've used them as a reference. There are a few trivia books and a guide for "young fans." But there's never been a guide written by fans for fans and fans-to-be. My goal in this Binge Watcher's Guide is to have plenty in it both for those who want to re-experience the series and those coming to it for the first time. Not only will I give you the heads up on Easter eggs to look out for and behind-the-scenes info, I also provide tips on how to run a Potter-themed binge-watch party (complete with recipes!) as well as special advice for parents introducing their kids to the movies for the first time.

So get ready to push your luggage trolley through the wall at Platform 9 3/4 and away we go!

Cecilia Tan
Cambridge, Massachusetts

The Zeitgeist

It all started with one little book. As it did for many Americans, *Harry Potter and the Sorcerer's Stone* came into my life in 1998. I had no idea at the time that all things Potter would become a huge phenomenon. A love of Harry Potter is now something passed down through families, like allegiance to a sports team. And each new generation gets to rediscover Harry's journey anew.

But back in 1998, no one had any idea that a children's fantasy book would launch a global phenomenon that would eventually include not just books but millions of fans, multiple theme parks, a Broadway play, and a blockbuster Hollywood movie franchise. At first there was just that book, which kept selling, and selling, and selling. It was released in the UK in June 1997, in the USA in September 1998, and it snowballed until it hit number one on the *New York Times* Bestseller List in August of 1999. That is an unusually long climb to the top of the list, and as more and more readers jumped onto the bandwagon, *Sorcerer's Stone* STAYED at the top of the list for so long that other publishers began to cry foul! It simply wasn't fair to expect mere Muggle books to be able to compete with a magical one, and in 2000 the *Times* split out the children's books into their own list.

So right from the get-go, Harry Potter was bending the rules and sometimes breaking them. Eventually the books grew to be so highly anticipated that book warehouses had to embargo the shipments and the UK and US publishers had to sync up their schedules. Bookstores everywhere began to host midnight launch parties for those who could not wait even one extra minute post-embargo to find out what trouble Harry, Ron and Hermione got into next. The book parties were glorious, full of costumes and candy and Sorting ceremonies and games—like Halloween crossed with the best childhood birthday party you never had.

One thing to remember about those days was that 1998 was the start of a terrible downturn for US bookstores. The chains like Barnes & Noble and Borders had started putting independent bookshops out of business at a frightening rate, and Amazon had grabbed 10% of all book sales in the country. As an author whose books would live or die by those bookstores, I can tell you it was nerve-wracking to watch. But every time a new Harry Potter book came out, it was like a Pepper-Up Potion, infusing embattled bookshops with new life and bringing customers into the stores for months afterward. Like Christmas in July.

That midnight party energy soon flowed right into the film franchise. The film rights supposedly went for a cool one million British pounds, even though no one knew how the series would end! Unheard of! At the time when the first film debuted—November 2001—only four books of the seven had been released.

There was so much anxiety about whether these films would be any good. How could they possibly live up to the expectations of literally millions of readers? By then, over five million hardcovers and six and a half million paperbacks had been sold, and the books had been translated into over 50 languages. People the world over were in love with Harry Potter and everyone had an opinion about how they thought Hogwarts should look, how Harry should sound, and what parts of the books should be kept in the films. Let's face it. "The book is better than the movie" is a common refrain. We can all name some books whose highly anticipated film adaptations turned out to be duds (sorry, *Dune*). There was a lot at stake. Many fans were not sure that making movies out of the Harry Potter books was actually a good idea at all.

Think for a second about some of the challenges facing these filmmakers. They would have to:

- Adapt some of the most-beloved books of all time, books that were so crammed full of details and plot twists there would be no way they could include them all and keep the films under two hours.

- Work with child actors. Actors who, by the way, would have to grow up along with their characters and would hopefully be just as winsome, handsome, and charming as high school seniors as they were as high-voiced 10 year-olds. That or re-cast every few years.

6

- Fight film industry biases against fantasy movies. Fantasy was considered "risky." (At the time the *Lord of the Rings* movies had not yet been made.)

- Invent and use a ton of CGI effects to make the wizarding world believably magical. One crummy or less-than-believable effect can ruin a film. (Looking at you, *Eragon*.)

- Set up character arcs for their entire cast... without knowing how the actual plot of future films would turn out, because the books *hadn't been written yet.*

In short, the filmmakers were doing something that had never been done before, and which no one was really sure they could pull off. Would they even get to adapt all seven books?

Spoiler alert: They did. The movies were massive hits. Throughout this *Binge Watcher's Guide* we'll be talking about all the challenges that were met and surpassed, about making true magic with each successive film, and the magic carpet ride that living through the release of the films truly was. But there was more going on than just great filmmaking and great source material.

One fact I think gets lost in most talk about the films is that the first one hit theaters only two months after the September 11th attacks. It was a time when the world looked suddenly like a much darker place than it had before. I think it was a world that really needed some escape, to believe in some innocent and good-hearted heroes, a world that needed some magic. People certainly flocked to the theater in droves to see it! *Harry Potter and the Sorcerer's Stone*, despite being released so late in the year, turned out to be the number one box office movie of 2001. It had the largest domestic (US) opening weekend of that year, was the top-grossing PG-rated film, and would become the number one box office film worldwide that year. It would go on to be nominated for three Oscars and, according to *Box Office Mojo*, has come close to a lifetime worldwide gross of almost (*Dr. Evil voice*) *One Billion Dollars.* (It's at $975 million as of 2019.)

Sorcerer's Stone was the start of something huge, but it would get even huger once the fandom got organized. In 1998 only 41% of adults in the US "went online," according to the Pew Research Center. Phones were not "smart" yet. (You also couldn't buy Slytherin hoodies at Hot Topic or order merch from Universal Studios.) But it wouldn't be long before midnight movie launches were selling out complete megaplexes—like those midnight bookstore parties but for thousands of people at a time.

I think it's not a mere coincidence that the rapid rise of the Internet matched the explosive growth of Harry Potter fandom. Pioneering blogging platform Livejournal launched in 1999 and would eventually grow into a major hub of Potter fandom. By 2001, when the *Sorcerer's Stone* movie came out, Internet usage in the US had grown to nearly 54%, passing the 50% mark for the first time—although only 7% of users had broadband and most were still using dial-up modems. Facebook (2004) and Twitter (2006) didn't exist yet. Livejournal and Yahoo groups were the main ways the fandom coalesced, shared fanfic, and began organizing real-world get-togethers, while websites like Mugglenet and The Leaky Cauldron became major hubs for news and information about all things Potter, including the film's stars. Harry Potter fandom didn't have to wade through *Variety* or *The Hollywood Reporter* to find out the celebrity gossip about Alan Rickman or Daniel Radcliffe; like wizards and *The Daily Prophet,* we had our own, dedicated sources—online.

That meant though, that every rumor, every leaked photo from the set, every interview, was instantly circulated among millions of fans. No film franchise before ever had such scrutiny on it. I think ultimately it was all to the good, though. As the filmmakers grew accustomed to the near-instantaneous nature of the 24/7 Potterhead news cycle, they learned how to prime the audience's anticipation for the films nearly as much as the books did. That's quite a trick when the majority of the audience already knows the plot because they've read the book! The gradual release of teasers for an upcoming film is now a commonplace technique, but at the time it was groundbreaking. The hype machine probably reached its most hysterical pitch in the lead-up to Harry's first kiss, which takes place in the fifth movie, *Harry Potter and the Order of the Phoenix.* Harry's love interest, Cho Chang, was brilliantly cast with Scottish 17-year-old Katie Leung.

Which brings us to another thing that, in retrospect, makes the Potter franchise seem prescient. These days there is a tremendous hue and cry whenever a film's cast lacks racial and ethnic diversity, especially a genre film. But the Potter films had diversity baked in from the start, thanks to J.K. Rowling's varied cast of students that had always included characters like Cho Chang, Parvati and Padma Patil, Lee Jordan, and Angelina Johnson.

I saw the effect of this diverse representation firsthand when I started attending Harry Potter conventions. I had been going to multi-fandom conventions since the late 1980s, including "Worldcon," the World Science Fiction Convention, the con where the Hugo Award is given. Worldcon moves from city to city, mostly within North America with periodic jumps overseas to places like Finland and Ireland. I had not realized just how overwhelmingly white Worldcon attendees were, though, until I walked into my first Harry Potter convention.

Walking about the crowded lobby at Terminus, I was instantly struck by how many East Asian, South Asian and black faces I saw. The convention was also about 95% female, and I found myself getting into conversation after conversation with women there, asking them how they joined the fandom and why they had chosen to travel all the way to Chicago for the event. And time after time they said it was simple really: the Harry Potter universe was one where they saw themselves included. They didn't have to fight for a place at the table because "the canon" had already provided them one. The books do have some problematic elements, but they prove to me without a doubt that representation matters.

Films are an even more important medium for racial and ethnic diversity than books sometimes, though, because readers can gloss over or forget a character's skin color while reading. On film, they can't. (As in the controversy over the casting of *The Hunger Games.*) The films embraced the diversity of the canon and that only resulted in even more fans on the bandwagon than before.

The net result of this wide appeal is that these eight films—the first of which was released in 2001, and the last of which was released almost exactly ten years later in 2011—stand as the dominant film franchise of the decade. I don't just mean in terms of money (which is an impressive $9.2 billion total box office gross, which doesn't even include DVD or streaming sales). They set an ambitious template for blockbuster franchises that would follow like the Marvel Cinematic Universe (launched in 2008 with *Iron Man*), the current phase of Star

Wars sequels (beginning with *The Force Awakens,* 2015) and other book series adaptations (like *Twilight,* 2008, and *The Hunger Games,* 2015). The Potter series defines film excellence in the Aughts and is a huge piece of the establishment of the ubiquity of Harry Potter in the 21st century.

Harry Potter is no longer "just" a book or "just" a movie. As I mentioned before, Harry Potter has become something that is passed down from generation to generation, like sports fandom to a team, and that is shared among family and friends and part of our common experience of growing up. It's woven into the fabric of our culture. When I say Harry Potter is everywhere now, I'm not exaggerating. Amazon sells over 30,000 products relating to Harry Potter. Google Scholar Search turns up almost 20,000 academic papers that cite the Potter books. (By contrast, Jane Austen's *Pride and Prejudice* turns up around 2,000, and *Alice in Wonderland* only about 200.) On Fanfiction.net, fanfic is posted relating to over 2,400 books and series. Over 800,000 of those fics are Harry Potter, about 58% of all entries on the site. (Next in line is *Twilight* with about 16%, and third is Percy Jackson with a mere 5%.) There are unofficial Potter-themed bars, coffee shops, and restaurants.

And then of course there are the official establishments: you can go to a Universal Studios theme park and actually eat in the Three Broomsticks or Leaky Cauldron and, of course, visit Hogwarts, all built out and decorated to be film accurate. Not very many other movies can boast that their settings have been turned into real-life immersive tourist attractions (though I hear you can visit Hobbiton in New Zealand), especially not ones that caused a 14% spike in attendance at Universal Studios (LA)—nearly one million additional visitors over the previous year. Hogwarts Castle is giving Cinderella's Castle a run for its money as far as being the favorite iconic childhood destination in Orlando, Florida.

So you could say these movies are more than "just" movies. However, we get to enjoy them just like any other movies, in our living rooms, on our devices, on cable TV and via DVD. When the opening sequence begins to roll on the quiet, nighttime street of Privet Drive, you can forget all the momentous cultural impact and be carried away into the simple pleasure of entering the wizarding world once again.

Before You Watch

Before you hit "play," there are things to know that I believe will enrich the viewing experience and make it all the more magical. I recognize that many people like to watch movies spoiler-free. This is pretty hard to do with a series that's as famous, ubiquitous, and old as this one, but if you're truly spoiler-averse, I would say skip these chapters until after you've watched the films.

I've organized the book into sections. The "before you watch" section includes a chapter on the casting of the main characters, tips and ideas for throwing a binge-watch party and advice from parents on introducing kids to the movies.

Then come chapters for the individual films, each of which has a section on casting notes for that installment, filmmaking notes and things to look for, a plot recap and "book lore." The plot recap is a scene-by-scene guided tour. (Your tour guide may occasionally be irreverent, but know that it comes from a place of love.) In the book lore sections you'll find some things that are in the book, but which were glossed over or left out of the film. You should be able to watch the films without knowing all those details, but they're in this book to increase your enjoyment and understanding.

Plot recap and book lore are packed with spoilers, by necessity.

Throughout the book I'll use shortened versions of the book and movie titles, dropping "Harry Potter and the..." and just going with the rest. I'll bop back and forth between calling the first installment *Sorcerer's Stone* and *Philosopher's Stone*, since which title you got depends on which country you are in. (Personally I think it was a little silly that the US publisher insisted that American children wouldn't read a book with the word "philosopher" in the title, but hindsight's 20/20.) I'll also refer to the main characters of Harry, Ron and Hermione as "the Trio," which was the term screenwriter Steve Kloves used in the scripts. (J.K. Rowling's own shorthand was to call them "HRH," which in the UK also stands for Her Royal Highness, so that amused her.)

At the end of the book we'll wrap up the tour with a couple of analytical essays, including my pick for "if you only watch one film..." and my recommendations on what to watch next when you're done.

Casting

As I mentioned in "The Zeitgeist," at the time they were made, no movie series had ever attempted to do what the Harry Potter films did, which was—among other things—take a cast of children and hope to follow them to adulthood on screen over the course of a decade.

One of the stipulations J.K. Rowling placed on the sale of the film rights was that the actors had to be British. She didn't want a Hollywood studio to shoehorn Tom Cruise in as Snape or Johnny Depp as Sirius. (We'll talk about *Fantastic Beasts* later... much later.) Indeed, several of her picks, such as Robbie Coltrane for Hagrid, were absolutely perfect—and yes, the studio did try to convince her that Robin Williams (!?) should play the Hogwarts gamekeeper instead.

Another major character she handpicked an actor for was Severus Snape. Alan Rickman was far older than the character he would play. He was 53 when he was cast to play the 31-year-old Snape—and was 63 when they had to film the flashbacks to 21-year-old Snape in the final movie. But Rowling knew the film franchise needed someone who could play the heavy with a great deal of nuance. Even those of us who had obsessively read the four books that had been released up to that point knew very little of Snape's background, much less what the plot held in store for him. Rowling told Rickman several things about his character that would later be revealed and swore him to secrecy.

Maggie Smith was another actor who appeared much older than her character as described in the books, but in recent years J.K. Rowling released more information about Professor Minerva McGonagall via her Pottermore website. Supposedly McGonagall's birthday was October 4, 1935, making her less than a year younger than Dame Maggie Smith who was born in December 1934. (However McGonagall appears as a Hogwarts professor in the *Fantastic Beasts* films, as well, which supposedly take place in the 1920s, before she would have been born. Like I said... let's not talk about *Fantastic Beasts* right now.)

With Richard Harris, another Rowling-approved casting choice, the producers couldn't go wrong. Dumbledore is meant to be over a hundred years old (born 1881) and the bearded, white-haired Harris did a terrific job embodying the benevolent and humorous Dumbledore depicted in the early books, although he did get one note from the author. At one point in the script some dialogue appeared in which Dumbledore thinks back to a pretty girl he remembered. Rowling nixed the line and told the actor (and screenwriter) that Dumbledore wouldn't say such a thing because he was gay. (She wouldn't tell the rest of us until after all the books were published.)

Unfortunately Richard Harris passed away of Hodgkin's lymphoma in 2002, after finishing filming for *Harry Potter and the Chamber of Secrets*, which was his last appearance on film. He was replaced by Michael Gambon, who played a much more subtly mysterious Dumbledore, which was appropriate to the plot and to the way he gradually reveals to Harry that there is more going on behind the scenes than Harry knows.

But enough of the good guys. Let's talk about the characters people love to hate.

The Best for the Worst

It's a Hollywood trope that villains should have British accents, and the Harry Potter series has enough baddies to fill out a Quidditch team. One of the great pleasures of these films is seeing veteran Brits like Alan Rickman chew the scenery with absolute aplomb. When Snape says "Turn to page 394" you can practically see the loathing dripping from the words. Herewith, the seven best of the worst—or the worst of the best—of the characters we love to hate from Harry Potter.

7. Richard Griffiths as Vernon Dursley

Americans might not have been as familiar with Richard Griffiths as British audiences, but like most of the actors on this list, he was an award-winning thespian, and you can sense the absolute glee he pours into the awfulness that is Harry's uncle-in-law. Dursley's menace is ultimately played for humorous effect, which gives Griffiths license to play the role to the hilt. He and Fiona Shaw, who played Aunt Petunia, had great chemistry as a terrible twosome, a husband and wife who bring out the worst in each other. Shaw would later describe the movies as terrific fun for her, with the only downside being that whenever she meets new children they have a tendency to hide from her or burst into tears.

6. David Tennant as Barty Crouch Jr.

At the time of his villainous turn in *Harry Potter and the Goblet of Fire,* David Tennant hadn't yet has his run as the tenth incarnation of Dr. Who, but now fans who know him from that and later work may be shocked to see him play "against type." Tennant is wonderfully, snakishly psychotic as Death Eater Barty Crouch Jr. complete with flickering tongue. The only reason he doesn't rate higher on the list is his performance is fairly short and mostly in flashback.

5. Kenneth Branagh as Gilderoy Lockhart

It's probably unfair to say it wasn't a stretch for Kenneth Branagh to play an egotistical, good-looking narcissist who loves being the center of attention, but I'm saying it anyway. He is delightfully cracked as two-faced fame-hound Gilderoy Lockhart, who blusters his way through his incompetence and hides his corruption with an over-the-top smile and reliance on his good looks. The scene where Lockhart and Snape demonstrate wand dueling is priceless. What's amusing is that although Branagh's performance seems utterly over the top, this is apparently the more restrained version. As Jason Isaacs told *Entertainment Weekly,* "I think [director Chris Columbus'] job consisted entirely of trying to stop me and Ken from trying to out-ham each other. ...Chris gave me a lot of 'Listen, I think they could see that performance in America from here without broadcast. Shrink it down to camera size'."(Another amusing note: Lockhart was the part Isaacs wanted to audition for.)

4. Helena Bonham Carter as Bellatrix Lestrange

Speaking of cracked, they don't come much more cracked than Bellatrix Lestrange, who was probably already not the sanest person before she did hard time in Azkaban, the wizarding prison. The books describe Bellatrix's slavish devotion to the Dark Lord and her mad taunting of Harry—Helena Bonham Carter nails both. She plays Bellatrix as deliciously deranged and dangerous—maybe a bit too literally? In an interview Matthew Lewis, who plays Neville Longbottom, described being awed by her performance, how she was an amazingly nice and sweet person, "and then the camera would come on and she would instantly turn into this raging madwoman!" What Lewis didn't say in that interview, but which was revealed in many others, is that during the scene where Bellatrix holds Neville hostage and threatens him in *Order of the Phoenix,* she got a bit too into character and accidentally punctured his eardrum with her wand!

3. Jason Isaacs as Lucius Malfoy

Jason Isaacs almost didn't take the part of Lucius Malfoy. He'd wanted the part of Gilderoy Lockhart, and having just played Captain Hook in a Peter Pan movie, he didn't want to be typecast as a children's villain. But once he took to the part, he really really took to it. First of all, the film producers were going to put him in short hair and a sort of pinstriped suit and he said, *no, this is all wrong.* A racist anti-Muggle like Malfoy is going to have long hair and an ostentatiously wizard-like wardrobe. Then there was his accent, which he based on a sadistic teacher he had in drama school, which "smacks of a sense of entitlement. ...A voice that made him drip with the millennia that his family had been in power—complete disdain and contempt for anybody and everything else." Isaacs also knew he had to bring his A-game if he wanted Malfoy to be more hated than Snape. "Nobody does sinister like Alan Rickman. I thought, 'If I'm going to do something, it'd better be unbelievably extreme.'" That sneer. Oh, that Malfoy sneer.

2. Ralph Fiennes as Voldemort

One of the things that is scariest about Voldemort is how unpredictable he is. Like Darth Vader in *Star Wars: A New Hope,* if you're on "his side" you may still end up a victim of his egomaniacal, psychopathic whims. Ralph Fiennes plays these "mood swings" to the hilt, and to give the actor the freedom to explore them, many of Voldemort's scenes were filmed as improvisations by Fiennes. There were apparently more than 20 takes of the Dark Lord's final speech after the Battle of Hogwarts—wouldn't you love to see them all? And that creepy, awkward hug with Draco? Also improvised and totally unexpected by the other actors. Tom Felton, who plays Draco, says the stunned look he wears in the scene isn't acting, it's absolutely real.

1. Imelda Staunton as Dolores Umbridge

And now, the absolute best of the worst, even Ralph Fiennes' manic uber-villain can't top the pitch-perfectly hate-able performance of Imelda Staunton as Dolores Umbridge. Her simpering back-of-the-throat giggle and her sadistic faux-sympathy when she makes Harry torture himself simply cannot be topped. Staunton says the "I Will Not Tell Lies" detention scene with Harry was the most difficult scene she's ever had to do. It left her "feeling bad for a couple of days... A horrible horrible feeling." The key to getting into the character, Staunton said, was that Umbridge believes she's doing good, that genocide and ethnic cleansing will be good for the wizarding world. As she told *Entertainment Weekly,* "She's not sort of twirling her mustache and saying 'Muahahaha,' it's the absolute and utter belief that actually it is going to help and that's, of course, so much more frightening." And that's why she tops this list. Brava, Imelda.

Casting the Kids

Finding the right children to play not only Harry, but Ron, Hermione and Draco as well, presented a huge set of challenges.

For one thing, the producers knew they had to catch lightning in a bottle. In a normal one-shot film, it's commonplace to cast a small 12- or 13-year-old for a 10-year-old, but that was just not going to work for a franchise expected to run for a decade. And what if there were delays starting filming? If it took two years to green light a script, the actors' voices might change and they might appear too physically mature to play their ages. Then they'd have to start the casting search over again. The timing had to be right, and the youngsters themselves had to be right.

Each successive film would kick off another round of massive auditions as new characters were introduced, looking for the perfect Luna Lovegood or Cho Chang. We'll talk about other characters as we come to each film's recap. The most important characters to nail had to be "the Trio" of Harry, Ron and Hermione. Frequent recurring characters Draco Malfoy and Neville Longbottom were going to be important to get right, too.

Actor Tom Felton often tells stories about auditioning for Harry Potter. He had already worked a little in film (*Anna and the King*) and went to an open casting call where there were hundreds of boys. At Salt Lake City Comic Con he told fans that hadn't yet read the books. "I remember vividly, Chris Columbus coming down the line saying, 'What's your favorite thing from the book? What are you most looking forward to seeing?' He only got to the second person next to me before I realized ****, I don't have an answer here. So the kid next to me was like, 'Gringotts. I'm so excited about Gringotts.' Then he came to me and I was like, 'Yeah man, I love those Gringotts. They are awesome. I can't wait to see them flying around.' I think that Chris Columbus knew straightaway that this kid could be a good Draco."

At one of his appearances at Dragoncon he revealed that the producers had him try on various roles and hair colors as he read first for both the parts of Harry and Ron, joking that they then tried him in a curly wig but he wasn't right for Hermione at all. "And then they tried me on blond and the rest is history." (Felton's natural hair is light brown.)

Matthew Lewis, who played Neville, was one of the more experienced child actors to join the cast. He had been acting in television since age five, following in the footsteps of his older brothers. The Leeds native is now noted for how incredibly good-looking he grew up to be, but his character is definitely meant to be a bit of a dweeby duckling before he grew into a rather heroic swan by the final film. His transformation into a heartthrob started rather earlier than the film producers were prepared for, so he was forced to wear false teeth and a fat suit. They eventually let him ditch the fake teeth but stipulated he couldn't fix his own crooked teeth until after filming was complete. "Which meant I had to go for 10 f***ing years without having anything done," he told an interviewer in 2013. "Looking back on it, it doesn't really bother me at all, but at the time, when you're going through puberty and you're on a film set with a lot of attractive girls... it was rubbish. It was really rubbish."

But, the Trio. What about the Trio? Casting director Janet Hirshenson told the *Huffington Post* that she thinks one of the most important things they looked for when casting the kids was what their parents were like. Parents who were grounded and supportive—but not pushy—is what they wanted. Chris Columbus, who had directed Macaulay Culkin in *Home Alone*, had experienced the kind of "stage parents" who pushed too hard. "[So] we auditioned the parents," he told *Entertainment Weekly*. "And my biggest question was, if the kid says, 'I wanna stop!' will you let them stop? And they all said yes, which is important to me."

Naturally red-haired Rupert Grint was a huge fan of the Harry Potter books. At age 10, he saw the open casting call and, with no acting experience to speak of, put together a video of himself rapping (yes, rapping) about why he wanted the role. At a 2011 con appearance with some other cast members he even sang/rapped a bit of it: "Hello there, my name's Rupert Grint! Hope you like this and don't think I stink. I'm four-foot-nine and age 11... That's all I can remember of it." Rupert felt he had a lot of similarities with Ron beyond red hair, including having a large family.

Emma Watson was another novice to the screen, having only acted in school plays before her audition for Hermione. She'd wanted to act since she was six years old and she impressed the producers immediately. Eventually they narrowed the choices down to half a dozen Rons and a handful of Hermiones. Emma was sure that another girl, one who'd done the Madeline movie, was going to get the part, but when they started screen testing different kids together, well. "For the Hermiones, as soon as Emma came on, there were six of us in the screening room. We just gasped. It was like, 'Oh my God.' Like, 'Whoaaa!' She took up the screen," said Hirshenson. Then came Ron. Columbus preferred another actor, but Hirshenson and the rest of the crew knew their pick. "We said, 'Look at that face on Rupert... That's Ron. Look at that face.'"

Harry, though, what about Harry? The most important role in the series was one of the last to be filled. They needed a boy who was green- or at least blue-eyed and small in stature. The director toyed with defying the "all British" casting rule and putting in an actor who had previously worked with him on the film *Stepmom*, Liam Aiken. They also considered an actor from *Billy Elliot*, but he was already too old. Columbus had seen one British kid he really liked, in the BBC One production of *David Copperfield*, but the child's parents had turned down an audition and the boy had apparently decided he didn't want to keep acting.

That boy was Daniel Radcliffe.

The Potter production team was familiar with his parents a bit through the entertainment business: Alan Radcliffe is a literary agent and Daniel's mum, Marcia Gresham, is a casting agent. Producer David Heyman went out to the theater one evening in London with some of the team, and they were seated *right in front of* young Dan, who was chatting away fearlessly with all these adults around him (and sort of wondering why these guys kept turning around to look at him). Columbus described him as an "old soul" and just knew he would be perfect for the part. In a video interview with J.K. Rowling and Daniel Radcliffe (where they interview each other), Dan tells the story of that night at the theater, and his parents hiding him behind a pillar during the intermission, while they tried to avoid talking to the film folks. "I don't believe in fate or destiny or whatever, but my parents do," he told the author. And that chance meeting got them thinking they should reconsider the gig.

Daniel and his parents were coaxed to give the audition a go after being assured that the filming would take place in England. At the time there was one other young actor in the running, and eventually it came down to screen-testing them both. Hirshenson told *HuffPost* the other boy was "terrific and vulnerable." But in the end they felt vulnerability wasn't enough. Harry can be quite spunky in the books and they felt only Daniel Radcliffe had the "stones" to play the full range of emotions.

From this point forward in the book I'm just going to call the Trio Dan, Emma and Rupert, because having watched them grow up, now they're as familiar to me as family. And by the time you're done binge-watching the series (and reading this book!) they will be to you, too!

Throw a Binge-Watch Party

This book being a Binge Watcher's Guide implies you might actually want to hold a marathon movie session. While I was getting ready to write this book, in the spirit of research I decided to throw a binge-watch party of my own. This chapter is a collection of tips, tricks and recipes that can enhance the Harry Potter binge-watching experience.

Timing

It turns out that the original eight Harry Potter films take about 22 hours to watch, which is a good length for a movie marathon. You could watch them all in one "day" if you started at 8:00 a.m. and then showed your guests out after breakfast the next day. When I threw my binge-watch party, though, I decided to host it in two 11-hour stints: noon to 11:00 p.m. on a Saturday-Sunday, with a short break for dinner each day. That worked better for my friends and my sleep schedule.

To MST3K or Not?

If you're going to do a watch party of any kind, one suggestion I got from several friends was this: decide whether you're going to ask everyone to be silent during the films or if you'll allow (or encourage) heckling, talking back to the screen, and general "MST3K"-ing. I've always felt part of Harry Potter fandom is a healthy engagement in both criticism and poking fun at the original material, and at my party we'd all seen the films before, so my watch party included some good-natured heckling. (If we'd had guests who'd never seen the films with us, though, we might have been more reverent.)

Party Menu

Like the books that they are based on, the Harry Potter films include a lot of chocolate, pastry and sweets, as well as traditional

English foods like meat pies and pasties (pasty rhymes with nasty), and made-up beverages such as pumpkin juice, butterbeer and firewhisky. These all make for great party foods, or at least their Muggle equivalents do.

Beverage

There are three beverages mentioned repeatedly in Harry Potter—well, four if you include tea—pumpkin juice, butterbeer and Odgen's Old firewhisky.

Pumpkin Juice

You can't buy pumpkin juice in the grocery store—at least not in the store near me—but you can make something that if you tell people it's "pumpkin juice" they'll probably believe you.

Back when J.K. Rowling was writing Harry Potter, the "pumpkin spice" craze hadn't yet begun—the Starbucks pumpkin spice latte wasn't introduced until 2003. She intended "pumpkin juice" to taste like, well, *pumpkin,* not the spices that are baked into pumpkin pie. But nowadays people are likely to imagine something "pumpkin-flavored" is nutmeg, clove and cinnamon flavored. To make a pumpkin-spice flavored drink, I brewed a black tea with pumpkin pie spices in with the tea leaves, and then I mixed the tea with orange juice and chilled it.

In the organic section of my local grocery they sell carrot turmeric juice that is bright orange, and doesn't "Carrot Turmeric" sound healthy? We tasted it and it was quite sweet (similar to orange juice) but would have substituted quite well.

I've also seen suggestions on the Internet that you can mix canned pumpkin puree with fruit juice but I was skeptical enough of this idea (wouldn't it need to be strained?) that I did not try it. (Fun fact: some cats love to eat canned pumpkin and it's a good source of fiber for them. Probably good for kneazles, too.)

Firewhisky

I've often wondered if the growth in popularity of Fireball Whiskey—a brand name of sweetened cinnamon-flavored whiskey—is related to the existence of firewhisky in the Harry Potter books. Originally introduced in the mid-1980s, Fireball wasn't particularly popular, but it's caught fire with consumers, now outselling Jameson Irish Whiskey and Patron Tequila in the USA. So, if you want to serve something that might be recognizable as firewhisky, Fireball is an easy one. It's also rather syrupy sweet and many of my cocktail-snob friends wouldn't drink it. Among some of the suggestions they gave me instead: soak cinnamon sticks (or habanero peppers!) in vodka and then use it to mix cocktails, or drop Cinnamon Red Hots candy into whatever you're pouring. It really depends on how adept at Potions you are.

Butterbeer

When asked what she intended butterbeer to be like, J.K. Rowling told *Bon Appetit* magazine in 2002, "I imagine it to taste a little bit like less sickly [sweet] butterscotch." In the books it can be served hot or cold, and it's clearly lightly alcoholic, enough to make Hermione tipsy in The Three Broomsticks and to make Winky the House Elf quite blotto.

Served hot: A hot steamed milk with butterscotch and caramel syrup with a little dash of scotch or rum if you want the alcohol would serve quite well. Another idea if you want more alcohol would be to just make hot buttered rum. Other kinds of hot toddies of course are delicious, too, but may move you quite far from the flavor profile... then again, what flavor did you imagine when you heard the word butterbeer? There is no wrong answer! The power of your imagination is what matters. Make something that is tasty and comforting for you.

Served cold: These days they serve a concoction at Universal Studios they call butterbeer and it is served either cold or frozen. It's basically like a cream soda Slurpee with a whipped topping. They told me at the park it has no beer and no dairy in it. When I asked how it was made I was told "magic." (Of course. Try making "frozen Coke" with cream soda and see what happens?)

I started throwing Harry-Potter-themed parties at science fiction conventions in 2010, when we thought the fandom might decline after the last movie came out (it didn't). I invented my own version of a slightly alcoholic drink made with canned whipped cream, cream soda and butterscotch schnapps. The magic part is to put the whipped cream in the cup *first,* then drizzle in the butterscotch, and pour the cream soda last. The partly dissolved whipped cream will foam up and look just like the head on a real beer. I usually finish the recipe off with a flourish of my wand, reciting the incantation "Vita Dulce, Vita Sana," which is Latin for "Sweet life, healthy life."

Meka, a friend I met through Harry Potter conventions, calls my recipe the "First Year," because she has come up with stronger versions appropriate for older drinkers. (In the wizarding world, 17 is the age of majority. In England the drinking age is 18, and in the United States although one must be 21 to *purchase* alcohol, some states allow consumption by those between the ages of 18 and 21).

Here are Meka's recipes:

Third Year:
1 shot whipped cream vodka
1/2 cream soda
1/2 butterscotch schnapps
Top with whipped cream

Seventh Year:
1 shot whipped cream vodka
1 shot vanilla vodka
1 shot birthday cake vodka
1/2 cream soda
1/2 butterscotch schnapps
Top with vodka infused caramel whipped cream

Snacks and Foods

You can always take the easy route and just put up a sign that says "Edible Wands" on a plate of pretzel rods (or pirouette cookies, or bread sticks, or Pocky...) but there are so many more things you could do. To keep things interesting throughout my two-day movie marathon, I served some foods that were themed to specific films.

Sorcerer's Stone/Philosopher's Stone:
If you're starting off with something sweet, you can't go wrong with baking a cake that says "Happy Birthday Harry" on it, like the one that Hagrid brings to Harry about 10 minutes into the first film. If

the cake sags a little, that's all right. Harry's cake gets a little squished in transit. It'll just seem more authentic.

While Ron and Harry share a compartment on the Hogwarts Express they get a visit from the Trolley Witch, who sells sweets and snacks on the train, including Chocolate Frogs, Bertie Bott's Every Flavor Beans and licorice wands. In one of my favorite joyous moments from the film, our previously deprived orphan Harry—having never had wizard candy before—buys one of each to share with Ron. So have some Bertie Botts—or at least generic jelly beans—on hand, along with some other fun candy to kick off with. "Licorice wands" sure sound like Twizzlers or something similar. If you don't want to track down the official chocolate frogs (now available from Universal Studios), how about chocolate turtles (a traditional chocolate, caramel and nuts candy in the US) instead? And although it isn't mentioned in the film, at Christmas, Harry gets a gift of homemade fudge. Hard to go wrong with fudge, even if it is also the name of the Minister for Magic.

When they get to Hogwarts, of course, Harry and the rest of the students experience the Welcome Feast, daily meals in the Great Hall, and the end-of-year Leaving Feast, so that gives one a lot of leeway for what to serve. At the first Welcome Feast Harry is wowed by the amount of food, which the book describes as including lamb chops, peas and bacon-wrapped steak! In the film we see the lamb chops as crown roasts, as well as corn on the cob and chicken drumsticks piled high—and Ron gleefully holding one in each fist. Whole roast chickens or turkeys can also be seen.

At Halloween the book describes the "scent of baked pumpkin" which could be done as a roasted pumpkin side dish or as a sweet pumpkin bread.

There is a scene in the film where Harry and friends visit Hagrid's hut, where they are served "rock cakes." They appear to be something like a raisin-filled scone if you could bake them until they were hard as rocks—hard enough that Harry fears for his teeth. One could presumably bake scones that were not quite so tough, though.

Chamber of Secrets
This film opens with a sequence featuring an amazing dessert prepared by Aunt Petunia. In the book it is described as a "huge

mound of whipped cream and sugared violets." The filmmakers depicted it as a two-tiered cake that befalls a literally sticky end—and which closely resembles the illustration on the cover of the Rolling Stones album *Let It Bleed*. There are a ton of recipes online for making your own candied violets or they can be bought ready-made, if you're going to tackle wowing your guests with such a thing.

Prisoner of Azkaban

This is the book and film in which a *lot* of chocolate is eaten, because it restores people after their chilling encounters with the Dementors. I made sure to have plenty of chocolate-covered toffee and other chocolate on hand to restore our souls! Dementors are scary AF.

This is a good time to introduce the idea of Cauldron Cakes. They are mentioned many times in the book, although no detail is given on what they are. Many fan recipes on the Internet suggest baking dark chocolate cupcakes, hollowing out the top so it looks like a cauldron, and filling with icing or flavored whipped cream. To get really fancy, make the handles of the cauldron out of thin black licorice or form them from melted chocolate on wax paper and let them harden.

Another variation is to bake individual-sized molten-chocolate cakes with liquid centers, but that's a recipe that has to be done *a la minute*, and you don't want to be fussing around baking when you're supposed to be watching a movie with your guests. I have, however, seen various brands of microwaveable molten chocolate cakes which might be a good choice.

And then there's the idea of doing your "Cauldron Cakes" as mug cakes. A mug cake is a thing you make by mixing up the cake ingredients in a coffee mug and then microwaving it to "bake" it and then eating it while still hot. They often have chocolate chips in them which melt deliciously. How about using a butterscotch chip instead for a butterbeer-like flavor?

Here's my recipe for Butterbeer Mug Cake:

Cecilia's Butterbeer Mug Cake

All mug cakes have variable cooking times depending on your microwave, so test them out before you try to do them at a party. Use regular size (eight ounce), straight-sided coffee mugs.

Ingredients:
4 Tablespoons flour
2 Tablespoons brown sugar
2 Tablespoons rum
1.5 Tablespoons salted butter
1/8 teaspoon ground nutmeg
1/4 teaspoon vanilla extract
2 Tablespoons butterscotch chips

Directions:
Melt the butter in the bottom of the mug until just melted. I recommend 10 seconds on high, then another 10 seconds, then five seconds at a time until if there's still a little solid in there, just swirl it around until it melts. Add the sugar, then the rest of the dry ingredients and mix with a spoon. Add the rum last. You should have a very thick but still cake-batter-ish mixture. Stir in the butterscotch chips last and then microwave for 45 to 60 seconds. Add 15 seconds more if it seems underdone.

This will result in a fluffy cake that is quite boozy. If you're making it for kids, I'd replace the two tablespoons rum with two tablespoons of milk (or almond milk) and a dash of baking rum flavoring.

There is plenty of room in the mug if you want to put vanilla ice cream (or butter almond or praline or caramel swirl...) on top. Unsweetened whipped cream with a drizzle of caramel sauce wouldn't go wrong either!

Goblet of Fire
We get a lot of food references in this book, including the chocolate éclairs that Harry, Ron and Hermione sneak from the kitchen, and "beef casserole" made by Hagrid—but as mentioned before Hagrid's cooking can be suspect.

This is also the book and film when the students from Beauxbatons and Durmstrang arrive to spend the year at Hogwarts. I decided that was a good time to serve some French pastries and macarons I picked up at the bakery. But I suppose it wouldn't be a bad time for some goulash as well, in honor of Durmstrang. (Although the exact location of Durmstrang is a secret, the name and other clues probably place it somewhere in the former Austro-Hungarian empire.)

Order of the Phoenix

There is a breakfast scene in this film where we can see racks of toast and plates of sausage. Ron is eating a rather large sausage off a fork while reading a colorful pamphlet. If you have freeze frame and high def you may be able to make out a nice little Easter egg: what he's reading is a pamphlet entitled "Cram It! How to Soar on Your O.W.L.s" (O.W.L.s are standardized tests for magical aptitudes). Both Hermione and Ginny seem rather put off, not by the pamphlet, but by the sheer volume of food Ron is ingesting. Sorry girls, but you should see how many pumpkin pasties my friends and I packed in during our binge-watch.

In this film, we see Cho Chang ask for a pumpkin pasty from the Trolley Witch, and they are mentioned a few times throughout the books. But what is a pumpkin pasty?

A pasty (or pastie) is a meat pie folded up so it can be held in one hand to be eaten. Kind of like an empanada (or a Hot Pocket).

An easy way to serve meat pies at a party is to just pick them up from a Chinese bakery, where there are numerous kinds of steamed buns with meat inside that can be eaten hot or cold.

But what about the pumpkin? I created my own recipe to add some pumpkin flavor to the filling. To save time before my party, I picked up pre-made fresh pizza dough at the grocery store so it only took about a half hour to prep the recipe. The prepped pasties can then be frozen overnight and baked on the day-of, or they can be baked right away. Here's the recipe:

Cecilia's Pumpkin Pasties

Filling Ingredients:
1 lb ground beef
1 small onion
1 tablespoon tomato paste mixed with 1/4 cup water
1/2 can pumpkin puree (unsweetened)
1 cinnamon stick
3 whole cloves or 1 pinch of ground cloves
1/4 teaspoon nutmeg
1/4 teaspoon ground cinnamon
Salt to taste

<u>Dough</u>:
1 pre-made grocery store pizza dough
1 beaten egg

<u>Dipping sauce</u> (optional):
1 cup plain yogurt
1 garlic clove, finely minced or well-crushed
Salt to taste
Paprika for garnish

This recipe makes about 20 pasties, but the number will vary depending on how small or large you cut the dough circles. I came up with it inspired by two things, empanadas and an Afghani pumpkin, cinnamon, and ground-meat dish called kaddo bowrani.

Heat some oil in a skillet or saucepan large enough to brown the ground beef. Start by sautéing the minced onion with all the spices in the pan, about five-10 minutes on medium. Once the onions are soft and translucent, pick out the whole cloves and the cinnamon stick, and then brown the beef in the pan. Once the beef is all browned and broken up into bits, mix the tomato paste and water together and then mix it in the beef. Add the 1/2 can of pumpkin puree. (I think small chunks of browned, caramelized pumpkin would also be good here, but pumpkins weren't in season. Kabocha or butternut squash might be great here, too.) Simmer the meat until there is no runny liquid and salt to taste. If you feel the pumpkin-spice flavor isn't strong enough, you can sprinkle more cinnamon and nutmeg, but be sure to taste it because if you get too much it can seem bitter.

Roll out the dough on a floured surface until it is 1/4-inch or less thick. Cut five-inch to six-inch circles in it using either a large biscuit cutter or a small bowl. Put a large spoonful of meat on each circle and fold over, crimping the edges to close. If the edged seem like they won't close, brush the egg wash lightly on the inside edges. Then use the rest of the egg wash to brush the outside of the pasties before you bake them. They will turn golden brown.

Bake at 400 degrees on an oiled sheet pan for about 20 to 25 minutes.

If you freeze them overnight, don't thaw the pasties first before baking, just put the frozen ones directly on the baking sheet, brush with egg wash, and bake for 30-35 minutes. If you opt for freezing them, make sure to put wax paper or parchment paper between them or they'll freeze together into a terrible mess.

Half-Blood Prince

In this film we see Ron chowing down on a bowl of red Jell-O (called jelly in British English) and Hermione whapping him and telling him once again to stop eating so much! Maybe we should take the hint.

Deathly Hallows:

Since these are the last two films, you may be getting toward the end of your binge-watch. The first place the Trio go once they're on the run from the Death Eaters is a cafe. They never get to have the cappuccinos they order, but that doesn't mean you and your guests can't have some coffee. There is also a lot of camping in the first film, but I don't recommend open flames indoors.

Watching with Kids

The Harry Potter books and movies are somewhat unique in that the earlier installments in the series are aimed at kids, but the later ones are really not. As Harry grows into wizarding adulthood (age 17), the themes of his story mature right along with him. In the films this is reflected by the choices of director. Chris Columbus, the American director of *The Goonies* and *Home Alone,* built his reputation as a deft helmsman of films for children starring children. His adaptations of *Sorcerer's/Philosopher's Stone* and *Chamber of Secrets* make great use of the winsome young actors at his disposal and hew very closely to the books. (Some critics seemed to think this was a bad thing, but I would say most fans disagree.)

The third film has Harry entering his teen years and the decision was made to bring in director Alfonso Cuarón. Cuarón had received critical acclaim for his Spanish-language film *Y Tu Mama Tambien,* a road movie that centers on two teenagers and their travels with a much older woman. The choice raised some eyebrows because *Y Tu Mama Tambien* was a somewhat raunchier film than the squeaky-clean Potter franchise, but Cuarón proved to be a strong choice. Film critics who had found the first two installments too, well, childish, praised the darker tone and character nuance in *Prisoner of Azkaban.*

But the fourth film, directed by Mike Newell (*Four Weddings and a Funeral*) is where the most serious shift in tone and style comes. *Goblet of Fire* is also the first of the films to get a PG-13 instead of PG rating in the US, and PG-12 in the UK. Spoiler alert: this will be the first of Harry's adventures to result not in triumph over evil, but a major death. Each of the final five films ends with a major death, and the challenges Harry faces grow progressively graver and more emotionally affecting. Are the latter films too scary or too intense for younger children?

I asked parents who are fans of Harry Potter for their advice on watching the films with kids, and one common theme arose in the responses I received: *read the books first.* Kristin from New Jersey wrote, "I had a rule that the child must read the book or listen to the audiobook first, so that we could process the material and the feelings before being overwhelmed by the film." Many folks including Todd from Connecticut agreed: "Read the books to the children first. Engage them in the story, the details. Then watch the movies. I say this from experience."

Amanda added, "Know your kid and what makes them scared. Understand how the story progresses, and that once you start it's hard to stop wanting to know what's next." You might think you can just say, "stop" after the second movie, but can you really tell a seven-year-old who is just *dying* to know what happens to wait a year or more to find out?

Several parents echoed the "know your kid" theme. Barbara Martinez, a Harry Potter fan I met while playing the game Wizards Unite, suggested this unique way of framing the discussion: "My children watched all of the movies—the best advice is to know your kids. Mine can get through even the scariest content if I prepare them for a scary moment, and ask them, 'if you were directing this movie and wanted this part to be scary, how would you do it? Do you think the director did a good job in making this part scary? Why do you think many people like scary movies?' Discussions like that help them manage the emotions, and not get derailed mid-movie." Discussing scary storytelling and film technique as Barbara suggests helps the child to draw the line between fantasy and reality.

Here's one tip that I learned as a child myself: sometimes it's better to let a child watch something that scared them again, rather than keep it from them. I was a very imaginative child and so I was good at scaring myself with things that "weren't real." If I watched a Godzilla movie on Saturday morning television, I couldn't get to sleep for weeks because I would lie awake worrying that a kaiju was going to step on our house. If I read a scary comic book about a vampire attack, I'd lie awake fearing vampires. My parents, who were trying to protect me, would ban me from watching whatever it was that had scared me, hoping that the effect would fade. It turns out that the thing that would make the feelings of fear fade most quickly, though, would have been to allow me to watch the scary part repeatedly. I eventually learned this myself by obsessively re-reading that vampire comic book. Since then I've read the advice of various child psychologists saying that the re-watch gives the child both a feeling of mastering their fear and also desensitizes them to the specific trigger.

One last tip if you're dealing with a child who has been scared by something they saw in a movie: don't ever say that it's silly to be scared of what's "only a movie." It may feel to them like you're not taking their fear seriously, and they won't trust you enough to tell you when they are scared by something in real life.

It's not a bad idea to talk over their reactions to each film as they watch, anyway, even if they don't seem scared. You'll learn more about what they find affecting and what they like, which could help in choosing films to watch as a family in the future.

1: Harry Potter and the Sorcerer's Stone

Film Data

    Title: *Harry Potter and the Sorcerer's Stone*
             (Harry Potter and the Philosopher's Stone)
    Release Date: November 14, 2001
    Director: Chris Columbus
    Screenplay: Steve Kloves
    Producer: David Heyman
    USA Opening Weekend: $90,294,621
    Running Time: 2:39

Here it is, the film that started it all. If *Harry Potter and the Sorcerer's Stone* (as it was called in the USA) had flopped, we might never have seen the rest of the series. Given that the books were already record-breaking, off-the-charts successes and well on the way to a reputation as canonized literary classics on par with *Alice in Wonderland, Peter Pan* and *The Wizard of Oz,* Harry Potter would survive just fine in print if the films didn't pan out. If the movie was terrible, J.K. Rowling might decide never to license the boy wizard for the screen again.

Of course that is not what happened. The film was a smashing success at the box office and was enjoyed by both kids and adults. Roger Ebert praised the film effusively in his review, summing it up well: "A lot of things could have gone wrong, and none of them have: Chris Columbus' movie is an enchanting classic that does full justice to a story that was a daunting challenge."

The critics who didn't like it (we see you *New York Times, Rolling Stone...*) mostly seemed to complain that the filmmakers were only *so* faithful to the book so that—*cha-ching!*—the film would make lots of money. Huh? This makes about as much sense as Yogi Berra saying, "No one goes there anymore. It's too crowded."

My take: anyone who doesn't like Harry Potter simply because it's already "too popular" is dead inside. I dare any of these Grinches to actually sit and watch the film with a 10-year-old and see if their hearts don't grow two sizes by the end.

Casting Notes

If you've already read the section on Casting in the "Before You Watch" chapter, then you already know how Dan, Emma and Rupert became Harry, Hermione and Ron, how J.K. Rowling hand-picked Alan Rickman and Robbie Coltrane to be Snape and Hagrid, and even how Tom Felton slithered into the role of Draco Malfoy. But there are a few other fun casting decisions to talk about in *Sorcerer's Stone.*

John Hurt as Ollivander

What? *That's* John Hurt? Yes, the same John Hurt who died so memorably of the chest-burster in *Alien.* I'll be honest. Under his film make-up I never even realized who played Ollivander until I was researching for this book. Hurt was completely convincing as the 90-plus year old wand maker. His character also recurs in the later films (although in some, his scenes ended up being cut). When he died in 2017 of pancreatic cancer, hundreds of Potter fans raised their wands to him in tribute outside Ollivander's shop at Universal Studios.

Warwick Davis as Professor Flitwick

Warwick Davis gets a lot of work as short characters and creatures. His first big break in show biz was as an ewok in *Star Wars: Return of the Jedi.* His grandmother had heard about a casting call for people "under four feet tall" and took him—then 2'11"—where he got the gig as a background ewok. When actor Kenny Baker—who was set to play the lead ewok Princess Leia meets—fell ill, Davis stepped in. The leading role of Willow in the fantasy film of the same name was written specifically for him. The Harry Potter crew found multiple roles for him in the series, but in this film we'll see him as a goblin bank teller at Gringotts and as Charms teacher at Hogwarts, Professor Flitwick.

Zoë Wanamaker as Madame Hooch

Here's another member of the cast decorated by the Queen of England for her acting prowess, even though she was born in America. Wanamaker was raised in England and received her CBE after becoming a naturalized citizen of the UK. Her Madame Hooch is one of my favorite characters in the films. As tough but stylish flying instructor and Quidditch referee, Wanamaker's rendition of Madame Hooch gives off distinctly butch phys-ed teacher vibes to me. She wasn't brought back in later films, perhaps both because Hooch's character barely appears and because she spoke out about how bad she felt the pay was on the film. She told *The Daily Telegraph* in 2001, "If they want me for a second [film], they'll have to up their rates." She has also been outspoken in recent years about the pay gap between male and female actors.

What to Look For

This will be our first look at so many iconic places in the Harry Potter universe, from Privet Drive to Hogwarts. Here are some things to look for:

Number Four, Privet Drive

Privet Drive is the suburban street where orphaned Harry grows up, raised by his Aunt Petunia and her husband Vernon Dursley, bullied by his cousin Dudley, and made to work like Cinderella, doing housework and wearing hand-me-down clothes. The nearly identical houses represent the conformist lifestyle the Dursleys aspire to, where everything is neat and orderly and there is definitely no magic. The main feature of the house described in the books is the Cupboard Under the Stairs which serves as Harry's bedroom.

J.K Rowling wrote on Pottermore that she was astonished to visit the Number Four, Privet Drive film set and discover that, unwittingly, the set builders had recreated exactly a house she had lived in as a child—a house she hadn't even realized she was picturing. "Although [in the books] I describe the Dursleys' house as big and square... whenever I wrote about it I was unconsciously visualizing the second house I lived in as a child, which on the contrary was a rather small three bedroom house in the suburb of Winterbourne." Was it magic? "As I had never described my old home to the set designer, director or producer, this was yet another of the unsettling experiences that filming the Potter books has brought me."

Platform 9 3/4

To get to magic school, Harry is instructed to go to Platform 9 3/4 at King's Cross Station, which confuses the heck out of him of course, since there is a platform 9 and a platform 10... but no Platform

9.75 so far as he can tell. Harry, you're not alone—train stations can be incredibly confusing.

And London has a *lot* of train stations. Counting stops on the underground and the above-ground stations for the many, many different British rail companies—trains having been a huge part of the English economy since the 1800s—there are over 350 in London alone. King's Cross is at an intersection where multiple train stations meet. When I went to London in 2011 for a Harry Potter convention, I stayed overnight at a hostel about two blocks from King's Cross, so of course I walked over to see if I could find Platform 9 3/4 for myself.

What I found was that the cathedral-like station described in the books is more likely St. Pancras station across the street. I've also seen speculation that J.K. Rowling was picturing Euston Station. She has also said she picked King's Cross because her parents met on a train to Scotland from there—but that can't be accurate since the trains out of King's Cross don't go to Scotland (well, except for the Hogwarts Express). Maybe Jo's parents tell their meet-cute story that way though, or they use "King's Cross" to refer to the area of the station and not the specific station? It's fine, though, really—in fiction one combines elements of reality for fiction's sake. No one could have predicted that thousands of people would later go looking for the "real" King's Cross.

For the film, they decided to be literal to the name in the book and use King's Cross station itself, which simplifies things a lot.

Turns out I wasn't the only person who went looking for the spot where Harry pushed his luggage trolley through the wall to get to the magically hidden train platform. For several years after the film's success, there was even a luggage trolley "stuck" in the wall where Platform 9 3/4 would be. When I went looking for it in 2011, the station managers had just moved it outside the station to better accommodate the crowds of people trying to take pictures of themselves pushing it. Even going by there at nearly midnight, I still found a line of people waiting to take selfies. The tourist attraction only continued to grow, and after a renovation of the entire station was complete, an actual Platform 9 3/4 official Harry Potter gift shop opened in 2013.

Hogwarts Castle

There are several aspects of the castle described in the books that the filmmakers needed to emphasize, including the moving staircases, talking portraits lining the walls, and of course the Great Hall. The big dining hall is the setting for many important scenes throughout the whole series, so they couldn't just borrow a room in a castle or at Oxford for a couple of days. The Great Hall set was built in its entirety at Leavesden Studios. (Now that Leavesden is a tourist attraction all its own, you can visit it. Or just build your own out of Lego. Harry Potter Lego sets are a thing.) One thing to notice that is never mentioned in the films, but which can be seen in one corner of the Great Hall, is a large brass contraption with four upright glass tubes. This is the magical house points counter, which keeps track of which house has earned the most points toward the annual House Cup. In the books the counters are described as giant hourglasses and they are located in the Entrance Hall, not the Great Hall.

Easter Eggs

Like the House Point Counter seen in the Great Hall, many of the Easter eggs in the first film are nods to content in the books that a filmgoer might not be aware of, and some even those who read the books might not have known. Some might have been told to the filmmakers by J.K. Rowling while others they may have invented themselves.

What has Neville forgotten?

Neville Longbottom's grandmother sends him a gift by owl: a Remembrall, which is a small crystal ball that fills with red smoke whenever Neville's forgotten something. Neville is dismayed to see it turning red right away, but he can't remember what it is he's forgotten. Can you figure it out? Neville's the only student in the scene without his Hogwarts robes on.

Minerva McGonagall: Quidditch star

In the scene where Harry first learns to fly a broom, he goes racing off when Draco—in a bit of Slytherin mischief—picks up Neville's dropped Remembrall and chucks it into the sky. McGonagall is the head of Gryffindor House (Harry's dormitory) and after she sees him make a spectacular catch, she immediately recommends him for the position of Seeker on the Gryffindor Quidditch team. Harry is confused by the fact he seems to have such strong flying skills despite never having done it before, and Hermione points him to a Quidditch trophy plaque that has Harry's dad's name on it. In the shot of the plaque, you know who else's name appears? McGonagall's.

By the way, it's a small change, but in the books, Harry's father was said to be a chaser, not a seeker, on the Quidditch team.

Moviemaking Magic

The Harry Potter movies are definitely filmmaking wizardry of the highest order, bringing together cutting edge effects for the time with strong storytelling. *Sorcerer's Stone/Philosopher's Stone* set the template for all the films to come and is probably the most faithful adaptation of all seven books. Here are some of the bits of movie magic you might want to know about, even where sometimes things went wrong.

Emma's Lost Tooth

The kids were so young while filming the first installment that Emma lost one of her baby teeth right in the midst of filming. She had to be fitted with a fake tooth so she would look the same in all her scenes. What's a bit ironic here is that Hermione's character is described in the books as having rather prominent front teeth!

Neville's Teeth

Another actor who wore fake teeth was Matthew Lewis. In order to make Neville appear as nerdy as possible, not only did Lewis wear fake teeth, his ears were taped to protrude and he wore padding to make himself appear chubby.

Pranksters

Emma Watson told Katie Couric on the television documentary special "Behind the Magic," which aired shortly before the movie debuted, that she and Rupert would prank Dan by sticking signs to his back when he wasn't paying attention which said things like "Kick Me." "And people would kick him!" she said. "And he'd ask why are you laughing, what's so funny, and we'd just be like oh nothing, nothing."

David's Promise

Producer David Heyman promised Jo Rowling that he would be faithful to the book. "That was of paramount importance to me and to Steve Kloves when he was hired [as screenwriter]," Heyman says in the DVD extras from *Sorcerer's Stone*. Although Harvard-educated Heyman is English, and his Heyday Films production company is based in England, not Hollywood, which helped convince J.K. Rowling that he was the right steward for the film rights. After years of being an executive for Warner Brothers and United Artists, he had founded Heyday just a few years before acquiring the rights to Harry Potter. He would ultimately produce all eight Potter films (and then go on to *Fantastic Beasts and Where To Find Them*).

Double-Duty

Staying true to the books meant making two versions of the movie, one for the countries like the U.S. where the book had the word *Sorcerer* in the title, and one for those like the U.K. that had the word *Philosopher* in the title. Lines of dialogue were filmed both ways, and two completely separate edits of the film had to be made. Personally I think the audience in the United States would have done just fine without the extra-magical "Sorcerer" in the title, but Scholastic, the book publisher in the U.S. disagreed, and the result was a lot of extra work for the filmmakers. By the way, the "philosopher's stone" wasn't something J.K. Rowling invented. She used many elements of ancient magical lore and mythology, from holly wands to centaurs, and the philosopher's stone came from alchemy. In the book, and film, it is used as it would be in alchemical lore, to create the elixir of immortality.

Steve Kloves

American Steve Kloves was brought in to write the screenplay. Kloves had proved his deft hand at adaptation of novels for the screen with his work on Michael Chabon's *Wonder Boys,* which received scads of award nominations for Best Screenplay. In the wake of that success, Warner Brothers sent him a catalog of novels to be adapted and *Harry Potter and the Sorcerer's Stone* caught his eye. Ultimately he would serve as screenwriter for all but one of the Potter films (*Order of the Phoenix*).

He called writing the screenplay for *Sorcerer's Stone* "one of the most challenging things I've ever done." As he explained in the DVD extras, "To condense the book is extremely difficult. There's a certain amount of care you have to take in selecting which moments you want to be in the movie so that they will represent the entire book." He worked on the screenplay for two years and was a little surprised that nothing he wrote was challenged by the film crew. "What everyone [did] was take on the challenge of being faithful to the book." So if he wrote he needed flying brooms, ghosts, or a dark stone corridor, the filmmakers would just come up with a way to make it happen. He had extensive access to J.K. Rowling, as revealed in a terrific "conversation"/mutual interview Steve and she did in 2011 that you can find on YouTube. Ultimately, the author would come to trust Steve's instincts on the characters and a kind of collaboration formed as the writing of the future film scripts took place.

Hogwarts Castle

In the film Hogwarts looks a lot like a cathedral, with its flying buttresses and grand archways of ancient stone. Why? "It's supposed to be a thousand years old," explained designer Stuart Craig. And the only buildings we still have today that are that old are cathedrals. "That was the key that unlocked the whole thing." Of course although everything looks like ancient stone, and they laid actual York stone in the floor of the Great Hall to give footfalls the right sound, almost everything else you see in the castle, from brickwork and sculpture to oak beams... is actually plaster.

Owl Post

Although there are between 700 and 800 visual effects used in the film, including the ghosts, the troll, Fluffy, and the flying keys, most of the owls (about 80%) you see are real. The filmmakers trained owls to drop packages in the Great Hall owl post scene and then composited the shots of multiple owls together, augmented by some CGI owls in the background.

A Real School on Set

Because of labor laws for child actors, all the kids who worked on the film, including the stars, their stunt doubles and stand-ins, and the secondary role actors, had to receive three hours of actual schooling and study per day on set. They were technically allowed a "nine hour" workday, but that day included those three hours, plus time off for meals and breaks, resulting in only about four and a half hours of actual camera time.

* * *

Sorcerer's Stone Drinking Game:

Drink any time anyone waves their wand or does a spell.
Bonus drinks: Every time someone says the full name "Harry Potter."

* * *

Book Lore

This is the first of our sections of "Book Lore," tidbits from the books that explain elements of the films that were either glossed over or left unexplained, as well as some that were left out entirely. I've placed them before the plot recaps, but in some cases you'll want to watch the film first and then come back to "book lore" for more explanation.

The Mirror of Erised

When Harry first encounters the magical Mirror of Erised, the camera pans across what looks like some kind of runic engraving or lettering at the top, but the words don't look like English. But they are. It goes by too quickly in the film to be read, but it says "erised stra ehru oyt ube cafru oyt on wohsi"—which if read backwards, or in a mirror, says: "I show not your face, but your heart's desire."

The Headless Hunt

Another veteran Brit of stage and screen, Sir John Cleese plays the part of the Gryffindor House ghost, Sir Nicholas de Mimsy-Porpington, called "Nearly Headless Nick" by the students. "My application to join the Headless Hunt has once again been denied," he complains, when Percy asks how he's been. Hermione demands to know what his nickname means and he demonstrates that he was almost decapitated... but not quite. His head is still just barely attached. What he doesn't explain is his comment about the Headless Hunt—who or what is that? They are a band of decapitated ghosts who ride together on ghost horses, carrying their heads. Later in the films (Prisoner of Azkaban) we see a member of the Headless Hunt "crash through" a window on his horse, head in hand.

The Bloody Baron

Each of the Hogwarts Houses has a ghost. Another of them—this one from Slytherin house—is shown only in a brief cameo as the ghosts fly into the Great Hall. The Bloody Baron is presented in almost a comedic way, laughing while swooping down the Slytherin table, but in the books he is highly feared by the students and even the other ghosts: he is supposedly the only one who can keep Peeves the Poltergeist in line.

Peeves? Who's That?

Actor and "post-punk" comedian Rik Mayall played the part of Peeves, a particularly mischievous Hogwarts ghost (poltergeist), but in the end he was deemed unimportant to the plot and ended up on the cutting room floor. (Some DVDs have a deleted scene of him, though.)

Hagrid's Flying Motorcycle

In the opening sequence of the film, Hagrid first delivers orphaned baby Harry to the doorstep of the Dursleys on a flying motorcycle. What's not mentioned in the film is that this particular flying motorcycle actually belonged to Sirius Black, Harry's godfather, who was blamed for Harry's parents' deaths. When Hagrid returns 10 years later to rescue Harry from the Dursleys' clutches, essentially acting as Harry's "fairy godmother," he is actually standing in for Harry's magical godfather.

Plot Recap

"Yer a Wizard, Harry!"

The best thing about this being a first-in-series film is that when we meet Harry, he knows nothing of the wizarding world, and neither do we. So for the most part we get to learn stuff as Harry learns it. Unlike in a book, a film can't really pause to explain much, leaving the audience guessing about a lot of things while they are carried along by the action. That's fitting because that is pretty much how Harry gets dragged through his first couple of years in the wizarding world, often leading him to leap into trouble without full knowledge of what the heck is going on. (A big laugh line in a later movie has Harry's mentor say to him "You're probably wondering why I brought you here," and Harry replies, "Actually... after all these years, I just kind of go with it.")

Of course the first big revelation is that Harry is a wizard in the first place. J.K. Rowling packs a ton of tropes from fairy tales, mythology and fantasy classics into this tale. As I previously mentioned, Harry is Cinderella: an orphan forced to cook and clean for the family who took him in. But he is also Frodo: raised in mundane circumstances, inheritor of a magical legacy, thrust out into a larger world he is ignorant of in order to do battle with evil—while being advised by a good-natured yet conniving, grey-bearded wizard Gandalf/Dumbledore.

Wait, you want more parallels between Harry and Frodo? How about both have scars that hurt throughout their quests—Harry's on his forehead, which he was left with after Voldemort attacked him as a baby, Frodo on his shoulder, where he was struck by a Ringwraith. Both Harry and Frodo have faithful sidekicks (both of whom are coded as being from a lower economic class to the hero). Both are facing an evil wizard who spends time disembodied (Sauron stays that way, Voldemort doesn't) and who tempts them to join the dark side. Both end up traipsing around in the wilderness a lot before their final confrontation with evil, while carrying a piece of jewelry that could cause them to turn evil with enough exposure: Harry with the locket Horcrux and Frodo with the One Ring. (And in both cases our hero has to destroy the magical object in order to destroy the evil wizard.)

But let's not talk about the end. We're at the beginning. Harry's life with the Dursleys is miserable and they're getting ready to ship him off to some grim state-run school. In one deleted scene, his Aunt Petunia is shown dyeing one of his cousin's old school uniforms gray so Harry can wear it in the coming school year—you can also see her doing it in the background of one of the shots that made it into the film. Before that fate can befall him, Harry's "fairy godmother" arrives in the form of a half-giant on a flying motorcycle. Hagrid takes Harry off to start his life as a student at Hogwarts, the "best" (and apparently only) wizarding school in the U.K. Harry then has to go on the best back-to-school shopping spree ever, starting with a trip to his literal pile of gold at the goblin-run bank, Gringotts. (Hagrid also picks up a package for Headmaster Dumbledore while at the bank.) Pockets stuffed with galleons, our young hero then acquires his magic wand, as well as school uniform, spell books, quills and an owl. Owls are the closest thing to mobile phones in the wizarding world; they're used for sending (handwritten) texts.

In a move that will become typical of the adults around Harry throughout the series, Hagrid then hurries off (to deliver the package he picked up at the bank) without adequate explanation of what Harry is meant to do next. Luckily, Harry overhears Molly Weasley and she guides him on how to get onto the magical Platform 9 3/4 to catch the train to Hogwarts. On the train Harry becomes fast friends with her son Ron, who is Harry's age. They also meet Hermione Granger, who is a bossy know-it-all despite the fact she was Muggleborn and didn't grow up around magic. Having already read all their schoolbooks, Hermione is a super-useful character because anytime the audience needs to know something, she can just crack out a quote from *Hogwarts: A History*.

Among the things Harry learns early on is that he doesn't even know his *own* history, much less that of Hogwarts. His Muggle relatives told him that his parents were killed in a car crash. Harry finds out that they were in fact killed by the worst evil wizard in a century, a wizard so bad they just call him "You Know Who." Harry also learns the reason everyone in the wizarding world knows Harry's name is because Harry survived that attack and is therefore famous. "The Boy Who Lived" is an epithet that gets attached to Harry as a result. Harry's like, *whatever, I'm just trying to humbly muddle through life as an 11-year-old kid remarkably untraumatized by being locked in a closet for most of my childhood.*

One of the things Harry *is* explicitly told is that evil wizards—like You Know Who—are sorted into Slytherin House at Hogwarts. Harry soaks up this information along with the fact that a very snotty, stuck-up rich boy named Draco Malfoy insults his new friend Ron for being from a poor family. When they arrive at Hogwarts all the first years are sorted into the four Houses (dormitories) and Draco is sorted into Slytherin almost instantly. So when Harry's turn comes, he silently wishes *not Slytherin, not Slytherin...* and lo, he is put into Gryffindor, which was the House of his parents, and where Ron is also sorted. Hermione is also sent to Gryffindor, and Harry gains three other boys as dorm mates.

The film moves quickly into introducing Harry—and us—to his classes (and teachers) for the year, which include Potions, taught by an absolutely insufferable bastard known as Professor Severus Snape. Snape absolutely drips with disdain for Harry, who has no idea why Snape is such an utter pill. All he knows is that Snape is the head of Slytherin House, which is where all the evil wizards come from, right? So maybe he hates Harry because he hates goodness? (Remember, Harry is 11 and not really into nuanced thinking, yet.)

At this point Harry is ready to really begin his adventures, having acquired a best friend (Ron), a rival (Draco), an antagonist (Snape), a father figure (Dumbledore), and a nemesis (You Know Who, aka He Who Shall Not Be Named, aka Voldemort). Oh, yeah, and a source of exposition (Hermione).

Harry turns out to be an average student at best, though perhaps a bit more adept than his dorm mate Seamus Finnigan, whose fiery Irish personality lends an overly incendiary effect to his spells. But one thing Harry excels at right off the Beater's bat is flying a broom, which is the main skill needed for the wizarding sport of Quidditch. (There is intense competition among the Houses for the Quidditch cup.) Harry discovers his flying talent and lands a place on the Gryffindor team completely by accident because he's such a relentlessly good-hearted hero-type. You see, Draco flies off with Neville's dropped Remembrall and without a second thought, Harry flies after him trying to get it back. Draco flings it into the sky and Professor McGonagall witnesses Harry snatching it out of the air. Rather than giving him detention for being a reckless maniac, she takes him straight to Gryffindor's Quidditch Captain, Oliver Wood— a sixth year who is hunky in a champagne-supernova sort of way.

The two things to keep in mind about Hogwarts as we go along are 1) they don't teach common sense at this school, and 2) there are lots of *rules*.

Lots and lots of rules, and the students are very wary of getting caught breaking them, since it could mean losing House points, unpleasant detention with the creepy Mr. Filch, or—at worst— expulsion. Harry, Hermione, and Ron are on their way back to Gryffindor tower one evening when one of the Hogwarts mysteriously moving staircases deposits them at a third floor corridor that all students have been forbidden to enter. Mr. Filch's cat, Mrs. Norris, sees them and they fear they'll be caught, so they make a run for it and end up stumbling upon a rather gigantic three-headed dog. Whoopsie. No wonder students are forbidden to go to that area. But what's a dangerous beast like that doing in the school, anyway? Hermione points out it's sitting on a trap door. It's a guard dog. But what's it guarding?

Ron isn't too keen on Hermione at this point in the tale, and he's had about enough of her know-it-all-ness when she shows him up in Charms class with her vastly superior Wingardium Leviosa (levitation spell). On their way out of class he gripes to Harry and Seamus that she's "a nightmare. No wonder she hasn't got any friends." Hermione overhears him and rushes off to go cry by herself in the girls' lavatory. (Many crucial scenes in the series will take place in bathrooms. I'm sure there must be many thesis papers in literature written explaining why.)

She still hasn't turned up by that night's Halloween Feast, when turbaned, stuttering Professor Quirrell bursts into the Great Hall to raise the alarm that there is a troll in the dungeon. He promptly faints, and Dumbledore sends the students back to their dormitories for safety while he and the staff go to deal with the troll.

Harry realizes that Hermione didn't get the warning, and instead of telling someone in authority about it (because common sense is not something they've learned at Hogwarts, plus Harry's penchant for leaping into hero-type situations) he runs off to find her himself, taking Ron with him. Of course it turns out the troll has left the dungeon and has wandered into—you guessed it—the very bathroom where Hermione has been contemplating starting her own podcast called Loneliest Nerd in the World, or maybe Bookworms Need Friends, Too. The boys end up rescuing her from the troll and Ron even gets to use that levitation charm to take the troll out with the troll's own club. Nailed it!

A squad of teachers arrives immediately after, and Professor McGonagall demands that the boys explain why they aren't in their dormitory where they were explicitly sent. Before they can even try to explain, Hermione tells McGonagall that they aren't to blame: she is. "I went looking for the troll," she says. "I thought I could handle it, but I was wrong." (Gasp! Hermione admitted she was wrong? Don't get used to it; it never happens again.) "If Harry and Ron hadn't come looking for me, I'd probably be dead." McGonagall is shocked that the teacher's pet showed such terrible lack of judgment and deducts five points from Gryffindor. However she gives it back and more, five each to Harry and Ron, and from that moment forward the three of them are fast friends.

Harry meanwhile notices that Snape's trouser leg is torn and he's bleeding. What could he have been fighting if not the troll? Harry comes to the conclusion that the package Hagrid picked up at Gringotts must be the thing that the giant three-headed dog is guarding. Snape must have let the troll in as a diversion, but he got bitten trying to get past the dog to steal whatever it is. This makes logical sense to his 11-year-old brain—Hermione's, too. However it's time for the big Gryffindor-Slytherin Quidditch match so they'll have to deal with Snape later.

Quidditch is sort of like rugby if it were played on flying brooms, with a ball that's trying to maim the players. Partway through the match, Harry's broom starts trying to buck him off, which is definitely not usual. Hermione sees Snape staring at Harry and chanting spells under his breath. She determines if she can break his line of sight, she can stop him from hexing Harry's broom. She does it by sneaking under the stands where Snape is sitting with the other teachers and then lighting his robes on fire.

That does the trick, and proves to the Trio that Snape is out to get Harry. But what to do about it? They decide to enlist the help of Hagrid, and tell him about the hexed broom and about how Snape tried to get past the three-headed dog on Halloween. "Oh, you mean Fluffy?" Hagrid says. The three of them are horrified to find out this ravening beast has a name. Hagrid says they shouldn't be concerned about Fluffy and they shouldn't be concerned about Snape either. Oh and by the way, whatever Fluffy's guarding is strictly between Dumbledore and Nicholas Flamel! (Hagrid, you may have noticed, has a way of saying things he's not supposed to.)

This sets our Trio off on many trips to the library trying to figure out who Nicholas Flamel is. The name sounds familiar but even Hermione has no idea who he is. When she leaves for Christmas holidays, Harry and Ron—who have stayed behind at Hogwarts—decide to sneak into the Restricted Section of the library using a mysterious gift Harry gets for Christmas: a magical cloak that turns the wearer invisible. (Harry also gets other gifts, which is heartwarming and something he's never experienced before, him being a deprived orphan and all.) Harry's clandestine trip into the Restricted Section under his cloak doesn't find him anything about Nicholas Flamel, but after a close call with Mr. Filch, he does run into Snape threatening poor Professor Quirrell! Snape is clearly up to no good.

While detouring away from Snape, Harry then encounters a large, ornate, freestanding mirror. But this is no ordinary mirror. In it he sees not only his own reflection, but his parents! *They're standing right beside him, smiling at him approvingly!* It's the most amazing thing he's ever seen. He brings Ron to the mirror to show him, but what Ron sees is himself as Head Boy and Quidditch captain. This is the Mirror of Erised—which is Desire spelled backward—and it shows what a person wants most. Harry gets kind of addicted to sitting in front of the mirror and pining for his lost parents, until Dumbledore catches on, gives Harry a speech about love and socks, and then tells him he's moving the mirror where Harry can't find it. *Okay, fine.* (Heavy sigh.)

In the spring Hermione finally finds Nicholas Flamel in a book. Turns out he's the "only known maker of the Philosopher's Stone." (Or

"Sorcerer's Stone"... supposedly the dialogue was recorded with both versions for the different markets, but in my U.S. DVD she definitely says "Philosopher's.") This stone can turn any metal to pure gold and can be used to make the Elixir of Life, which grants immortality. (J.K. Rowling didn't make that part up: alchemists did.) The Trio conclude the stone must be what Fluffy's guarding and they go sneaking off that night to Hagrid's hut on the edge of the forest to try to pry more information out of him. They get a bit distracted by the fact that Hagrid is in the midst of hatching a contraband dragon egg. The hatchling promptly burns off half of Hagrid's beard and Hagrid names him Norbert. (An entire subplot about Norbert was cut from the film.)

When they get back to the castle, it turns out Draco has tattled on them: students are not supposed to be out after dark. The joke's on Draco, though, as he has to serve detention with the Trio since he, too, was out of bed. Rather than polish trophies with Mr. Filch, though, this time they are sent with Hagrid to look into some trouble in the forest. (Another Hogwarts rule forbids students from going into the forest... but I guess two wrongs make a right?) Draco and Harry are sent off together, and they find the corpse of a unicorn. Something has been drinking its blood. They meet a helpful Centaur of Exposition (since Hermione went off with Ron in another direction) who tells them "drinking the blood of a unicorn will keep you alive even if you are an inch from death... but it will be a cursed life." Harry asks, "But who would choose such a life?" Exposition Centaur points out that there is one person who would, and by the way, Harry Potter, do you know what's hidden at the school right now? Harry puts two and two together and concludes that Voldemort himself—that's right, You Know Who— is living off unicorn blood and would like nothing better than to get the Philosopher's Stone to make himself truly immortal. Snape, therefore, must be working for him and trying to return him to power.

And if Voldemort returns, surely he'll try to kill Harry, to finish the job he started when Harry was a baby!

"And here I've been worrying about my Potions final," says Ron.

Hermione, trying to be the voice of reason, reassures Harry that he's safe as long as Dumbledore's around, since Dumbledore was the one wizard Voldemort feared. The next day, though, Dumbledore is called to London on urgent business of some kind, and Harry's scar starts to hurt. The pain turns the wheels in Harry's head faster, and he realizes that it was just too weird that Hagrid always wanted a dragon and then one day someone just turns up with a dragon egg? The Trio find out that Hagrid told this stranger—whose face Hagrid never saw—far too much about Fluffy: most crucially Fluffy's weakness is that he falls asleep with just a bit of music.

They try to enlist the aid of Professor McGonagall, but she just scolds them to stay out of affairs that are not their business. Harry decides they have no choice but to take things into their own hands to prevent the stone from falling into Snape's. That night they sneak out to get past Fluffy only to find that Fluffy is already asleep—someone's beaten them to it. They forge on anyway. Fluffy was only the first line of defense. There are multiple traps and challenges to be surpassed, requiring each of their talents (although there's a logic puzzle for Hermione to solve in the book that didn't make it into the film). Before they can reach the final chamber, they have to play a giant game of wizard chess (Ron's specialty) and in order to win it, Ron, playing the part of a knight, has to sacrifice himself so Harry can go on ahead.

In the final chamber, Harry finds the Mirror of Erised. And staring into it, trying to figure out how it's hiding the stone, is the Hogwarts professor who is trying to get the stone for Voldemort. But it's not Snape. It's Quirrell.

"No... *Snape,* he was...!" Harry tries to insist, half to himself.

"He does seem the type, doesn't he?" says Quirrell, whose stutter and mousy demeanor are completely gone. Quirrell then goes into full villain gloating mode, explaining it was he who was trying to kill Harry during the Quidditch match, "Even with Snape muttering his little counter-curse." Quirrell confesses to letting the troll in on Halloween, as well. But he's stymied by the fact that he can see himself holding the stone in the mirror... but can't figure out how to get it. He forces Harry to look in the mirror and tell him what he sees. Harry lies and tells him he sees himself winning the House Cup, while what he actually sees is his own reflection winking and slipping the stone into his trouser pocket... And he feels the stone is actually there.

Quirrell then takes off his turban so his "master" can speak to Harry directly. And there at last is true evil, the face of Voldemort, sticking out of the back of Quirrell's head. Creepy AF.

You Know Who pulls out all the villain clichés of course, somehow (magically) knowing that Harry has the stone, and giving

Harry the option to join him rather than die horribly. Harry, of course, would rather die horribly and isn't shy about letting Voldemort know it. But Voldemort tempts him: "Would you like to see your mother and father again? Together, we can bring them back." If only Harry would give him that little ol' stone. Harry's tempted at that moment: after all, the Mirror is sitting right there and he can see his parents in it. But then Voldemort oversells the point, and tries to tell Harry there is no such thing as good and evil. It's totally the wrong thing to say to an 11-year-old with a hero complex who lacks a nuanced view. "You liar!" shouts Harry, and then Quirrell has to try to kill him to get the stone.

Spoiler: It doesn't work. When Quirrell tries to touch Harry, he turns to ash. Harry's kind of horrified, but, well, it worked, whatever it was...? Voldemort's disembodied soul flies off, and Harry passes out. When he wakes up in the hospital wing, Dumbledore is there to answer the final riddles: The reason Harry could get the stone out of the mirror is because only someone who wanted the stone, but not to use it, could retrieve it. And Quirrell/Voldemort couldn't stand Harry's touch because Harry's dying mother imbued his very skin with the power of... Love. Yeah, Love. There you go. (Later in the series we'll find out that's a massive oversimplification, but whatever, that's the explanation a traumatized 11-year-old gets.)

Then there's a celebratory Leaving Feast in the Great Hall where Dumbledore awards the House Cup to Slytherin for having accrued the most points on the year... except then he decides at the last second to award points to Harry, Ron and Hermione for their parts in defeating the Ultimate Evil... and oh, by the way, a few for Neville, too... and voila! Gryffindor wins! (Even my eight-year-old nephew found the sudden switcheroo a bit unfair to the Slytherin kids, but well, I guess we're not supposed to have sympathy for the Obvious Bad Guys, at least not from the point of view of an 11-year-old who lacks nuance.)

Final emotional coda: on the train platform, getting ready to send all the kids back to London, Hagrid gives Harry a photo album with pictures of Harry's dead parents in it. That's right. Harry's made friends, learned magic, and defeated evil, but being an orphan still sucks.

2: Harry Potter and the Chamber of Secrets

Film Data

    Title: Harry Potter and the Chamber of Secrets
    Release Date: November 15, 2002
    Director: Chris Columbus
    Screenplay: Steve Kloves
    Producer: David Heyman
    USA Opening Weekend: $88,357,488
    Running Time: 2:44

And now we move on to the sequel, *Harry Potter and the Chamber of Secrets*. For Movie No. 2 Chris Columbus returned as director and Steve Kloves as screenwriter. Hewing closely to the book and relying heavily on the Trio's luminous little faces had brought them a smash hit in the first installment, setting new box office records worldwide, so why mess with success?

Some at Warner Brothers worried that there would be a large drop-off in popularity from the first film because this time the media did not go into a frenzy over it. They needn't have worried. *Chamber* took in $88.4 million on its US opening weekend, putting it third on the all-time list (behind *Sorcerer's Stone* and *Spider-man*) and opened on a record-setting 8,515 screens at 3,682 theaters. In the UK, *Chamber* surpassed the box office records set by *Philosopher's Stone*. "There was no loud, thunderous buzz from the media," said Jeff Goldstein, executive vice president of Warner Brothers. "It was the public themselves. That's why it was difficult to project." By the end of the year, it was the second highest grossing film worldwide in 2002, behind only *Lord of the Rings: The Two Towers,* and number one in the U.S.

Many critics seemed to love it as much as the ticket-buying public. "The first movie was the setup, and this one is the payoff," wrote Roger Ebert. "[*Chamber*] leaves all of the explanations of wizardry behind and plunges quickly into an adventure that's darker and scarier than anything in the first... What a glorious movie." *The Telegraph* (UK) raved that it was "so very much better than its uninspired predecessor... sadder and more shadowy, too."

The detractors had similar complaints to the first go-round. In fact, the *LA Times*' Kenneth Turan wrote, "It's likely that whatever you thought of the first production—pro or con—you'll likely think of this one." As with the first, Turan felt *Chamber* was too slavish to the book and didn't become a truly great film on its own merits and he looked forward to Alfonso Cuaron putting his stamp on the third film, which was already in production.

Some reviewers felt the confrontations with scary monsters were *too* scary for kids, and some simply thought Dobby the House Elf was far too annoying. (Did filmmakers learn nothing from the debacle known as Jar Jar Binks?) But even the detractors were charmed by the new additions to the cast and liked the faster-paced action.

Casting Notes

Kenneth Branagh as Gilderoy Lockhart

Roger Ebert called master thespian Kenneth Branagh's casting as everyone's favorite narcissistic egomaniac, Gilderoy Lockhart, "delicious." Lockhart is an over-the-top character and Sir Kenneth clearly has a grand time hamming it up. Rowling writes with a bit of satire at all times and Lockhart's characterization is her way of spoofing on the shallowness of celebrity culture. Branagh himself was once Britain's "golden boy" after a run of successes for stage and screen (*Henry V, Hamlet*, etc.) in the early 1990s—complete with marrying his frequent co-star Emma Thompson, then having an affair with Helena Bonham Carter while filming/directing *Frankenstein*. You can basically see Branagh spoofing himself in the character, and it's grand fun.

Jason Isaacs as Lucius Malfoy

We already talked a bit about Isaacs being cast as Lucius in "Before You Watch," but there's more to tell, oh, yes. Isaacs was bitten hard by the Potter bug after his audition, when he sat down to read some as research and ended up sucked in. "I read the first four books in one sitting—you know—didn't wash, didn't eat, drove around with them on the steering wheel like a lunatic. I suddenly understood why my friends, who I'd thought were slightly backward, had been so addicted to these children's books." He reportedly looked at Tom Felton's portrayal of Draco in the first film, as well, and started digging into what kind of a bully Lucius would have to be to turn out a son like that. He drew on his own experiences growing up Jewish and being targeted for harassment at school and by neo-Nazi members of the National Front, getting into the heads of his tormentors and their anti-Semitic and white supremacist attitudes.

By all accounts he had a grand time playing haughty, uppercrust Lucius, not only in this film, but in the future ones in which Lucius appears. "All [Rowling's] characters are rounded," Isaacs told the Associated Press in 2011. "They all have destinies they are struggling with or bonds that they're breaking or internal challenges. There's no character in Potter which is off the shelf. These are delicious characters to play."

Mark Williams as Arthur Weasley
A veteran character actor who had been in *101 Dalmatians, Shakespeare in Love* and many other films, Mark Williams joined the cast as the patriarch of the ginger-haired Weasley clan. In many ways, Arthur Weasley is the counterweight to Lucius Malfoy and Williams plays him that way: warm, open, curious and quirky, versus Lucius's icy disdain.

Shirley Henderson as Moaning Myrtle
Shirley Henderson was perhaps a bit old (age 36) to play the part of a schoolgirl, except that as a ghost she would look, well, ghostly. Plus she's petite in size (5-foot-0), and her main identifying feature—her girlish voice—would serve her very well in the role. Henderson had been acting professionally or over a decade when she was cast, with such lines on her resume as films like *Trainspotting* and *Bridget Jones's Diary*. In the books Myrtle may come across as a mopey goth, but Henderson plays her to the hilt, every bit as campy and over-the-top as Branagh's turn as Lockhart.

Other new additions to the cast this film include three Hogwarts staff members: Gemma Jones as school nurse Madam Pomfrey, Miriam Margolyes as herbology teacher Professor Sprout and Sally Mortemore as librarian Madam Pince.

What to Look For

Growing Up Fast
What a difference a year makes. From the first moment Dan opens his mouth in his first scene, you realize his voice has dropped. In fact all three of the Trio (as well as Tom Felton as Draco) have gone from squeaky child voices to throaty tweens seemingly overnight.

Changes at Hogwarts
The basic layout of the castle has remained the same as in the first film, but we get to see a new area we haven't before: the "dungeons" near to the Slytherin common room. We see the same Gothic-architectural corridor when Harry and Ron attempt to spy on Draco and in a flashback of Tom Riddle's.

The Burrow
When Harry arrives at the Weasley home with Fred, George and Ron, he gets his first look at a wizarding house, and so do we! A pan is washing itself in the kitchen sink and a pair of knitting needles are working on a sweater. That's not CGI, by the way: the knitting needles are mechanical, built by the props department. Another thing Harry sees there is what looks like a grandfather clock but it doesn't tell time. Three hands with Ron, Fred and George's faces on them move to point at the word "Home." You can see they had been pointed at "Lost." Some of the other options visible are School, Quidditch, Dentist and Prison. (And the book tells us there is also a "Mortal Peril" setting.)

Tom Felton Ad-Lib
There's a scene where Harry is in disguise as Draco's goon, Goyle. He notices Harry-as-Goyle is still wearing glasses and when he demands to know why, Harry whips them off and mumbles, "Reading."

Draco, without missing a beat, sneers: "I didn't know you could read." This line was ad-libbed by Tom and it was too good a moment to cut!

Post-Credits Scene

At the very end of the credits there's a shot of the window at Flourish and Blott's bookstore, showing a new book by Gilderoy Lockhart entitled *Who Am I?* And featuring a photo of Lockhart looking around wonderingly while wearing a straitjacket. (He must have had a multi-book contract with his publisher?)

* * *

Chamber of Secrets Drinking Game:

Drink any time Gilderoy Lockhart brags,
exaggerates or lies about anything.
Bonus drinks: Every time a book is opened.

* * *

Book Lore

The Decree for the Reasonable Restriction of Underage Sorcery
This old wizarding law comes up in several of the installments, including this one. Back in 1875, the Ministry for Magic supposedly banned all magic use by those under age 17 when outside of school. This apparently doesn't include accidental magic (like that time Harry made the glass disappear from the reptile house in the zoo). In the first film Harry is told of the rule, but is not given its full name. When he is saying goodbye to Hagrid at the end of the year, Hagrid tells him if his cousin Dudley tries to bully him, he ought to threaten to give Dudley a pair of pig ears (to match the tail Hagrid gave him the first time they met). "But Hagrid, we're not allowed to do magic outside of school," Harry says. Hagrid points out that's true... but Dudley doesn't know that.

But how strictly is the decree enforced? And how is it monitored? If both the books and the movies are any indication, we see numerous examples of the decree being broken, such as when Hermione fixes Harry's glasses on Diagon Alley, and the book gives many other examples (such as we hear of Sirius using sticking charms as a teenager to decorate his bedroom). Are these just continuity errors or is this a law that is only selectively enforced, like jaywalking?

In the book version of *Chamber of Secrets*, when Dobby the House Elf levitates the pudding at No. 4 Privet Drive, the Ministry not only detects the charm, they send Harry an official warning of illegal use of a hover charm. They apparently can tell magic was used inside the house but they don't know by whom. This is how the Dursleys find out that Harry isn't allowed to use magic outside of school. In the film, they skip this, but by the third film, it appears the Dursleys learned of the rule somehow. It's a little baffling, then, that *Prisoner of Azkaban* opens with a shot of Harry practicing a spell ("Lumos Maxima!") under his bed covers.

Two installments later (*Order of the Phoenix*) Harry will actually get expelled from Hogwarts for casting a spell in front of Dudley (to save his life) and have to go to the Ministry for a hearing to appeal the expulsion, and in the final book and seventh movie (*Deathly Hallows Pt. 1*) a plot point will turn on the fact that until he turns 17, Harry still has "The Trace" on him, a Ministry tracking spell that detects Underage Sorcery. It would appear that although the consequences for breaking the law can be severe, the decree is very inconsistently applied... or possibly just inconsistently written.

Justin Finch-Fletchley

You never hear the full name of this Hufflepuff student in the film, but Justin Finch-Fletchley is a Muggleborn in Harry's year. Played by Edward Randell, Justin features in several deleted scenes, including one where he introduces himself to Harry right before the dueling incident, and another where he and some other Hufflepuffs are debating whether Harry is the Heir of Slytherin or not. Justin's character appears in the books many times, but this is the only film where his character is named or given any dialogue.

Plot Recap

"Spiders, why spiders? Why couldn't it be 'follow the butterflies?'"

The second installment in the Harry Potter series begins as is traditional: with Harry having spent the summer at the Dursley home, being treated like utter crap. At least now the Dursleys have been ever-so-slightly shamed into giving Harry "Dudley's second bedroom" to live in, instead of the cupboard under the stairs...? As the film opens, Harry is under orders to stay quiet in that room while Uncle Vernon entertains an important client and his wife, and he's moping quite a bit because he hasn't heard from Ron or Hermione all summer. He's not allowed to let Hedwig out specifically because he might "send messages to [his] freaky little friends." Shades of last summer, when the Dursleys did everything they could the keep Harry's Hogwarts letter from reaching him...

But it's not the Dursleys' fault that Ron and Hermione's letters haven't been reaching Harry. A two-foot-tall house elf named Dobby shows up to warn Harry not to go back to Hogwarts. House elves, it turns out, are the slaves of the wizarding world, and when they defy their masters they have to punish themselves. Also, they aren't allowed to wear clothes. Yeah, that sounds like we're getting into either *50 Shades of Grey* territory or maybe something much darker than that, but Dobby is mostly played for laughs, with the same kind of hapless comedy that made Jar Jar Binks an annoying waste of CGI in *Star Wars: The Phantom Menace.* Anyway, Dobby is being a very rebellious elf indeed by coming to warn Harry that Hogwarts will not be a safe place this year, and he's not above trying to take measures into his own hands, like intercepting Harry's mail all summer so that Harry would think no one liked him and maybe he wouldn't *want* to go back.

With logic like that, arguing with a house-elf is like arguing with a Flat-Earther, which is to say, there's really no arguing with Dobby. Harry tries anyway—or at least tries to stop Dobby from hitting himself with a lamp. (House elf logic means Dobby has to punish himself... Told you it didn't make much sense.) Dobby's behavior makes quite a ruckus, invoking Uncle Vernon's ire. It boils down to this: Harry is desperate to keep the elf quiet, and the elf is desperate to make sure Harry doesn't go back to Hogwarts, for Harry's own good.

Dobby uses elf magic to levitate the fancy dessert that Aunt Petunia made and drop it on the head of one of the dinner guests, knowing full well that this will get Harry grounded. The repercussions are swift. Vernon puts bars on Harry's window and locks on his door, and vows he'll stay there 'til he rots.

Fortunately, Harry's got friends with magical means at their disposal. Ron shows up with his twin brothers Fred and George in a flying car, they make a daring rescue of our hero, and take him back to The Burrow, the wonderfully ramshackle Weasley homestead. There Harry meets Ron's little sister, Ginny, who is so shocked to see Harry she runs away without even saying hello. (She's been talking nonstop about Harry all summer, apparently.) Soon enough, all of their Hogwarts letters arrive with their back-to-school shopping lists and Molly and Arthur gather the whole Weasley brood (including Ginny, their youngest, who will be going to Hogwarts for the first time) for the trip to Diagon Alley.

You may have wondered during the first movie why wizards send their kids to school via train. Don't they have magical ways of getting around? Well, flying brooms aren't really that practical, and a flying car isn't either—you can get into big trouble with the Misuse of Muggle Artifacts office of the Ministry, and if you're seen you could break the International Statute of Secrecy! So the Weasleys introduce Harry to something called Floo Powder, that lets you travel via a magical network connecting fireplaces all over Britain. Harry botches his first attempt and overshoots Diagon Alley, emerging soot-covered in a creepy curio shop.

Foreshadowing Alert: Several of the items Harry sees in the curio shop will become important four movies from now. These filmmakers were really planning ahead! (And so was J.K. Rowling.)

80

Turns out Harry has landed in Knockturn Alley, which is where the creepiest witches and wizards conduct their business. Hagrid comes to the rescue ("just looking for flesh-eating slug repellent") and drags him away from a very dodgy crowd.

* * *

Easter Egg: As Hagrid leads Harry out of Knockturn Alley, they pass a rack of second-hand books on sale in the alleyway. A full set of the hardcover editions of the Harry Potter books released up to that point can be glimpsed!

* * *

By the time Harry catches up with the Weasleys, they are in the bookshop Flourish and Blotts, where they meet two new characters. One is Draco's father, Lucius Malfoy, who says some snotty and condescending things to Mr. Weasley and the gang, insulting their secondhand textbooks and ratty clothes. (You can see little Draco trying to muster even close to the same level of disdain and he can't quite manage it. Like a lion cub trying to roar.)

The other newcomer is none other than the man who'll be filling the post at Hogwarts that was vacated when Professor Quirrell was turned to ash. Being professor of Defense Against the Dark Arts at Hogwarts is basically like being Spinal Tap's drummer. This year Dumbledore has hired the flamboyant adventurer and prolific author Gilderoy Lockhart to fill the post. Lockhart practices the wizarding version of gonzo journalism, gallivanting about the world dealing with werewolves, hags, ghouls and the like and then writing bestselling books about his experiences like *Travels with Trolls, Voyages with Vampires,* and *Year with the Yeti.* His latest book is an autobiography entitled, simply, *Magical Me.*

He's in Flourish and Blotts doing a book signing, and upon seeing Harry, he seizes the opportunity for a photo op. All the women and girls are quite taken in by the smarmy charm of the foppish Lockhart, but Harry can't wait to get away from the tireless self-promoter.

The next day the whole family heads off to King's Cross Station so everyone can catch the Hogwarts Express as usual. Family attention is focused on Ginny who is going for the first time, so no one notices when Harry and Ron are mysteriously blocked from going through the barrier at Platform 9 3/4. Of course, Harry being Harry, trying to get some adult in authority to fix the situation would never occur to him. He and Ron instead decide that, now that they have surely missed the train, their best course of action is to take Mr. Weasley's flying car all the way to Scotland.

Unfortunately when they get to Hogwarts they crash land in a murderous tree called the Whomping Willow, which nearly smashes them to bits, breaks Ron's wand, and does quite a lot of damage to the car, which ejects the boys and their luggage and then flees into the forest.

The boys are in deep trouble now, receiving not only a tongue-lashing from Snape and detention from McGonagall, but also a "howler"—a rather loud magically scolding letter from Molly that excoriates Ron in front of the whole school when owl post is delivered at breakfast. As if Ron didn't have enough trouble, what with having to fix his wand with Spell-o-tape (a joke on Sellotape, a brand of cellophane tape sold in the UK). Then it's off to classes, including re-potting baby mandrakes in Herbology, and their first Defense Against the Dark Arts class with their new professor, Gilderoy Lockhart. For a first lesson, Lockhart frees a cage full of cornish pixies who wreak utter havoc on the classroom. When he tries a spell to control them, it's not the slightest bit effective, and he bolts from the room, with a parting word to the Trio, "I'll just ask you three to nip them back into their cage, eh?" (Hermione, of course, is actually up to the task.)

I should say something more about those mandrakes. You can never tell when J.K. Rowling puts something in a book just to be a joke (like the vampire who seems very disappointed in his goblet of red wine) or if it's going to become important to the plot. This is one reason she had to be very closely in touch with the screenwriter and the director. Sometimes entire characters—like Peeves—end up cut. But those mandrakes. We're going to need them.

Of course a new school year means a new Quidditch season, and Wood, Harry and the rest of the team head out to the pitch for practice only to find the Slytherin team has beaten them to it. The snakes have shiny new brooms courtesy of the daddy of their shiny new Seeker: Draco. In the confrontation between the teams Draco calls Hermione the m-word. ("Mudblood" is an offensive term for Muggleborn witches and wizards used by the pureblood supremacists.) Ron, incensed that Draco would say such a thing to Hermione, tries to hex him, shouting "Eat Slugs!" Unfortunately because of his broken wand, the hex backfires, and Ron begins to vomit up slugs instead. Oh, magic is a cruel and ironic mistress sometimes.

Hagrid's the obvious choice to go to for help with a problem of the emetic nature. While Ron is purging, Hagrid exposits—in case it wasn't obvious—that purebloods like the Malfoys are awful and bear ill will toward Muggleborns. Got it.

* * *

"Fame is a fickle friend, Harry.
Celebrity is as celebrity does. Remember that."

* * *

Now, remember how the boys earned detention for their car escapade? Harry serves his with Professor Lockhart, helping him answer his fan mail and listening to Lockhart natter on with vacuous advice. After they've been at it for hours, though, Harry thinks he hears a creepy voice but he can't figure out where it's coming from. As he leaves Lockhart's office the voice starts to sound like Arlo Guthrie in "Alice's Restaurant." (It's saying "Kill! Kill!") Harry, being totally reckless about danger as usual, follows the voice through the corridors of the castle until he comes to a huge puddle of water, a bunch of spiders fleeing and a petrified cat. Oh, and also some graffiti on the wall that reads: "The Chamber of Secrets has been opened. Enemies of the heir... beware."

The fact that it's written in blood should be a bit concerning.

The cat is Filch's companion, Mrs. Norris, and Filch immediately blames Harry for her "murder" (although she's merely petrified). Now, you'd think that the first conclusion Filch would jump to is that this is a schoolboy prank—probably the work of the Weasley Twins. But no, he and everyone else take it all really seriously. "You'll be next, mudbloods!" Draco exults. Dumbledore sends everyone back to their dormitories for safety, "Except you three." (Apparently Dumbledore remembers the last time he sent everyone back to their dorms for safety, the Trio were, of course, immediately found taking on a mountain troll by themselves.)

The incident sends our three heroes into full on Scooby-Doo mode. As soon as they are out from under any adult supervision, they set themselves to solving the mystery of who the Heir of Slytherin could possibly be. Their number one suspect, of course, is Draco Malfoy. Hermione hatches a plan to brew Polyjuice Potion, which takes a month to make but will turn you into another person for an hour. With this they'll be able to impersonate Draco's inner circle.

Meanwhile: Quidditch. A big Gryffindor/Slytherin match, of course. You'd think that Harry's biggest concern in this game would be his rival Seeker (Malfoy) but no, this time a Bludger—a game ball that usually attacks players randomly to make the game exciting and dangerous—is tampered with to hone in on Harry alone. It breaks his arm, but it being Harry, he still catches the Golden Snitch (the fluttery little ball which means instant win for whichever team's Seeker gets it). Hermione destroys the rogue bludger (shouldn't that have been the referee's job?) but Lockhart tries to fix Harry's broken arm with a spell. Instead of mending the bones, though, the spell removes the bones from Harry's arm completely. Harry has to spend the night in the hospital wing, painfully regrowing them.

During the night Harry thinks he hears the "Kill! Kill!" voice again, but before he can go investigate, Dobby shows up. Harry learns that Dobby was (of course) behind him and Ron missing the train, and he was also (of course) behind the rogue bludger, all in the service of trying to get Harry to leave Hogwarts, because—as Dobby warned at the end of the summer—Hogwarts isn't safe anymore. And why does Dobby care whether Harry is somewhere safe or not? Turns out Dobby has a case of hero worship. "Dobby remembers how it was before Harry Potter triumphed over He Who Must Not Be Named! We house elves were treated like vermin, sir! Of course... Dobby is *still* treated like vermin..." Before he disappears using elf magic, Dobby lets slip that this isn't the first time the Chamber of Secrets has been opened.

Two seconds later Harry learns the same thing anyway, because Dumbledore and some other members of the staff carry in the latest victim of petrification: this time an annoying first-year named Colin Creevy who never goes anywhere without his camera and who *also* has a bad case of hero worship for Harry. He's still got the camera plastered to his face. Harry, while pretending to be asleep, overhears Dumbledore inform the staff that the Chamber of Secrets has been opened again, and that Hogwarts isn't safe.

That's right, this school, which has a murderous willow tree outside its gates, is surrounded by what's basically Mirkwood, and which has been known to be marauded by violent mountain trolls on occasion... *NOW* it isn't safe...??

Of course, far as we can tell, although the staff has been warned to keep everyone safe, Hermione, Ron and Harry have no trouble just wandering off to a secluded girls' lavatory to work on the Polyjuice potion. No one ever uses that bathroom because it's where the ghost known as Moaning Myrtle resides. Myrtle is a bit... high-strung.

The one step that Dumbledore takes to supposedly increase Preparedness for Danger is to let Professor Lockhart start a dueling club. Lockhart gathers the students in the Great Hall and, up on one of the tables, gives a demonstration of how wizard dueling works, using none other than Professor Snape as his "sporting" partner. "Don't worry! You'll still have your Potions Master when I'm through with him," Lockhart enthuses smarmily. When Snape nearly puts him through a wall with a powerful "Expelliarmus!" Lockhart decides students should do the next demonstration, and he calls on Harry and Ron.

"Weasley's wand causes devastation with the simplest of spells," Snape warns, and chooses Draco instead. Of course. A dramatic showdown by these rivals is just what the screenwriter ordered. Draco attacks Harry by conjuring a large cobra, which starts menacing a hapless Hufflepuff named Justin. Harry tells the snake to clear off, but—surprise!—Harry speaks snake. To everyone else in the room it sounds like he's goading the snake to attack Muggleborns because you know who else spoke snake? Salazar Slytherin. (Oh, and also You Know Who.) Harry doesn't even realize he's doing it when he speaks in Parseltongue and is a bit freaked out.

Not nearly as freaked out as everyone else, though. Now the whole school is convinced that he's the Heir of Slytherin.

Of course it's also Harry—walking by himself back to the dorm when he can't stand all the whispering behind his back in study hall—who discovers the next victims of petrification: the ghost Nearly

Headless Nick and Justin. Filch and McGonagall send Harry straight to Dumbledore's office, where Harry assumes he'll be expelled. There, while waiting for the headmaster, he has a chat with the Sorting Hat, which had almost put him in Slytherin... did the hat know something that Harry doesn't about himself? He also meets Fawkes, Dumbledore's pet phoenix, and learns—after Fawkes alarmingly bursts into flames—that phoenixes, well, they do that. Dumbledore also exposits that their tears have miraculous healing powers and they can carry very heavy loads. (At some future point we'll also learn that Fawkes gave two feathers to be made into wands. One is Harry's. The other is... you guessed it... You Know Who's.)

But the real reason Harry has been summoned to the headmaster's office is so Dumbledore—after assuring Harry that he doesn't believe the attacks are his doing—can ask Harry if he has *anything he'd like to tell him.* Harry probably wants to tell him Lockhart's a bumbling fool, Malfoy's a racist and there's a house elf trying to kill him in the name of saving him, but...? All joking aside, Dan does a great job of acting in this scene, while Harry starts to question his own sanity, but ultimately goes with his instincts to trust himself and his friends over anyone else. He tells Dumbledore, no, he's got nothing to say. Dumbledore is fine with that, and sends him on his way with a simple "off you go." (We never find out what Filch's reaction is to Harry not being expelled after all.)

Christmas break is approaching and the Polyjuice Potion is finally ready. Hermione plucked a hair off the robes of Millicent Bulstrode before she left for the holidays and Harry and Ron get hairs off Draco's two dim-witted goons, Crabbe and Goyle (as well as taking their uniforms). Up in Myrtle's bathroom, they each put their designated hairs into the potion and voila! Harry becomes Goyle, Ron becomes Crabbe, and Hermione... accidentally pulled a cat hair off Millicent's robe. Whoops.

The two boys go on without her. They're not even sure where the Slytherin Common Room is, but they run into Percy Weasley, a school prefect, patrolling the dungeon corridors. Before they can get into too much trouble or give themselves away, Draco shows up, demands to know what Percy is doing down there (Wait, what *is* Percy doing down there? In the book he's sneaking about with a girlfriend...) and hurries them away. A fairly hilarious scene ensues in the Slytherin common room where it turns out Harry and Ron are terrible actors, but they do learn that 1) Draco doesn't know who the Heir of Slytherin is, 2) the last time the Chamber was opened was 50 years ago, 3) a Muggleborn student died that time, 4) Draco is an entitled little twit. (Well, they already knew that.)

A few days later, Hermione's still laid up the hospital wing getting her accidental feline transformation reversed. The boys find another huge puddle of water on the floor. This time it doesn't lead to a petrified cat, ghost or student, but just to Moaning Myrtle's bathroom where—being the ultimate mopey goth that she is—Myrtle's flooded everything in a fit of pique because someone "threw a book at her" while she was "sitting in the U-bend thinking about Death." In other words, someone tried to flush a book down the toilet. Harry discovers it's a blank diary with the name Tom Marvolo Riddle on it. He takes it back upstairs and on a whim starts writing in it. The ink disappears and new words appear: magic! If he writes a question, Tom Riddle answers it. Harry asks about the Chamber of Secrets and finds himself sucked into a sepia-toned replay of an episode in Tom Riddle's life, 50 years earlier.

Tom is in Slytherin student robes, watching the body of a young woman being carried away. A young-looking Dumbledore appears, and Tom asks if the rumors are true. "If they close Hogwarts, I don't have a home to go to." He pleads with Dumbledore, if the person responsible for the attacks was caught, would the school remain open? Instead of answering, Dumbledore asks if there is anything Tom wishes to tell him?

Tom replies, exactly like Harry had when he was asked, no, there's nothing. And Dumbledore's reaction is the same, too: "Off you go."

Harry follows Tom down into the Slytherin area of the dungeons, then, and witnesses a confrontation between Tom and a young Hagrid (!) whom it appears Tom has been helping to keep something hidden. "I don't think you meant it to kill anyone but... The dead girl's parents will be here tomorrow," he says, threatening to turn Hagrid in. "The least Hogwarts can do is make sure the thing that killed her is slaughtered." Hagrid insists that it wasn't Aragog, that his pet didn't kill anyone. "Monsters don't make good pets, Hagrid," Tom warns, before he tries to kill a spider the size of a large cat. The spider escapes, but Hagrid doesn't. "They'll have your wand for this," Tom warns. "You'll be expelled."

And now you and Harry know why Hagrid doesn't have a wand (unless you count that pink umbrella he carries... and which he asked Harry back in the first film not to tell anyone about). Harry of course tells Ron and Hermione that Hagrid was the one who opened the Chamber of Secrets all those years ago, and Hermione thinks that can't possibly be right... Before they can investigate further, though, someone ransacks Harry's things in Gryffindor tower: The diary is the only thing taken.

It's not clear if they tell anyone about the ransacking, but the next day something happens that is so serious that even Quidditch is canceled. Hermione herself is found petrified near the library. She was holding a mirror in her hand. Apparently when it's just a supporting character like Justin who gets attacked, everything goes on as normal, but when it's a main character, *whoa,* then all of a sudden actual safety protocols are put in place: 6:00 p.m. curfew for all students. Teachers will escort students to lessons. No exceptions.

No sooner are these rules spoken by Professor McGonagall to the gathered Gryffindors than Harry makes himself an exception. They've got to go talk to Hagrid. If he let the monster loose last time, he'll at least know how the Heir is doing it, right? Time for the Invisibility Cloak to go into action!

Ron and he go down to Hagrid's hut to try to get some answers, but they have to hide again before he can tell them anything because Cornelius Fudge, the Minister for Magic himself, is there to arrest Hagrid and take him to Azkaban prison because obviously since he was blamed for the attacks 50 years ago, he must be blamed again now. Dumbledore seems powerless to stop the arrest. (It's unclear why the Minister for Magic is there alone to handle this, without even a member of Magical Law Enforcement to accompany him. Budget cuts?) To make matters worse, Lucius Malfoy shows up to tell Dumbledore that he and the other 11 governors of Hogwarts have decided it's time for Dumbledore to step down as headmaster. Dumbledore says he'll go, but that "help will always be given at Hogwarts to those who ask for it." Dumbledore seems to know Harry and Ron are there, and this message is for them. Perhaps admonishing Harry for not confiding in him earlier...?

Hagrid also has a message for the general air in the room before he goes off with Fudge: follow the spiders. Just like the spiders fleeing the scene of the first petrification, Harry and Ron see a line of them fleeing Hagrid's hut. Fun fact: Rupert is actually arachnophobic, so it was easy for him to act terrified in the next scene.

The boys follow the trail of small spiders all the way to the lair of Aragog, who is now a giant spider about the size of a Jeep Grand Cherokee. Also a fount of exposition. Aragog tells them that he is not the monster they're looking for. Hagrid's innocent and always was. The girl who died back in Riddle's day was killed in a bathroom while Aragog never saw any of Hogwarts other than the box Hagrid kept him in. What's attacking people at Hogwarts is "an ancient creature we spiders fear above all others." While they converse, thousands and thousands of spiders of varying sizes (from lapdog on up to horse-sized) are gathering around. Aragog helpfully explains that although the spiders wouldn't harm *Hagrid,* there's no way to keep them from attacking fresh meat like Ron and Harry. Run away! (See, I told you the forest was Mirkwood.)

Harry and Ron (and Hagrid's dog, Fang) are quickly surrounded and about to be eaten when they are rescued by none other than the flying Ford Anglia the boys had crashed into the Whomping Willow back in September. After a few close calls, the apparently sentient car gets them safely back to Hagrid's hut and then hurries back into its adopted arboreal habitat.

The boys go to visit Hermione, still petrified, in the hospital wing, because they just can't piece all the clues together on their own but maybe her mere presence will help them think. Harry realizes that she has a piece of paper crumpled in her hand, though! It turns out to be a page about the Basilisk. Guess what that is: an ancient creature that spiders fear and which is apparently a giant snake, which is why Harry can hear its voice! And it kills by looking you in the eye. Harry figures it out then: those who are petrified didn't actually look it directly in the eye, they only saw it through a camera, or through a ghost, or reflected in a puddle. Or in a mirror, like the one Hermione was carrying.

And Hermione wrote a word on the page as one last clue: Pipes. The basilisk has been getting around using the plumbing. Harry has one last brainstorm: the girl who was killed in a bathroom has to be Moaning Myrtle. Before they can go talk to Myrtle, though, they hear Professor McGonagall announcing that all students are to return to their dormitories, and all teachers are to head to the second floor. One guess where Harry and Ron go!

The Heir of Slytherin has written another message on the wall: *Her Skeleton will Lie in the Chamber Forever.* This time instead of being petrified, a student has been taken, and not just any student, but Ron's little sister, Ginny.

Snape and McGonagall are beautifully savage to Lockhart when he arrives. "Weren't you just saying last night that you've known all along where the entrance to the Chamber is?" Snape asks him. "That's settled then," McGonagall says. "After all, Gilderoy, your skills are legendary." Lockhart goes off to his office to "get ready" while the rest disperse, and Harry and Ron go to tell him about the basilisk.

What they find, though, is Lockhart packing to flee the castle. Lockhart unabashedly tells them "my books wouldn't sell half as well if people didn't think I'd done all those things [myself]!" He's a complete fraud. The only magic he's actually good at is memory charms. That's how he takes credit for the adventures and successes of others, by wiping their memories of what they'd done, and then putting the stories into his books. He picks up his wand to do the same to Ron and Harry of course, but they've got the drop on him, and they march him down to Moaning Myrtle's bathroom.

Myrtle tells them the night she died she heard a boy's voice speaking "a kind of made up language" (Parseltongue) and when she came out of the stall to tell him to get out of the girls' lavatory... she died. The last thing she saw was a pair of yellow eyes and she points them to the sink where she saw it. Why look, there's even a wee snake embossed on it! Harry speaks some Parseltongue to it and the entrance to the Chamber opens. This isn't the time to be wondering how Salazar Slytherin, a founder of Hogwarts who lived about 900 years before the introduction of indoor plumbing to Great Britain, could have created an entrance to the basilisk's chamber in a bathroom that couldn't have existed yet? Maybe some Heir of Slytherin did the remodeling?

When they get down to the Chamber the first thing they find is a shed snake skin 60 feet long. Oh my. Lockhart seizes Ron's wand and gloats: the world will know the tale of how the boys lost their minds when they saw Ginny's mangled body and Lockhart was too late to save them! But Ron's wand being what it is, the Obliviate spell backfires, wiping out Lockhart's memory of who he is, and starting a slight cave-in that separates Harry and Ron, blocking the tunnel with rubble. While Ron works on clearing the rubble, Harry runs on ahead to try to find Ginny.

He finds her unconscious and cold, and she's not alone. Tom Riddle is there! Tom explains that Ginny herself is the Heir of Slytherin. She's the one who opened the Chamber, painted the messages in blood, and petrified the cat. She had been writing in the diary and Tom would write her back. She was so seduced by Tom's ideas, eventually he could put her in a trance and make her do things. She tried to stop, even flushing the diary down the toilet that one time, but now... she'll die. He's been sucking the life force out of her, and once she's dead, he, who was just a memory preserved in a diary, will be *alive!*

* * *

"Lord Voldemort is my past, present, and future."

* * *

Meanwhile, though, Riddle has gained a new goal other than merely completing Salazar Slytherin's goal of purging the school of Muggleborns. He's learned all about Harry from Ginny—who you may remember was kind of obsessed with Harry even though she hadn't yet met him. Tom wants to know how infant Harry could have possibly defeated Voldemort, the most powerful wizard in the world.

Harry, meanwhile, wants to know why the heck Tom Riddle cares about Voldemort?

Oh. It's because Tom Marvolo Riddle *is* Lord Voldemort, as Tom shows Harry via a fiery anagram. Tom wasn't going to "keep my filthy Muggle father's name," so he came up with a new handle and then went on to terrorize the wizarding world... at least until about 11 years earlier when the attack on Harry backfired somehow. Thanks to the diary, Ginny, and current events, though, Lord Voldemort has a chance to give it another go.

By the way, Tom has picked up Harry's wand, so there isn't much Harry can do other than argue with him (which works about as well as arguing with idiots on Facebook). Harry does go on a bit of a rant about how great Dumbledore is, though, which summons Fawkes the phoenix. Cool. Fawkes brings Harry the Sorting Hat, which seems less than helpful—although the bird does peck out the basilisk's eyes so at least the giant snake won't be killing anyone with a stray look. So there's that. A sword magically appears in the Sorting Hat, though, which is a bit more helpful for fighting with—in fact, that seems to be the kind of "help" that Dumbledore was hinting at back at Hagrid's, which will be given at Hogwarts to "those who ask." An epic battle ensues, and eventually Harry does vanquish the creature, but not before being bitten. Another bad thing about basilisks: super-poisonous venom. He nearly collapses beside Ginny, a fang sticking out of his arm, being slowly overcome by the poison. She's nearly lifeless lying there on the stone, the diary clutched in one hand.

Tom Riddle gets in one more good gloat about what a silly little girl Ginny is, to be taken in by a book. Harry is dying, but that pisses him off, so he grabs the diary in one hand and the bloody basilisk fang in the other and stabs it into the pages. Ink pours like blood from the hole and Tom himself begins to come apart. Harry stabs the book over and over until Tom is gone, destroyed by the venom of the creature he had summoned. This, my friends, is what is known as a comeuppance.

Ginny wakes up the moment Tom is gone. "Oh, Harry," she confesses, "It was me, but I didn't mean it. Riddle made me do it."

Harry tells her it's all right, and that she should get herself back to Ron. He doesn't tell her that he's dying. He's basically planning to just expire right then and there. Fawkes comes swooping back then and he tells Fawkes he was brilliant, "but I just wasn't fast enough." Fawkes calls out like a bird of prey, which I suppose is Phoenix-speak for "cry me a river, Harry" or maybe "shut up, dumbass, didn't you listen to what Dumbledore said?" Fawkes in fact drops a few tears into Harry's wound and, of course! Dumbledore told Harry that phoenix tears have miraculous healing powers. Harry is saved, and Fawkes is strong enough to fly them all—Ron and Lockhart included—right out of the Chamber entirely and into the moonlit night.

Of course, the movie doesn't end there. We still have to have our celebratory emotional coda (like the medal ceremony at the end of *Star Wars: A New Hope*) and tie up our loose ends. The boys are next seen, still bedraggled from being in the Chamber, being dressed down by Dumbledore. Naturally, although they've broken more than enough school rules to get themselves expelled, he's giving them special awards for service to the school. He then sends Ron off to the Owlery to send release papers for Hagrid to Azkaban. Then he gives Harry a second chance to tell him if he has anything on his mind. This time Harry takes the hint and tells Dumbledore, *yes, I'm getting kind of freaked out by all the parallels between me and Tom Riddle aka Lord Voldemort.*

Dumbledore explains: when Voldemort was vanquished the night he tried to kill Harry as a baby, he must have unintentionally transferred some of his powers to Harry. Being a Parselmouth was one of them. He and Harry also seem to share "a certain disregard for the rules." But only intense loyalty to Dumbledore could have called Fawkes into the Chamber to aid him, and only a true Gryffindor could have pulled the sword of Godric Gryffindor from the Sorting Hat. Dumbledore's lesson is that Harry chose to be a Gryffindor and "it is not our abilities that prove who we truly are, it is our choices."

Then who should arrive at Dumbledore's office, livid at Dumbledore's return, but Lucius Malfoy. Dobby is with him and Harry realizes Dobby belongs to the Malfoys. Dobby has known the Chamber of Secrets would be opened since the summer, which means Lucius must have been behind the whole thing. Dumbledore tells Lucius to go stuff it. (I'm paraphrasing, obv. He actually says the governors came to their senses when Ginny was taken and several of them only signed the suspension papers for Dumbledore because Lucius had threatened to curse their families.) Dumbledore clearly also knows that Lucius was behind the whole thing, and gives him a subtle, veiled warning when Lucius pretends ignorance and asks who the culprit was. "Voldemort," Dumbledore says simply, holding up the diary. "And I do hope no more of [his] old school things find their way into innocent hands."

Lucius smacks Dobby a few times on his way out. Harry has seen quite enough, and he's not into veiled or subtle. He asks Dumbledore for the diary, chases down Lucius, and tells him he forgot something. He hands the diary to Lucius, who again pretends ignorance. "I don't know what you're talking about."

"Oh, I think you do, sir." Harry replies. "You slipped it into Ginny Weasley's cauldron that day in Diagon Alley." In the bookshop, when Lucius was disparaging the secondhand textbooks the Weasleys were buying. Lucius now thrusts the ruined diary into Dobby's hands and turns to go. Harry urges Dobby to open it.

Inside the pages is a sock. "Master has presented Dobby with clothes!" Dobby exclaims. "Dobby is free!" Yep, the difference between eternal slavery and freedom in the wizarding world all stands on a technicality. Lucius is so incensed he draws his wand and starts to curse Harry. "Avada—!" He gets no farther, though, because Dobby blasts him with his own magic. Take that, you pompous, evil viper.

Lastly, we have the restoration of the status quo: the baby mandrakes that were planted in act one have finally grown up enough to make the anti-petrification cure, and so Hermione and all the other victims of the basilisk are revived in time for a feast in the Great Hall and the announcement by Dumbledore that "as a treat" all exams are canceled! (Hermione is of course crushed by this news.) Plus, Hagrid's back! Cue the hugs and applause!

3: Harry Potter and the Prisoner of Azkaban

Film Data

Title: Harry Potter and the Prisoner of Azkaban
Release Date: June 4, 2004
Director: Alfonso Cuarón
Screenplay: Steve Kloves
Producers: David Heyman, Chris Columbus, and
          Mark Radcliffe
USA Opening Weekend: $93,687,367
Running Time: 2:22

Year Three is here, and Chris Columbus moves to the producer's chair and installs Alfonso Cuarón to direct Harry's transition into his teenage years. Film critics the world over, many of whom felt Columbus was too much of a bland "corporate sentimentalist" and only relied on the books so much because he lacked imagination(??), rejoiced. In general critics felt that this was the best of the Potter films yet because of directorial flourishes Cuarón brought to the adaptation and the increasingly nuanced performances coming from Dan, Emma and Rupert.

As the *LA Times* wrote, "One of the benefits of Cuarón's direction, his expertise with younger actors, means that the constant determination and occasional fury exhibited by the characters, especially Harry and Hermione, are completely convincing." Harry is 13 now, the equivalent of an American eighth-grader, and the films recognize that while Harry retains an innocent, noble-hearted core, he has, as Roger Ebert put it in his review, "developed an edge."

So has the plot itself, darker than in the previous film, which is saying something given that this is the first film in which some aspect of Voldemort himself doesn't directly confront Harry. From *The Atlantic*: "Cuarón's *Prisoner of Azkaban*, while a touch less faithful to the details of Rowling's oeuvre, captures far better its mood, the constant sense of wondrous discovery and lurking danger."

This time instead of learning more about the Dark Lord, we find out much more about the previous generation: Harry's parents and their friends who were destroyed by their fight against Voldemort. Harry's simplistic picture of his father as a freedom fighter begins to grow more detailed while he grapples with new knowledge about his parents' relationships and rivalries. "Happily, the film's young leads are up to this delicate task. Daniel Radcliffe may not be quite ready for Hamlet yet, but he carries off an air of worried introspection with assurance," reads the review in the *Telegraph* (U.K.). "Rupert Grint's

Cecilia Tan

Ron Weasley is as much loyal friend as mere comic foil. And Emma Watson pulls off a good trick—Hermione Grainger (sic) evolves from irritating swot into a rigorously bright if impatient young woman."

Casting Notes

Gary Oldman as Sirius Black

The latest in the cast's long line of decorated legendary thespians, Oldman plays the part of rebellious and battle-scarred Sirius Black here with a somewhat manic, dangerous edge. This is fitting as we, and Harry, are supposed to think he's a murderer and the man who told Voldemort where to find Lily and James (his best friend) in order to kill them. Rowling writes Sirius as sort of a punk, describing him as a leather-jacketed rebel; indeed, he would have been 16 years old when the Sex Pistols hit the UK punk scene. How interesting that one of Oldman's first movie roles was to play Sid Vicious in the 1985 biopic *Sid & Nancy*

Emma Thompson as Sybil Trelawney

If you look at Emma Thompson's résumé and compare it to that of ex-husband Kenneth Branagh, who played Gilderoy Lockhart in the previous Potter film, you might notice that she's actually done far more than him and been even more highly lauded. (In 2018 she was appointed a Dame Commander of the British Empire, one step above Branagh's Knight Bachelor in the British orders of chivalry.) In this film she gets to flex her comedic muscles as the hapless professor of Divination, Sybil Trelawney, who wears such thick glasses her eyes appear hugely magnified. "These parts are very rich and fun to play," she told *USA Today*. In a later Potter film, her sister Sophie will be employed in the role of Ministry official Mafalda Hopkirk.

David Thewlis as Remus Lupin

In 2007, after the final Harry Potter book was released, J.K. Rowling told the world that Albus Dumbledore was gay. David Thewlis reportedly expressed surprise. "I always thought [Lupin] was the gay one," he told *CityNews* Toronto. Rowling has said she had intended lycanthropy—a disease that inspires fear, loathing and discrimination that those who suffer from it don't deserve—to be a kind of wizarding stand-in for AIDS, but that the metaphor was supposed to end there. Thewlis and director Alfonso Cuarón interpreted it a bit more literally, conceiving of Professor Lupin "like a gay junkie."

Michael Gambon as Albus Dumbledore

Richard Harris, who played the role of Dumbledore in the first two films, passed away just before the second film's release, requiring a re-cast. Michael Gambon took over the role just at the point in the story where Dumbledore's motives and methods start to become more questionable. Gambon embraces Dumbledore's wily complexity, preserving his whimsical side while adding an inscrutability that serves Dumbledore's hidden motives well.

Lenny Henry as Shrunken Head

Here's another decorated actor, Lenny Henry, CBE, but can you even say he's "cast" in this movie? He's the voice of a shrunken head puppet created for the film that does not exist in the books. When Harry takes the Knight Bus, the head is a rear-view mirror ornament which gives pun-laden commentary throughout the scenes in a "funny" Jamaican accent. If this was an attempt to "diversify" the cast, it was a poor one. Henry has criticized British television and movies for being too white. In a speech to the Royal Television Society in 2013 he decried the state of roles for non-white actors: "When you can cast an Asian girl, and she is not playing the victim of an arranged marriage, or cast a bloke with dreadlocks not playing a drug dealer, then we will have something to work on." Lenny Henry deserved better than this.

What to Look For

Deviled Easter Egg

There is a shot right after the Opening Feast when all the Gryffindors are heading back to their dormitory on the moving staircases. The walls are covered with portraits, of course. As Seamus is trying to get the Fat Lady to open the portrait door, on the lower right one of the portraits is of none other than Lord Voldemort himself, who hasn't even truly appeared in the series yet!

Changes At Hogwarts

The courtyard at the main entrance now has a fountain we haven't seen before, but more conspicuous is there is now a huge pendulum swinging back and forth in the doorway from a gigantic clock overhead. Is that safe? No, it's foreshadowing.

What Happened to Professor Flitwick?

Warwick Davis, who played Professor Flitwick in *Sorcerer's Stone*, is credited in this film just as "wizard," for playing the part of the choirmaster. The producers wanted to keep him involved even though Flitwick wasn't in the script. In later films they decided they liked the look of the choirmaster better than the original gray-haired and heavily-makeup dependent Flitwick, so they just changed the name of the character to Professor Flitwick. Maybe the professor had an accident with an aging potion or something.

Hermione Punches Draco

Tom Felton told the audience at Salt Lake City Comic Con that in the scene where Hermione punches Draco in the face, the punch wasn't real—there was no actual contact, it was just staged to look like there was. But a few months before the shooting of the scene, they were rehearsing, and "I went up to her in the kids' play area, just mucking around. At the time, it was written as a slap, and I said, 'So we're gonna do the slap. Let's work on it now and make sure it looks really professional and looks very realistic.' She was like, 'Okay.' And she just slapped me across the face!" The punch/slap is canonical, by the way. It's in the book.

* * *

Prisoner of Azkaban Drinking Game:

Drink whenever something (bird, hippogriff, animated parchment, etc) or someone (usually, but not always, Harry...) flies through the air. Bonus drinks: Any time someone compares Harry to one of his parents.

* * *

Book Lore

Snape's history with the Marauders, Patronuses and more

A lot of stuff is going on in the ending of this book—so much that the audience may get left behind in the rush of revelations. In the final act of *Prisoner of Azkaban,* there is a confrontation among Snape, the Trio, Professor Lupin, Sirius Black and eventually Peter Pettigrew. That is a lot of players to be keeping track of, especially since each of them seems to have their own motive. They also each know far more about each other than Harry does—and far more than the audience does. Although we learn a lot about what the connections are between Sirius, Remus, Peter and Snape, the movie never comes around to explaining even a fraction of what is in the book.

So if you're wondering why on Earth Snape would say "Revenge is sweet!" when he catches Sirius, or why Harry sees a glowing stag protecting him from the Dementors, or how Professor Lupin seems to know all about how to work the Marauders Map, or how Sirius knows that Peter Pettigrew is disguised as a rat... you could just read the book. Or you could keep reading right now.

First is one simple fix that could have been inserted with a line of dialogue: the Patronus Charm doesn't only create a glowing shield of light—when performed most powerfully it can create a kind of avatar that takes the form of an animal. The animal is an expression of something inside the spellcaster, often symbolic of what makes that person happiest. Harry's takes the form of a stag, but we need to know more about James before we can understand why.

Harry's parents, James and Lily, met at Hogwarts. James was part of a gang of four Gryffindors who called themselves the Marauders: himself, Remus, Sirius and Peter. Sirius was such a rebel against his Slytherin family that he got himself sorted into Gryffindor, and the four of them got into plenty of trouble together. They were also powerful wizards who not only created the Marauders Map to aid them in their various schoolboy endeavors, the three who weren't werewolves also secretly became Animagi. It's implied they did this in a kind of solidarity with Remus. As we learn in the film, Sirius can turn into a big black dog, and Peter into a rat. What they don't tell you is that James could turn into a stag—and that's the form Harry's Patronus takes. As it reads on the map, the names are Messrs. Moony, Wormtail, Padfoot and Prongs—Lupin (werewolf), Peter (rat), Sirius (dog) and James (stag).

So, what's that all got to do with Snape? Severus Snape is the same age as the Marauders. When he catches Harry sneaking around in the middle of the night, he tells him he's "just like his father. Arrogant, strutting about the castle." Harry denies that he's arrogant or strutting, but how does he know what James was like? James probably *did* strut about the castle given that he had a map that let him sneak out with impunity. But what does Snape have against Sirius? What is his "revenge"? That has to do with a dangerous prank Sirius played on him.

Lupin, in the film, says Dumbledore has "already done so much" for him. That goes all the way back into his school days. Dumbledore, who was headmaster by then, planted the Whomping Willow to hide the secret passage to the Shrieking Shack, and built the shack to be an impenetrable safe space where Lupin could go once a month for his werewolf transformation. The reason the Willow doesn't attack our heroes on their way out of the passage the way it did on their way in is that there is a way to make it stop—pressing a spot on one root.

When they were students at Hogwarts, Sirius told Snape how to stop the Willow, knowing that Snape's curiosity would get the better of him. Snape then went into the passageway not knowing that a deadly werewolf, the transformed Remus, would kill him if he reached the Shack. James saved Snape's life by dragging him out of there. This is how Snape knows that Lupin is a werewolf, and the incident only made Snape hate all the Marauders even more than before.

Plot Recap

"A child's voice, however honest and true, is meaningless
to those who've forgotten how to listen."

Here we are again my friends, for the start of Harry Potter's hormonal teenage years and Year Three at Hogwarts. We open, as is traditional, with Harry having spent a miserable summer living with his Muggle relatives. This time Vernon's sister Marge has come to visit, and when she goads Harry with disparaging comments about his dead parents, Harry's instinctive magic goes into action, inflating her like a parade balloon and sending her floating out across the Surrey sky. Hilarious as this is to us (and maybe ever-so-slightly to him), Harry is a teenage rage-ball now, and he grabs his trunk and wand and gets himself away from that terrible house. Unfortunately, this means running off without getting a permission slip signed by Uncle Vernon, but screw that.

Harry doesn't really know where he's going, and as he gets farther from No. 4 Privet Drive, his rage cools. Just as it's dawning on him that it's now the middle of the night and he's not sure what to do next, he thinks he sees a huge black dog growling at him from the bushes. As he draws his wand to deal with the threat, though, he's nearly run down by a triple decker bus—yes, triple—which turns out to be the Knight Bus, "emergency transport for the stranded witch or wizard." Like many forms of magical transportation, the Knight Bus is a wacky, harrowing ride, but it does take him to The Leaky Cauldron. While on the bus, Harry sees the conductor reading a copy of *The Daily Prophet*. The front-page story is about the murderer Sirius Black who has just escaped from Azkaban (wizarding Alcatraz).

* * *

Easter Egg: In the establishing panning shot of the Leaky Cauldron interior, a wizard in the foreground is magically stirring his tea and reading a book. The book is Stephen Hawking's *A Brief History of Time*. This is a double Easter egg, though, as the wizard is played by Ian Brown, front man of the rock band Stone Roses.

* * *

At the Leaky Cauldron, Harry is welcomed by none other than Cornelius Fudge, the Minister for Magic himself, who tells him his inflated aunt has been located, deflated, and her "memory modified," so "No harm done!" Fudge seems unusually jaunty and warm to Harry—or maybe it's just that the previous time Harry saw him was when Fudge had showed up to drag Hagrid off to Azkaban, which didn't leave a good impression.

"But Minister, I broke the law," Harry says. Fudge laughs it off. "Oh, come now, Harry, the Ministry doesn't send people to Azkaban for blowing up their Aunts!" However, the Minister does scold Harry a little for running off—very irresponsible, given that there is "a killer on the loose."

"What's he got to do with me?" Harry wants to know.

"Nothing, of course!" says the Minister. Yeah, right.

Next morning, it's time to go off to Hogwarts. Hermione and Ron turn up at the Leaky, fighting like an old couple over the fact that her cat (half-kneazle, actually) keeps chasing Ron's rat around. (Hogwarts students are allowed an owl, a toad, a rat or a cat.) The rest of the Weasleys soon follow, and Mr. Weasley takes Harry aside to tell him something the Ministry doesn't want him to know: "You are in grave danger."

What, again?

Arthur tells Harry a crucial piece that Fudge did not: Black is undoubtedly coming to try to kill Harry (!) to finish off the job that his master, You Know Who, failed to accomplish. "Promise me you won't go looking for Black," Mr. Weasley begs.

"But why would I want to go looking for someone who wants to kill me?" Harry asks. And as with so many other communications with adults in the wizarding world, Harry gets no answer. (Apparently Harry hasn't figured out what everyone else in the story has: he's the hero.)

On the train to Hogwarts, the Trio get into a train compartment with a man asleep under his coat—apparently a new Hogwarts professor—and Harry confides to the others that Sirius is coming after him. Before they can talk much about it, the train comes to a mysterious stop in the pouring rain on a bridge across a chasm, the lights go out, and the windows begin to ice up ominously.

And then a dark-robed ethereal creature, scary AF, comes after Harry and starts sucking the life force right out of him. Harry succumbs to unconsciousness as he hears a woman's screams (the screams of his dying mother). The sleeping professor suddenly wakes up and drives the creature away with a brilliant light from his wand. When Harry comes to, the professor gives him a piece of chocolate, which he says will help him recover from the attack. Only Harry was directly attacked and passed out, though Ron says he felt like he was never going to be able to feel happy again. The professor explains the creature was a Dementor, a guard from Azkaban, searching for Sirius Black.

At the Opening Feast, he is introduced as Professor R.J. (Remus) Lupin, this year's new Defense Against the Dark Arts teacher. (When everyone gives the new professor a rousing round of applause, Snape, seated right next to Lupin, can be seen clapping exactly twice with zero enthusiasm.) In other announcements, Hagrid will now be teaching Care of Magical Creatures—oh and by the way, the Dementors are going to stick around all year to "guard" the school until Sirius Black is captured. "Dementors are vicious creatures. They will not distinguish between the one they hunt and one who gets in their way."

Great. So just when our main characters are entering their hormonal teenage mood swing phase, a bunch of Grim-Reaper types that literally embody depression are going to be hovering overhead.

Next comes the portion of every school year where we meet our new teachers and class subjects. Harry, Ron and Hermione are taking Divination together, taught by the myopic, hippie-dippy Professor Trelawney. Hermione is quickly convinced that Trelawney (and the entire subject of Divination) is rubbish. But Ron gamely tries to read Harry's tea leaves. They form into the shape of a menacing black dog—like the one he saw on the roadside in Surrey?—which is apparently a bad omen known as The Grim.

Next is Magical Creatures with Hagrid, which features a book that bites Neville and some disparaging comments by Draco that Harry is just too much of a rage-ball to let pass. Draco loves to taunt Harry about "fainting at the sight" of the Dementors. The day's lesson turns out to be to introduce the class to a hippogriff named Buckbeak. Half-horse, half eagle, hippogriffs are fierce and easily offended, and, as Hagrid explains, offending a hippogriff might be "the last thing you'll ever do." Of course Harry ends up being the one to touch the hippogriff (you have to be polite and bow first) and before he knows it, Hagrid has planted him on Buckbeak's back and sent him on unexpected flight around the lake and castle.

Of course when they get back, Draco, not impressed at all, marches right up to the beast and gets himself kicked by the hippogriff and has to be taken to the hospital wing. In the next scene, a study session in the Great Hall—as the ghosts of the Headless Hunt ride through—Draco can be heard telling Pansy Parkinson that he could have lost his arm and he "couldn't possibly do any homework for weeks." (He appears to be fine, just a bit bandaged...) No one is getting much studying done anyway, since Seamus bursts in with a copy of the *Daily Prophet* reporting that Sirius Black has been sighted not far from Hogwarts.

* * *

"This class is ridiculous."

* * *

Next up in the lesson plans: Defense Against the Dark Arts. Professor Lupin has a wardrobe set up with a boggart in it. As each student faces it, the boggart turns into whatever that person fears most. The spell to counteract the boggart is "Riddikulus!"—picture the boggart in the most ridiculous circumstance and laugh your fears away. Neville sees Professor Snape... and with some helpful suggestions from Professor Lupin, pictures Snape wearing Neville's grandmother's clothes and hat. Ron sees a spider... wearing roller skates. Parvati Patil sees a giant cobra turn into a clown. (The clown is pretty terrifying, too, actually...)

When it is Harry's turn, what comes out of the cabinet is a Dementor, and Harry freezes, unable to defend himself or react. Professor Lupin jumps between them and the Dementor disappears, replaced by a moonlit sky. Harry is going to need some remedial lessons, it would seem.

Now, remember that permission slip Harry didn't get signed before he ran away from No. 4 Privet Drive? It was to allow third-year students to visit Hogsmeade Village, the charming wizarding town not far from Hogwarts Castle. It's just as well Harry can't go, since while all his friends go off to buy candy and drink butterbeer, Harry gets to have an important talk with Professor Lupin about why the boggart became a Dementor.

"What you fear most is fear itself," Lupin tells him. Dementors force you to relive your worst memories and feed off your pain. Harry tells him he thinks he heard his mother's death screams. What Harry doesn't know is that Professor Lupin was a good friend of his mother's. Lupin gently breaks the news that he knew both Lily and James and it's clear his fondness for them belongs to Harry now, as well.

When Ron and Hermione get back, they're full of tales of the village, including Honeydukes candy shop and the Shrieking Shack, the most haunted building in Britain. But trouble is afoot right in Hogwarts; Sirius Black got in somehow, despite Dementors at every gate, and slashed up the Fat Lady's painting on the entrance to Gryffindor tower. Students spend the night in the Great Hall while the castle is searched. Harry, being the typical insomniac eavesdropper that the plot requires, overhears Snape and Dumbledore talking. Snape doesn't trust someone on the staff and wants to warn Harry. Dumbledore says nah.

When we next enter the Defense Against the Dark Arts classroom, Professor Lupin is not there, but Professor Snape is acting as substitute teacher. He gives no explanation other than to say Lupin is unable to teach at this time, and immediately begins teaching them about werewolves. He even assigns homework over the weekend of an essay on how to recognize one. Which is rough, since it's Quidditch time!

Even rougher is the fact that during the match, Harry gets flat out attacked by Dementors. He once again relives the moment of his mother's death while falling from his broom hundreds of feet in the air. Oh, and the broom gets destroyed by the Whomping Willow. Ouch.

The next day Professor Lupin is back, and Harry and he go for a stroll in the woods (but not the forbidden part of the forest, I suppose). Lupin tells him Harry's more strongly affected by the Dementors because he's had some truly terrible experiences and the other students really haven't. "You are not weak. There are true horrors in your past." He promises he'll teach Harry a way to fight the Dementors, but after the holidays. "For now, I need to rest."

The rest of the students take their Christmas trip to Hogsmeade and Harry is determined to go along. He tries to follow the group through the snow in his Invisibility Cloak, but Fred and George Weasley, Ron's twin older brothers who are first-rate troublemakers themselves, stop him... so they can show him a better way. The give him something they "nicked from Filch's office" called The Marauders Map, which shows where everyone is at Hogwarts at all times. It also shows the seven secret passageways out of the castle, one of which goes straight into Honeydukes' cellar in the village. Brilliant!

The combination map and cloak get Harry into the charming little village. He catches up with Ron and Hermione looking at the Shrieking Shack—the most haunted building in Britain, they repeat once again—but before he can reveal himself, Malfoy and two of his minions appear and try to start bullying them. Normally Crabbe and Goyle would be Malfoy's two sidekicks, but instead it's Crabbe and an unnamed Slytherin boy. Apparently Josh Herdman, the actor who played Gregory Goyle, injured his arm and was unable to film the rest of the movie. (In the final two films, it'll be the other way around, with Goyle on hand, but Crabbe will be written out after actor Jamie Waylett is charged with drug possession.) Invisible Harry gives the Slytherins a good scare.

Back in the village, Harry sees Cornelius Fudge arriving at the Three Broomsticks, hears his name taken in vain, and naturally decides to snoop. In an upstairs room, Professor McGonagall tells Rosmerta that the Potters went into hiding when You-Know-Who was after them and the one who knew where they were was Sirius Black. Black not only led Voldemort to them, but he also killed another friend of theirs, Peter Pettigrew, that night. That's the murder he was sent to prison for. Oh, and by the way, did you know that famed killer Sirius Black not only now wants to kill Harry, he's actually Harry's godfather?

That's the last straw for Harry, who storms off. Hermione and Ron find him crying in the snow. Harry vows that when Sirius shows up next, he'll be ready to avenge his parents. (*Such* a teenage rage-ball.)

With spring comes the thaw and Remus Lupin's promised lesson in how to get rid of Dementors. Lupin teaches Harry the Patronus Charm, a kind of psychic shield that is made of a person's happiest memories. The problem is Harry doesn't have a lot of happy memories to draw on, so the charm fails at first. (But with a lot of chocolate and determination, he eventually makes it work.)

Meanwhile, Ron and Hermione are fighting again: Ron thinks her cat finally tore his rat, Scabbers, to pieces. But they set aside their differences to try to console Hagrid who has come back from the Ministry with bad news: Buckbeak has been sentenced to death for scratching Draco on the first day of school.

* * *

"Messrs. Moony, Wormtail, Padfoot and Prongs offer their compliments to Professor Snape and request he keep his abnormally large nose out of other people's business."

* * *

One night, Harry is up late, looking at the Marauders Map, when he sees something impossible: Peter Pettigrew's name on the map. He gets out of bed (breaking a major school rule, of course) and goes to find this man, since after all, *he's supposed to be dead,* and supposedly was a friend of his parents. When he gets to the corridor, though, he finds no one, even though the map makes it seem like they must have just passed each other. Before he can search further, he is caught by Professor Snape.

"How extraordinarily like your father you are," Snape tells him. "He, too, was exceedingly arrogant." He makes Harry turn out his pockets. The map appears blank until Snape tries a revealing spell on it, and then it shows him a message telling him to "keep his abnormally large nose out of other people's business." Snape is incensed and about to take, or perhaps destroy, the map, but Professor Lupin intervenes.

Lupin takes Harry (and map) off to his classroom and points out that in the hands of Famed Murderer Sirius Black, the map would be a map right to Harry. "Your parents gave their lives to save yours, and wandering around the castle at night, unprotected, with a killer on the loose, seems a poor way to repay them!" He tells Harry he won't cover for him again and sends Harry back to his dormitory. "And don't take any detours, or I shall know." Since he is keeping the map. Harry agrees, but he tells Lupin that he saw Peter on the map, even though they both know that can't be possible.

What Harry doesn't know at this point (and the audience is never told!) is that Lupin, along with James, Sirius and Peter, were known as the Marauders, and they're the original creators of the map.

Daytime finds us back in Professor Trelawney's class, and for once it isn't Harry who stalks off in a huff. This time it's Hermione: she's had enough of this Divination rubbish. She knocks her crystal ball off its stand and takes off. After class, Harry brings the crystal ball back to the classroom. As he sets it back on the stand, in it he thinks he sees the face of Sirius Black calling his name, and then Trelawney suddenly appears and speaks a true prophecy: that the one who betrayed his friends will return tonight, innocent blood will be spilled, and master and servant will be reunited once more. Eek! Harry is good and freaked out by this.

He doesn't have time to talk about it with Ron and Hermione, though, as it's the day of Buckbeak's execution. They go down to Hagrid's hut to support him, but run into Malfoy, Crabbe and not-Goyle trying to spy on the execution from afar. Hermione is so angry that she draws her wand on Draco, then puts it away only to turn around and punch him smack in the nose. (After the Slytherins run off, she says, somewhat sheepishly surprised at herself, "That felt good.")

They have some tea with Hagrid and talk. Hagrid surprises Ron by handing him Scabbers. Before we can find out where Hagrid found him, Harry gets pelted with a stone through the open window. He looks out and sees Dumbledore, Fudge and the Executioner on their way down. "It's late!" Hagrid exclaims, like some huge Lewis Carroll reference.

He hurries them out the back door because it won't do for them to be seen "outside of the castle *at this time of night,* especially you, Harry." (This comment doesn't exactly make sense, since it's clearly not yet night, and Fudge even says the execution is to take place at sundown, which hasn't happened yet. But anyway.)

They run back to the point where they'd met Malfoy and his goons earlier, where they can only just see the executioner exit the hut, the massive swing of his axe as he hits something in the pumpkin patch, and then the crows flying up at the impact. As they cling to each other in sadness and outrage... Ron's rat bites him and runs off.

Ron chases Scabbers; Harry and Hermione chase Ron. Ron catches Scabbers but Harry and Hermione stop short, realizing that he's now sitting under the Whomping Willow. But Ron points at the danger behind them: The Grim! A big mangy-looking black dog has appeared right behind them and is growling menacingly.

The dog leaps right over them, though, and attacks Ron instead, dragging him toward the Willow and down a tunnel underneath the roots. They try to follow but the Willow begins Whomping them. Eventually they make it down the hole, and into a secret passage that leads right to the Shrieking Shack. And there they find out that the black dog is not an omen at all... It's Sirius Black. He's an Animagus, he looks not quite sane, and he's out for blood.

But whose? The Trio keep assuming it's Harry he wants. "If you want Harry, you'll have to kill us, too!" Hermione cries, throwing herself between Black and Harry.

"Only one will die tonight," Sirius replies.

"Then it will be you!" Harry shouts, putting Sirius at wand point. But before he can do anything more, he is disarmed by a well-placed Expelliarmus from none other than Remus Lupin... who embraces Sirius like a long-lost brother.

"Let's kill him!" Sirius enthuses.

"No!" Hermione is having none of it. She's figured out already that Lupin is a werewolf—because of the essay Snape made them write.

Lupin gives his wand to Sirius and tells him to go ahead and kill him, but "Harry has a right to know why" first.

Harry thinks he knows, of course. He thinks Sirius betrayed his parents. "You're the reason they're dead!"

Emotions are running very high, so Lupin's explanation comes out quite hot. "Someone did betray them but it was someone that I believed until quite recently was dead." Who?

Sirius literally spits the answer out: "Peter Pettigrew! And he's right here in this room!"

He is? Before that mystery can be unraveled by our Trio, though, along comes Snape, who disarms Sirius, and exclaims, "Vengeance is sweet." So, wait a second, you're telling me that not only is there a ton of unfinished business between Sirius and Remus, and between Sirius and Peter, there's a history between Sirius and Snape, too? Sirius really got around back in the day.

Before we can really find out what all went on between Sirius and Severus in their school days, though, Harry gets hold of Hermione's wand, hits Snape with an Expelliarmus so strong it knocks him out, and then demands the full explanation. What in the name of all that is magic is up with Peter Pettigrew? He's an Animagus, too, you see. He's Ron's rat, Scabbers. Remus and Sirius force him back into his human shape to prove the story. He's a sniveling, pathetic wreck. Harry realizes they shouldn't kill him—yet, anyway—as he's the only proof that Sirius didn't commit murder. Harry decides they should take Pettigrew back to the castle.

But there are complications still to come. After Harry and Sirius have a little bonding moment—Sirius tells Harry that he's his godfather and that if Harry wanted, he could come live with him instead of with his aunt and uncle—Remus and Pettigrew emerge from the tunnel under the willow. But their timing is terrible: the full moon is just rising and Remus transforms into a werewolf. Pettigrew turns back into a rat and flees. As a werewolf, Remus has no memory of who he is, and turns to attack Harry, Hermione and Ron. Snape emerges from the tunnel then and puts himself between the kids and the werewolf, who attacks again. This time Sirius in his dog form intervenes, and the two of them fight and go chasing each other away. Harry being Harry runs after them. It looks like Sirius is injured, but before the werewolf can finish him off, Harry distracts him. And before the werewolf can finish *Harry* off, a distant howl distracts *him.* (See, I told you there were complications.)

The werewolf runs off toward the howl, and Harry runs to where he saw Sirius, now back in human form, fall down. But the Dementors are coming. Their quarry is in sight, and they swarm over them. Harry tries the Patronus charm, but the Dementors are too strong. They begin to suck out Sirius' soul.

Harry looks up, though, and from across the lake he thinks he sees his father cast the strongest Patronus charm he's ever seen, one that takes the form of a shining stag. Then, as he has after every other encounter with a Dementor, Harry passes out.

He wakes up in the hospital wing. Hermione tells him Sirius has been captured and the Dementors are about to perform the soul-sucking Kiss once again. Then Dumbledore comes in. Can't he save an innocent man? No, Dumbledore says, but he tells them where Sirius is being held. The bell in the tower begins to chime and he speaks to Hermione. "You know the laws, you must not be seen. If you succeed tonight, more than one innocent life will be spared."

Ron often speaks the no-nonsense questions the audience is wondering and this scene is no exception. What the bloody hell was that all about?

Hermione has been using a Time-Turner all year to take double classes. Ron has been doing double takes all year wondering how it is she seems to suddenly turn up. Given that he can't walk because of the dog bite on his leg, it'll have to be Harry and Hermione who go back in time to fix everything, though.

They return to Hagrid's hut to retrace their steps and Hermione realizes when Dumbledore said that more than one innocent life could be spared, he meant Buckbeak. They hide in the pumpkin patch and see Fudge and the executioner coming. But shouldn't they see themselves hurrying out the back right now? Hermione then throws the stone that hit past-Harry in the head and made him look out the window in the first place. Present-Hermione and Harry then free Buckbeak. But what next?

They see Lupin and Snape both descend into the tunnel to the Shrieking Shack, and then they wait to see what happens. Harry tells Hermione rather wistfully about Sirius wanting them to live together. Then comes the werewolf attack, and it's present-Hermione who howls to divert Lupin from killing past-Harry. And it's present-Buckbeak who then saves present-Harry and Hermione from the werewolf.

But the Dementors. Now is when they swarm Sirius and Harry on the side of the lake. "This is awful," Hermione says. "You're both dying." Harry tells her not to worry, he saw his dad show up before and he will show up again. But no one comes. Harry finally charges forward and conjures the stag Patronus himself. That works! Harry knew he could do it because he realizes *he already saw himself do it before!*

They then fly Buckbeak up to the tower to rescue Sirius, who gets one more tender, bonding moment with Harry before he has to flee off on the hippogriff's back—two condemned beasts on the lam together. Harry and Hermione run back up to the hospital wing just as the bell is tolling and voila, they close the loop. Mission accomplished.

Although Harry doesn't feel like it is. The next day, he goes to see Professor Lupin and finds he's packing up to leave. Everyone knows he's a werewolf now and he expects the angry letters from parents will begin arriving any minute demanding his resignation, so he's already tendered it to Dumbledore. "None of it made any difference," Harry laments. Pettigrew escaped and Sirius is still wanted for murder. No, says Lupin, it made a great deal of difference. "You uncovered the truth and saved an innocent man from a terrible fate." And now that he's no longer a Hogwarts teacher, Lupin can give Harry back the Marauders Map.

Harry gets one more thing, as well. Remember his destroyed broom? He goes down to the Great Hall to find all the Gryffindors clustered around a package for him. Just like the last broom that mysteriously appeared as an anonymous gift in *Sorcerer's Stone* (we're pretty sure it came from Professor McGonagall), this one also showed up with no card... just a hippogriff feather. This broom's a Firebolt, the "fastest broom in the world." Harry wastes no time in hopping on, and whoosh! Off he goes into the sky, his face pure joy.

4: Harry Potter and the Goblet of Fire

Film Data

    Title: Harry Potter and the Goblet of Fire
    Release Date: November 17, 2005
    Director: Mike Newell
    Screenplay: Steve Kloves
    Producers: David Heyman
    USA Opening Weekend: $102,685,961
    Running Time: 2:46

"It's rare that one is able to herald the fourth picture of a franchise series as the best to date," reads the review of *Goblet of Fire* in *The Telegraph* (U.K.). "These days, the novels are getting saggier and more bloated (at more than 750 pages in length, the last one was longer than *Crime and Punishment*), but ever since Christopher (*Home Alone*) Columbus vacated the director's seat, the film adaptations have been getting progressively sharper and more interesting."

Well. Interestingly enough, with British-born Mike Newell at the helm—the series' first British director—critics found themselves not only captivated by the increasingly darker action, but by American teen-movie textures more reminiscent of John Hughes than anyone else. The first of the Potter films to gain a PG-13 (rather than PG) rating, features a 14-year-old Harry who "finally [has] full-blown adolescence to contend with." (Roger Ebert) The same Harry who faces down dragons with aplomb finds it much more difficult to work up the nerve to ask a girl to the Yule Ball.

Critics were largely charmed by this entry into the series. Even one of the more lukewarm reviews, from *The Guardian,* said: "It looks like another handsomely made, good-natured and high-spirited family movie... [W]hat confident entertainments the Harry Potter films are, speaking boldly and intelligently to their fanbase. The Star Wars prequels were ropey; the Matrices died of embarrassment... It may yet be that the Harry Potters will outpace even Peter Jackson's revered Tolkien epic." (This was before *The Hobbit* was attempted.) The *LA Times* was finally fully won over, saying that the film "successfully re-created the sense of stirring magical adventure and engaged, edge-of-your-seat excitement that has made the books such an international phenomenon." And David Edelman of *Slate* wrote that he "couldn't be more pleased with what the screenwriter, Steven Kloves, and the director, Mike Newell, have wrought this time," though he emphasized that he left his 7-year-old at home because "it's scary, kids."

I call this film the "turning point" of the series because of how it ends. The climax of *Goblet of Fire* is the return of Voldemort to full power, and it stands at the pinnacle right at the halfway point of the eight films. Everything before the restoration of the main villain has only been preludes, and everything after this will be focused on his defeat.

Casting Notes

David Tennant as Barty Crouch Jr.

He wasn't yet known for his run as the Tenth Doctor in *Dr. Who* when he took his turn in a Potter film, but David Tennant was on his way to taking his place in the pantheon of British acting greats in sci-fi/fantasy films. He told *Entertainment Weekly* that what he enjoyed most while filming *Goblet of Fire* was "sitting around in a circle telling wonderful stories [between takes.] There was something really fabulous about Michael with his enormous beard, Alan wearing his wig and Maggie in her witch's hat. I just thought, 'This is what acting's all about, isn't it?'"

Robert Pattinson as Cedric Diggory

This London-born actor came to the Potter franchise in an unusual way. He'd played the part of Reese Witherspoon's son in *Vanity Fair*, but his part had been cut from the film entirely. "I went to the screening, and no one had informed me that I was cut," he told *W Magazine*. "The casting director... felt so guilty... that she gave me first run at the part in *Harry Potter*, so I was quite glad I got cut, in the end." After Potter, he wasn't really sure how seriously he wanted to pursue acting, but at age 22 ended up landing the life-changing lead role in *Twilight*.

Katie Leung as Cho Chang

Katie Leung won the part of Cho Chang through open auditions, beating out about 3,000 other hopefuls. Scottish-born of Chinese descent, she told the magazine *What's on Stage* that before the audition she really hadn't considered a career in acting, "Perhaps the reason was that I didn't see anybody who looked like me on television." But when her father saw an ad for the auditions, he said he would take her. "I didn't want to miss the opportunity of being in London and I only expected to gain experience from it, so it came as such a surprise when I won the part," she told the *Pacific Citizen* newspaper. "The auditions took place within a period of around two months and it involved drama workshops and a screen test, which was incredibly terrifying but such an amazing experience!"

Miranda Richardson as Rita Skeeter

Miranda Richardson almost didn't play Rita Skeeter. Rosamund Pike (*Gone Girl*) was originally signed on, but she backed out when she found out she would have to be committed to appear in future Potter films. Richardson told the BBC that Rita would be "very outrageous in appearance; a fashion victim it's safe to say, who cares more about her nails than anyone in the world."

Brendan Gleeson as Alastair "Mad Eye" Moody

Brendan Gleeson's four sons were so excited about their dad being offered the part of Mad-Eye Moody that he pretty much had to take the part. "They all roared when they heard. 'Dad's going to be Mad-Eye Moody. Wa-hey!' After that, it was never not going to happen," he told *The Guardian*. "Robbie Coltrane told me I should forget about walking through airports again [but] as unconventional as my looks are, they're not quite as unconventional as Mad-Eye Moody's, so I've kind of gotten away with murder."

Ralph Fiennes as Lord Voldemort

Fiennes was another actor who had missed the Harry Potter book phenomenon, but when the film producers approached him, his nieces and nephews went bonkers. "[T]he clincher was that my sister Martha—who has three children who were then probably about 12, 10 and 8—she said, 'What do you mean? You've got to do it!'" he told British talk show host, Jonathan Ross. Once he took the part, Fiennes was all in on making Voldemort the perfect villain, down to collaborating with production designer Stuart Craig on the design of Voldemort's wand. He also delved deep into the sources of Voldemort's villainy.

"Young Voldemort was an orphan and denied any kind of parental affection or love, so he's been an isolated figure from a very young age," Fiennes told *The Hollywood Reporter*. "He's all about acquiring power and controlling and manipulating a lot of people," he said. "It can be thrilling and quite freeing to play, because all the rules disappear."

He conceived of Voldemort being a bit more energetic than as depicted in the books, playing the role with a kind of manic menace and unpredictable moods. To give him the most snake-like look required no prostheses, just makeup and motion-capture dots that allowed the filmmakers to digitally erase his nose.

What to Look For

New Mode of Magical Transportation

So far in each film we get introduced to some form of magical transportation that always has some odd mechanism or consequences, and which may seem less than practical. In film one, we had flying motorcycle and broom, two, Floo Powder, three, the Knight Bus, now in four we are introduced to the Portkey, which is a charmed object that, at a pre-set time or trigger, will teleport itself and anyone touching it to a pre-set place. You can make a Portkey from anything so they are often discarded objects like an old boot.

House Elf Cameo

Dobby and another elf named Winky play not insignificant roles in the *Goblet of Fire* book, but they're not in the film... unless you count a momentary cameo. You see them for just a flash as Harry and Hermione are making their way through the immense campsite around the Quidditch World Cup for the first time. The elves are riding llamas.

Quick Quotes Quill

Rita Skeeter, the muckraking writer who interviews Harry about the tournament, has a charmed green quill that transcribes what she and her interview subjects are saying, on a pad floating beside her. You might think this is done with CGI, but in many shots it's actually a practical mechanical effect, with the quill held to the parchment with a magnet.

Whatever Happened to Colin Creevey?

Colin plays a significant part in the plot of *Chamber of Secrets*. As the books progress, he continues his role as hero-worshipper to Harry, and even introduces a younger brother, Dennis, who is even more hero-worshipping than Colin. But neither of them appears in this, or subsequent films, and the role of cute Harry Potter superfan in *Goblet of Fire* is filled by an entirely original character, Nigel Wolpert. Supposedly the reason is that the actor who played adorable little Colin, Hugh Mitchell, went through such a growth spurt by the time filming began on *Goblet of Fire* he had to be replaced. Rather than re-cast the role, the filmmakers chose to replace him with an original character. Good thing that didn't happen to Dan, eh?

First Appearance of the Deathly Hallows?

In Dumbledore's office, after Harry sees the memory in the Pensieve, Dumbledore goes on a rant about how he has searched and searched for something he might have overlooked. As he says this he is looking into a glass curio cabinet at a three-dimensional representation of the soon-to-be familiar symbol: a circle within a triangle with a line running through the center. In Dumbledore's curios cabinet, it appears as a pyramid with a sphere suspended on a rod inside it.

* * *

Goblet of Fire Drinking Game:

Drink any time fire or flames are lit or flare up.
Bonus drinks: Every time Mad-Eye Moody sips off his flask
or twins speak in unison.

* * *

Book Lore

Priori Incantatem

At the end of the film Dumbledore "explains" what happened when Harry's and Voldemort's wands connected when they dueled by saying "Priori Incantatem." But he doesn't actually explain anything with that. Why did it happen? And what is it, exactly?

You may remember back in the first film when 11-year-old Harry goes to buy his first wand from Ollivander. The one Mr. Ollivander chooses for him to try he is told has a phoenix feather as the core. The phoenix was Fawkes, Dumbledore's bird. There is one other wand that also has a feather from Fawkes: Tom Riddle's/Voldemort's wand.

Because of the twin cores, the two wands connect in a battle of wills, and when one wand overtakes the other, it forces the losing wand to disgorge the last several spells performed. In the case of Voldemort's wand, the last spells it was used for were killing Cedric and Frank Bryce (the caretaker of the old house), and then—going back 13 years—Harry's parents. (In the book there is also a fifth victim, Bertha Jorkins, a Ministry employee who had stumbled upon Wormtail while vacationing in Albania.)

The ghostly forms that appear are not true ghosts, but more like an impression of their life force, retaining their shape and personality. They only last for a short time before they fade away, so their sudden attack on Voldemort is all they have time for.

Plot Recap

"Don't forget you have friends here, Harry. You're not alone."

You know you're in for a somewhat different experience in this film when, instead of opening at No. 4 Privet drive, we start with a creepy scene of an old caretaker checking on a mysterious light in the gothic mansion in his care and stumbling upon Lord Voldemort and his minions (including Wormtail and a giant snake) plotting. All we see of Voldemort is one tiny, wizened hand, but he is powerful enough to use the Killing Curse on the unfortunate old man.

But was it real? Harry wakes up from this vision/nightmare at the Burrow, where he's staying over along with Hermione, because Mr. Weasley is taking them on some kind of adventure that requires them to get up before dawn.

You also know it's going to be a bit different this film because both Harry and Ron are sporting boy-band haircuts, and one of the first new people we meet is "strapping young lad" Cedric Diggory, along with his father Amos, who works at the Ministry with Mr. Weasley. They hike through the woods with Amos to a "manky old boot" which is a Portkey—an object that will teleport the whole group (as long as they're touching it) to their destination, which it turns out is the Quidditch World Cup.

An immense campsite has spring up in the middle of nowhere for the event. Mr. Weasley ushers them to what appears to be a pup tent that might fit two or three people at most... so how did Fred, George, Ron, Ginny and Mr. Weasley all fit in there? Once inside, a wide-eyed Harry discovers it's an entire, multi-room pavilion and exclaims, "I love magic!" (We do, too, Harry.)

Our crowd has a brush with the Malfoys, who are on their way to sit in the Minister's box while the Weasleys are climbing all the way to presumably the cheapest seats at the very top of the stadium. Ron is rooting for Bulgaria, whose Seeker—a beefy-looking fellow named Viktor Krum—is the "best in the world."

"[Krum]'s more than an athlete, he's an artist!" enthuses Ron after the match, back at their tent. But the celebration is cut short as a group of masked, robed figures bearing torches—looking a lot like if the KKK wore black—march through the camp, throwing hexes and burning tents. Everyone attempts to flee, but Harry gets clouted on the head and knocked out.

When he comes to, the camp is dark and empty. A man Harry doesn't know casts an image into the sky of a glowing green skull with a snake coming out of its mouth. As anyone who has ever seen a Disney animated film knows: glowing green equals evil. Harry tells a Ministry official on the scene—Bartemious Crouch Sr., "Barty" to his friends—about the man he saw, and asks if the people in the masks were, by chance, Voldemort's followers? Yep, those were Death Eaters.

The terror attack is on the front page of the *Daily Prophet* as we next join the Trio on the Hogwarts Express. Harry suddenly notices a Ravenclaw girl named Cho Chang when she asks the trolley witch for a pumpkin pasty, because Harry is 14 now and it's time to start noticing that sort of thing. Meanwhile, he at least does write to Sirius to tell him about the attack, the nightmare, and the fact his scar has been hurting.

The Opening Feast is a bit different from previous years because this year Hogwarts will be home to the students from two other schools as well, Beauxbatons from France and Durmstrang from "the north." Ron just about faints when he sees Viktor Krum is one of them. They're here because it's time for the Triwizard Tournament, which is a magical contest that will confer eternal glory on the winner. Only students age 17 or older will be able to enter, though, as decreed by the senior Mr. Crouch—head of international magical cooperation for the Ministry. One champion will be selected from each school by a magical gizmo, the titular Goblet of Fire, which is a bit like the Olympic flame except blue. Students write their names on slips of paper and toss them in if they wish to enter.

Before Dumbledore can finish his introduction of Mr. Crouch, though, one last person bursts in to join the staff at the head table: a scarred, rough-looking figure with a gnarled walking staff, terrible limp, and one magical glass eye. The students whisper it's Mad-Eye Moody, a former Auror ("dark wizard catcher, mad as a hatter") who is Dumbledore's latest attempt to fill the once-again empty Dark Arts post. He's swigging from a flask and his magical eye swivels constantly, looking for danger.

In class, Moody gruffly introduces himself as "ex-Auror, Ministry malcontent, and your new Defense Against the Dark Arts teacher. I'm here because Dumbledore asked me, end of story, good-bye, The End! Any questions?" No one dares ask one, not even Hermione.

Moody plunges straight into the darkest of all Dark Arts lessons imaginable, going straight to the three Unforgivable Curses. These curses are so bad, some of the students haven't even heard their names, and supposedly to speak them out loud is, in and of itself, Unforgivable, against the law, the end. So Moody of course demonstrates them.

First is Imperio, the Imperius Curse, which lets the caster completely take over the mind of the one being cursed. He demonstrates on a spider, Engorgio'd larger than the size of his hand. He can make her jump from student to student, dance, whatever.

Then there is Crucio, the Cruciatus Curse, which causes unbearable pain. He tortures the spider then, which freaks out Neville Longbottom.

And last is Avada Kedavra, the Killing Curse. Moody kills the spider on Hermione's desk saying, "only one person has been known to have survived it. And he's sitting in this room." Harry, of course.

After the lesson, Moody seems to feel he should make it up to Neville for freaking him out like that, and he invites him to have a cup of tea.

Meanwhile, down in the Great Hall, students are putting their names into the Goblet. Cedric Diggory is cheered on by his Hufflepuff cohort. Fred and George, who are only 16, try to get past the Age Line and fool the Goblet by taking an aging potion, but it backfires. Krum enters, and he and Hermione notice each other. Hormones, I tell you.

When it's time for the champion selection, Dumbledore dims the torches dramatically and the Goblet flares up to spit out the first name. Viktor Krum is announced to great applause. The Goblet flares again: Fleur Delacourt! And a third time: Cedric Diggory! Dumbledore then unveils the Triwizard Cup and is just starting a speech about eternal glory when the Goblet flares once more. What is going on?

A fourth name floats out of the Goblet of Fire. One guess which. Harry Potter, of course.

* * *

"Speaking of your parents, were they alive,
how do you think they'd feel? Proud?
Or concerned that your attitude shows at best a pathological
need for attention and at worst a psychotic death wish?"

* * *

Everyone is incensed and confused by a fourth champion being named, including Harry, who swears he didn't put his name in. But the Goblet of Fire is a binding contract because *magic*. Barty Crouch Sr. decrees Harry has no choice. He is now a Triwizard Champion and must compete.

Ron is sullen. He doesn't believe that Harry didn't do it on purpose. Harry insists, "I don't want eternal glory! I just want to be—!" Himself, presumably.

There won't be much chance of that when gossip columnist Rita Skeeter enters the picture, arriving the next day with a photographer from the *Daily Prophet* to interview the champions. She sequesters Harry in a broom closet ("you'll feel right at home") and immediately begins asking him probing questions like, "Were your parents alive, how do you think they'd feel? Proud? Or concerned that your attitude shows at best a pathological need for attention and at worst a psychotic death wish?"

Harry catches a glimpse of what her charmed Quick Quotes Quill is writing down and insists, "Hey! My eyes aren't 'glistening with the ghosts of my past!'"

Speaking of ghosts of the past, it's high time Sirius wrote back to Harry. He owls a note they should speak face to face at 1:00 a.m. in the common room. Harry has no idea how this is going to work, but he goes down there at the appointed time. Sirius uses the fireplace to speak to Harry, with the coals and embers forming into his face. He asks about the dream Harry had: Wormtail, Voldemort and a third man were there, and the man was promising to *get to* Harry somehow. But it's just a dream, right? Sirius sounds rather skeptical as he assures Harry, yes, it's just a dream! But his name being put into the cup, the Dark Mark appearing, the Death Eaters... it's probably all related. "Hogwarts isn't safe anymore," Sirius warns.

Wait, has Hogwarts ever been safe? Why does anyone think that place is ever safe for anyone, much less Harry, who's come close to dying there at least once a year already?

The last bit of Sirius's warning: Igor Karkaroff, the headmaster of Durmstrang, was a Death Eater. And even the supposed good guys are heartless bastards, like Barty Crouch Sr., "who sent his own son to Azkaban." No, Harry is not in good hands and needs to be careful. As if it's possible to be "careful" while participating in a tournament that has maimed and killed competitors in the past.

The next day, Harry is hanging out by the lake with Neville. This is totally because Ron is still in a snit and not because it's a plot device for Neville to show Harry some cool things about magical water plants (from a book Professor Moody gave him the day they had tea). Ron, Hermione and Ginny come down to the lake so that Hermione can tell Harry that Ron was told by Parvati who was told by Dean who heard from Seamus that Hagrid is looking for him. Harry's response: "What?" Ron isn't speaking to Harry because he's still in a snit.

Harry eventually gets the message to meet Hagrid. Hagrid has a secret rendezvous with Madam Maxime, whom he is quite taken with—after all, he rarely meets a woman his size. He has Harry follow under his Invisibility Cloak to see what he intends to show her: several large dragons, caged in a clearing in the forest. Ron's brother Charlie, who works at a dragon sanctuary in Romania, helped bring them in. ("Didn't Ron tell you?" Hagrid asks.)

Harry finds sentiment around the school is against him; Cedric's supporters are wearing buttons that say "Potter Stinks." Just about the only people still saying hello to him are the Patil twins, Parvati and Padma, who go everywhere together. Harry pushes through his detractors to seek out Cedric and tell him what he now knows—the first task of the tournament involves dragons—and that the other champions have been tipped off, too. Cedric says thanks, "and I've asked them not to wear the buttons." Harry doesn't really care if the whole school's against him. After all, two years ago they thought he was attacking people and petrifying them. But the fact that his best friend didn't even tell him about the dragons does sting a bit. Harry runs into Ron on his way from talking to Cedric and calls him a "right foul git" and tells him "Stay away from me."

And who should he run into next but Draco Malfoy and his pack of Slytherins. Draco taunts Harry, Harry puts in a few choice words about Lucius ("he's vile and cruel") and then stalks away. Draco draws his wand as if to hex him, but Moody, who has watched all these exchanges Harry has been having, steps in, transfiguring Draco into an albino ferret and stuffing him down Crabbe's trousers. Moody gets chewed out by McGonagall for it, but once she's gone, he takes Harry to his office where they discuss what Harry should do to handle his dragon. "What are your strengths, Potter?"

Harry says he's good at flying but that he isn't allowed a broom. Moody fixes him with a stare from his one good eye and points out meaningfully: "You're allowed a wand."

The day of the task arrives. The champions go one by one from their tent to face their chosen beasts. Harry is last, and has the worst of the lot: the Hungarian Horntail. Each champion must steal a golden egg that the dragon is guarding, because it contains a clue to getting past the second task. The dragon is very rough on Harry, coming very close to killing him a few times before he can enact his plan to magically summon his Firebolt-brand flying broom to him. Harry's "Accio!" is quite strong, bringing the broom all the way from the castle down to the stadium. When he flies, though, the dragon breaks free of its chain and a stunt-filled chase around the towers of Hogwarts castle ensues. Eventually he and the dragon both crash into a bridge, leaving the spectators in stunned silence for long moments, before Harry finally rises out of the chasm on his damaged broom to swoop into the stadium and claim the golden egg.

Cut to the Gryffindor common room where Harry, triumphant and still quite sooty, is being carried on the shoulders of his cheering housemates, holding the golden prize aloft. But when he tries to open the egg, it just makes a horrible screeching sound. Harry gets the egg shut again as Ron comes in, asking, "What the bloody hell was that?" Fred and George shoo everyone away so the two friends can reconcile... now that Ron's worked himself up to it.

He tells Harry he now realizes that only someone "barking mad" would *want* to be in this tournament. "Caught on, have you?" Harry replies, still a bit angry. "Took you long enough." Ron says in his defense that he was far from the only person who believed Harry had put his own name in. And at least he warned Harry about the dragons. Harry points out that it was Hagrid who warned him, but Ron points out that the whole thing where he told Hermione to tell Harry that Seamus had told... etc. etc. was actually just Ron all along.

Now that they've made up, Harry (with his arm in a sling and still sporting some cuts and bruises from his dragon encounter) joins Ron and Hermione at breakfast the next day. Ron receives a package of what at first he thinks is a ghastly-looking dress for his sister, Ginny. But no, it's a set of dress robes for the upcoming formal occasion, the Yule Ball.

Next thing they know—in a scene that is not in the books but is wonderfully comical—the Gryffindors are being tutored by Professor McGonagall in the art of ballroom dancing. (Interestingly enough, the one who takes to it the best? Neville.) Next comes the challenge as big as decoding the mystery message in the egg: figuring out how to ask a girl to the ball. "They travel in packs," Harry notes, frustrated at his failed attempts to separate Cho Chang from her friends for a conversation.

In one of the movie's most sharp-witted scenes, the Gryffindors are in study hall, and Ron is obsessing over not having a date for the ball. He is being repeatedly scolded and thwapped by Snape for talking when he's supposed to be studying, but it's an emergency: even Neville's got a date already! Fred slips a note to Ron that warns him to hurry up. *Who are you going with then?* Ron whispers. Fred hits Angelina Johnson with a crumpled bit of parchment, points between himself and her, mimes dancing, while mouthing *want to go to the ball with me?* She says yes. That's sorted!

Ron, inspired by the example, turns to Hermione, "hey, Hermione, you're a girl..." Harry tries to stop him but it's too late. Hermione is not only rather offended that he seems to have just noticed, she storms off after delivering the gut punch: she's already got a date.

Harry finally gets his chance to ask Cho when he runs into her at the Owlery. She's thrilled to be asked by him! But almost sad to inform him she's already accepted a date with someone else. Ron meanwhile psychs himself up to ask Fleur Delacourt and rather overdoes it. Ginny and some of the other girls bring him into the common room looking like he just had a near-death encounter—he was so terrified he ran away before he even heard what she said. There's got to be a better way. Harry's racking his brain trying to think of what to do when the Patil twins come walking through, and say in unison, as usual, "Hi, Harry." All of a sudden, Harry has an idea.

Next we see all the well-dressed young couples beginning to promenade to the Great Hall. Ron is freaking out about how awful his dress robes look, but there's nothing for it. At least, he thinks, he's better off than Hermione, whom he is convinced was lying about having a date and is probably up in her room crying. They meet up with the Patils and Professor McGonagall hurries over to tell Harry and Parvati that they are expected to take part in the first dance: it's traditional for the champions to open the ball. Harry now sees who Cho's date is: none other than Cedric Diggory. He can't take his eyes off her and Parvati suddenly says, with a gasp, "She's beautiful."

Harry agrees, then realizes Parvati isn't talking about Cho. She's stunned by the appearance of Hermione, fully made up, hair tamed, in a gorgeous gown. And her date is none other than Viktor Krum.

An orchestrated dance ensues, with Harry the most awkward of the dancers, partly by design, and partly because Dan Radcliffe was busy filming other stunts while all the rest of the cast were learning the dance steps! (They worked on it for a few weeks while he only had a few days to try to catch up.)

Later, the ball dissolves into a rock concert (in a cameo appearance by Jarvis Cocker and the band Pulp!) that is meant to be wizarding rock band the Weird Sisters, though the band isn't named in the final cut of the film (supposedly because of a dispute with the Canadian folk band Wyrd Sisters). Professor Flitwick crowd surfs and everyone is having a grand time.

Everyone except Ron, who is miserably jealous over Hermione, and Harry, who sticks loyally by his miserable friend, and their two dates, who are trying hard to stick loyally by their boys, but oh boy are they miserable... and they eventually abandon them, too. Ron confronts Hermione with a load of rubbish about Krum being too old for her, and a Durmstrang, and on and on, until she finally tells him off. ("Next time pluck up the courage to ask me! And *not* as a last resort!") Ron still has his head up his ass, though, and Hermione breaks down crying on the stairwell. Sorry, Cinderella.

Meanwhile Harry's snuck away from the ball to spy on

Karkaroff and Snape. In a deleted scene Snape is rousting couples making out from their hiding spots while Karkaroff confronts him about the fact that the Dark Mark, which is tattooed on the arm of every Death Eater, is black and visible again. (The marks faded when Voldemort was vanquished.) Since this scene did not make the final cut, instead we have Harry and another vision/nightmare about Voldemort. In this one, he sees a graveyard and then another scene in the house, where the mysterious man he doesn't know is showing his Dark Mark tattoo to Voldemort, proving that his power is growing strong once again.

Once the ball is over, it's back to classes and getting ready for the second task. Hermione is still seeing Krum but she takes some time to try to help Harry who, two days before the task, still hasn't figured out the secret of his egg. But it won't be Hermione to the rescue this time. It's Cedric, repaying the favor for the tipoff about the dragon. He sends Harry to the prefect's bathroom and tells him to bring his egg and "mull things over in the hot water." Harry goes and takes a gigantic bubble bath and with a little help from Moaning Myrtle—who keeps trying to get a peek past the bubbles but who tells him what Cedric did—Harry finally opens the egg under water and hears a song sung by merpeople. There are merfolk in the lake. They'll be stealing something important from each champion, who will have an hour to retrieve it from under the water.

Harry, Ron and Hermione hit the library, trying to find a way for Harry to breathe under water for an hour, but late into the night they still haven't found a solution. Mad-Eye Moody comes along and tells Ron and Hermione they're being summoned to Professor McGonagall's office. He suggests Neville help Harry put his books back so Harry can get a good night's sleep. Neville's been totally turned on by the extra Herbology books Moody's been giving him, and can't shut up about magical plants. But it turns out of course he has the answer: Gillyweed will let Harry breathe under water for about an hour.

In the morning Neville gives Harry the gillyweed, and lo, it gives him gills and turns his feet into flippers. He swims easily through the lake toward the merpeople's singing voices. Fleur gets caught by the grindylows and has to quit the task. Harry finally comes to the "treasures" and discovers they are Ron, Hermione, Cho and Fleur's little sister Gabrielle. Cedric comes for Cho, and Krum for Hermione, but

Fleur doesn't come. Harry fights off the merfolk, who are only supposed to let him take one, and takes both Ron and Gabrielle back with him. As he nears the surface, the grindylows attack him also. He sends Ron and Gabrielle to the surface while he sinks to the bottom, finally mustering the energy for one last spell to propel himself out of the water. Fleur is incredibly grateful for him saving her little sister, and even gives Ron a kiss of gratitude ("you helped!" "yeah, a bit") and the judges decide to award Harry second place, since he would have been first if he hadn't displayed such moral fiber.

On the shore, Harry has a moment with Barty Crouch Sr. who sympathizes with him over his lost parents. Once you lose family you're "never whole again," he says. Mad-Eye Moody storms up, licking his lips, and confronts him. "Not trying to lure Mr. Potter into one of the Ministry's summer internships, are we? Last boy who went into the Department of Mysteries *never came out!*" Mr. Crouch looks distressed and runs off.

A bit later, after sundown, Hagrid and the Trio are walking through the forest, singing songs and reminiscing (no, I'm not kidding), when Harry stumbles upon a corpse. It's Barty Crouch Sr.

This sets off a furious argument between Dumbledore and Cornelius Fudge, who refuses to cancel the tournament because that would make him look like a coward to other magical leaders. Harry overhears this argument when he goes to Dumbledore's office. Dumbledore ushers the minister out, and asks Harry to wait in his office until he gets back. This leads—as leaving Harry alone in a room full of magical stuff tends to—to Harry getting bitten by sentient licorice and then falling into a glowing birdbath.

It's not a birdbath of course, it's a Pensieve, a place where a wizard can collect his thoughts—literally—by pulling the memories out of his head and letting them pool there. When Harry falls in, he is sucked right into an old memory of Dumbledore's: a hearing at the Ministry for Igor Karkaroff, presided over by Barty Crouch Sr.

Karkaroff, a convicted Death Eater, is turning state's evidence trying to get himself released from Azkaban. He spits out names: Evan Rosier. Nope, already dead. Augustus Rookwood, who works in the Ministry itself. They'll take it under advisement. Severus Snape. Dumbledore objects, stating that the council has already been well informed of Snape's former affiliation and that he has been working as a double agent under Dumbledore's supervision ever since. Mr. Crouch grows impatient. If Karkaroff can't give them anything juicier than that, they'll send him back to Azkaban.

He has one more name, he says, one of those who tortured Frank and Alice Longbottom (Neville's parents) with the Cruciatus curse until they went mad. One more name:

Barty. Crouch. Junior.

Who happens to be trying to sneak out of the hearing room right then. Harry recognizes him as the man from his dreams! Junior is seized by guards and dragged in front of his father, hissing and spitting almost like a snake. "Hello, Father!" he spits. "You are no son of mine," says Mr. Crouch and... Harry find himself back on his arse on the floor of Dumbledore's office.

Whoa. And there's Dumbledore, who doesn't seem at all perturbed that Harry has been swimming around in his memories, uninvited. He merely explains that's useful to be able to go back and search your memories this way sometimes. But although he's searched and searched, he can't find whatever small detail or thing he might have overlooked that would solve the mystery he's trying to solve right now: why are these terrible things happening around the tournament? What's the connection?

Harry tells Dumbledore that he's been having dreams that feature Barty Jr. and, as he did with Sirius, he asks, should I worry about these dreams? They aren't really happening, are they? And like Sirius, Dumbledore seems Very Concerned and yet he tells Harry, no no, don't worry about it.

Fine. Harry heads back to his dormitory only to stumble on Snape and Karkaroff. Karkaroff is showing Snape the Dark Mark and saying "it's a sign!" He rushes off when he sees Harry, but Snape lingers, accusing Harry of stealing the ingredients for Polyjuice. He shows him the vial of Veritaserum, one drop of which would have Harry spilling all his secrets. Too bad its use on students is prohibited.

Harry doesn't know who's making Polyjuice, but it isn't him. He's too busy getting ready for the third and final task. In this one, the four champions will search a giant hedge maze (kind of like the one in *The Shining,* only much, much bigger) for the Triwizard Cup, which Professor Moody has hidden somewhere deep within. First to touch the cup wins. They are warned, though, that what they will face in the maze will be their own fears, magnified. Harry and Cedric, who are tied for first place (not sure how they calculate that ranking, but just go with it) get to enter the maze first. Off they go while the Hogwarts band plays and the girls from Beauxbatons... do the Macarena. (No, I'm not kidding.)

It is scary in there. Fleur gets eaten by the roots of the hedges, and then at one point Harry meets Krum, obviously bewitched with his eyes clouded over, by the maze itself? He passes right by Harry, without saying a word or attacking him. But when Harry meets up with Cedric, and they cross paths with Krum, Krum attacks Cedric. Cedric fights back while Harry tries to tell him Krum isn't himself. Together they disarm him and leave him behind as they go for the cup. They see it, they run toward it, but the roots of the maze trip up Cedric. He calls for help. Harry hesitates, what the hell is going on? Is this supposed to happen? Cedric screams for help again, and Harry goes into action, blasting the attacking roots and freeing him. Again they run for the cup and Cedric tells him to take it. Harry should take it because he has won. Harry says no, they should grab it together. On the count of three...

They grab it. And the world spins off its axis and Harry realizes he's felt this before, when they grabbed the Portkey to the World Cup. But where is this one taking him and Cedric?

They land in the graveyard Harry's been seeing in his dreams. That can't be good. Harry urges Cedric to grab the Portkey and return to Hogwarts, but it's too late, Wormtail and a wizened creature that is Voldemort are there. They kill Cedric immediately, imprison Harry, and Wormtail drops the body of the creature into a large cauldron along with some of Harry's blood, a bone from the Riddle family tomb, and his own hand. This is very dark magic indeed and it resurrects the Dark Lord at last. He seems to be clothed by darkness itself as he rises.

This is the first time we've seen Voldemort in all his glory, a moment that has been building up for four entire films. The whole cast knew it was a momentous day. In the DVD extras, Emma Watson says, "I wasn't in that last Voldemort scene but I remember coming to the set. It's such a huge moment in comparison to the whole four films that have been made, seeing Voldemort for the first time. So I think everyone was really nervous and really wanted it to be right and a really good scene. I remember coming on set, and the tension and the quietness of the whole set was unlike any other set I've ever been on."

Using the Dark Mark on Wormtail's arm, the Dark Lord summons the Death Eaters to his side. Now that he has been reconstituted using Harry's own blood, he won't suffer the burn if he tries to touch him as Professor Quirrell did in *Sorcerer's Stone*. He intends to kill Harry as his first act upon his return, to remove his biggest obstacle in rising to power once again. He wants to duel, to prove his superiority in front of his followers, and to torture Harry until he begs to die. Evil stuff. He uses Imperio to make Harry bow to him and then softens him up with Crucio. He makes Harry pick up his wand and fight him.

As they duel, Voldemort tries to cast Avada Kedavra, while Harry tries to cast Expelliarmus, but their two wands connect. Spirit-forms of the last four people killed by Voldemort come out of his wand; Cedric, the caretaker and Lily and James Potter. Lily and James tell Harry they can hold off Voldemort for a moment, but only a moment, and he must get back to the Portkey. Cedric asks Harry to take his body back to his father. Harry agrees, breaks the connection with Voldemort, and leaps to Cedric's body as he summons the Portkey into his hand. He is instantly transported back to the Triwizard stadium.

He appears to great fanfare before anyone realizes that Cedric is actually dead. This is when it really begins to set in that the horror that is You Know Who has really returned, and how much darker the entire world—and the film series—will be from this point on. "He's back, Voldemort's back!" Harry tells Dumbledore. Harry is distraught, in tears, unwilling to leave Cedric's side, but it is the anguished cries of Amos, Cedric's father, that really rend the heart.

Mad-Eye Moody finally drags Harry away—saying, "you don't want to be here right now. I gotcha"—all the way back to his office in the castle. There Harry tells him the cup was a Portkey: "It was like falling into one of my nightmares." Moody asks if there were others there in the graveyard and Harry realizes that Moody knows far too much about the scene already.

But Moody is growing frantic. The flask he habitually swigs from is empty and as he searches the office he tells Harry he was the one who told Hagrid to show him the dragons. He told Cedric to open the egg under water and gave Longbottom the book of herbs. Harry realizes then that Moody has been orchestrating things all year. "*You put my name in the Goblet of Fire!*"

Yes, and now he's going to finish the job that the Dark Lord didn't... except that Dumbledore, Snape, and McGonagall blast through the door in the nick of time. Snape pours the Veritaserum down his throat and they find the real Moody locked in a trunk right there in the room. So who's been masquerading as him all this time?

Before their eyes he transforms back into Barty Crouch Jr. The villain of the piece is finally unmasked. But he is only a minion of the greater villain, who would have killed Harry were it not for the weirdness with the wands.

* * *

"The time is coming when we must choose between what is right and what is easy."

* * *

So, we come to the final gathering in the Great Hall, but unlike the celebrations, awards, gifts of brooms, and applause of the previous films, this one is a funeral for Cedric Diggory. Dumbledore tells all present that he was murdered by Lord Voldemort (and that the Ministry did not want that information to be divulged). Many noble words are spoken about a noble boy, but that is all they are now: words.

Then there is an emotional coda scene, where Dumbledore visits Harry in the dormitory, where he's packing to leave and everyone else is already gone. Dumbledore apologizes for putting Harry in grave danger this year (by not stopping the tournament and letting events play out). Harry doesn't really mind that, but he wants to know what the heck happened in the graveyard when his wand and Voldemort's connected? Dumbledore mumbles some Latin (Priori Incantatem) and says, "you saw your parents that night, didn't you?" Harry nods. Apparently that's explanation enough for them both. (If it's not enough for you, check out "Book Lore.")

Dumbledore does some more speechifying, but this time to Harry alone: "The time is coming when we must choose between what it right and what is easy." And also, "Don't forget you have friends here, Harry. You're not alone."

And then it's really time to say goodbye, as the Durmstrang ship and the Beauxbatons carriage are loaded up to leave. Hermione says to Harry and Ron what is really true: "Everything's going to change now, isn't it." But Harry isn't morose about it at all. "Yes," he says, like he knows they'll be up to the challenge of at least three more movies. (It turns out to take four.)

5: Harry Potter and the Order of the Phoenix

Film Data

Title: Harry Potter and the Order of the Phoenix
Release Date: July 11, 2007
Director: David Yates
Screenplay: Michael Goldenberg
Producers: David Heyman and David Barron
USA Opening Weekend: $77,108,414
Running Time: 2:18

The longest of the Harry Potter books made the shortest film at the time. *Order of the Phoenix* was a behemoth of a book—over 250,000 words—making it three times the size of *Sorcerer's Stone*. The movie, by contrast, was a mere 138 minutes (2:18), the shortest to date.* How did that happen? By necessity.

The time period between the 2000 release of book four and the 2003 release of book five is referred to in Harry Potter fanfic circles as the "three-year summer." During the long gap, the intense desire for more of Harry (and Draco and Sirius and so on...) drove an explosion in Harry Potter fanfic, coupled with the massive growth of the World Wide Web and blogging platforms. The anticipation had reached an all-time high, not least of all because *Goblet of Fire* essentially ends on a cliffhanger: Voldemort is back. Now what?

Order of the Phoenix, the book, probably took so long to write for several reasons. One is its sheer length, but note that the three-year summer coincides with the launch of the film series. Both of the first two movies were released in that time period. Although J.K. Rowling was not supposedly involved in the day-to-day film work, she was definitely involved to a greater extent than most novelists. Perhaps the film-related work, whether time-consuming or not, disrupted her creative flow. Perhaps the pressure of needing to meet book industry demands made writing the book an uphill climb; recall that each new Potter book release created a huge lift in a sagging industry.

Maybe it was also that this being the book that came right after the biggest turning point in the series, the return of Voldemort, it was simply the hardest to write. Many fiction writers express that the very middle of a book is the hardest part to get through. This book was the middle of the series, and the middle of this book goes on for a very, very long time. Which begs the question: why weren't massive rewrites done once the first draft clocked in at a quarter million words? Pressure to stay on schedule once the book release date was announced was intense. Rowling said in an interview at the time that there wasn't time to rebuild the structure. Harry has several painful lessons with Snape that, in a major rewrite, would probably have been condensed, but Rowling was never given that chance.

The filmmakers, on the other hand, had no choice but to restructure. This was the first (and only) of the Potter films to be adapted by a screenwriter other than Steve Kloves, who was so tuckered out after *Goblet of Fire* that he had to take some time off and handed the pen to Michael Goldenberg. A new director was also brought on board in BAFTA-winning Brit David Yates. Somehow they managed to tame the 900-page beast that Rowling's literary editors had punted to them. The result is a dark thriller that keeps to the action and (thankfully) spends much less time caught up in Harry's teen angst and alienation than the book does. Both the characters and the actors are older, and they know they are fighting the Ultimate Evil: in short, these movies aren't for kids anymore.

Roger Ebert didn't like that, much. "Whatever happened to the delight and, if you'll excuse the term, the magic in the Harry Potter series?" he asks in his 2 1/2 star review. The "innocence is gone" and he thought the plot was "so labyrinthine that it takes a Ph.D. from Hogwarts to figure out." Buddy, you should've seen the book.

Did it help or hurt that at the time the *Order of the Phoenix* movie came out (released on July 11, 2007) the final book in the series was set to land later that month? (July 21, 2007) *The New York Times* wrote, "Anticipation of that event may be stealing some thunder from this movie—a rare instance of the book business beating Hollywood at its own hype-producing game," but praised the film for being a "a sleek, swift and exciting adaptation." *The Hollywood Reporter* on the other hand, felt it was all a set-up for later movies—always a danger with "middle" installments—saying, "this book—and movie—is a watershed of backstory, revelations and plot clarifications before heading into the two remaining chapters. So while 'Phoenix' is a necessary film, it's quite possibly the least enjoyable of the lot so far."

The Telegraph also had negative things to say: "*The Order of the Phoenix* will, of course, do exceedingly well. Younger viewers, so desperate to lay hands and eyes on anything Hogwarts-related, are hardly going to pick holes. But holes there are—and very big ones, so let's just hope that Yates, who has also been signed up to direct the next film, makes a better job of things next time round."

The Guardian didn't think much of the plot or the writing, either, but called Imelda Staunton's turn as Dolores Umbridge "marvelous and genuinely unpleasant." The best thing about the film, though, is that the series "is shaping up to be an extraordinary real-time experiment for Daniel Radcliffe. Plenty of young actors complain that they did their growing up in public. For Radcliffe that is literally true. When the saga is finally complete... we will gasp at Radcliffe's remarkable stamina and maturity in the role." Indeed. "Eliot's Prufrock measured out his life in coffee spoons; British film writers measure out theirs by Daniel Radcliffe's growth spurts."

*The final film in the series, *Deathly Hallows, Pt. 2*, would end up 2:10.

Casting Notes

Gary Oldman as Sirius Black, Again

Yes, Gary Oldman was introduced as Sirius Black back in *Prisoner of Azkaban*. But two years later, after having recovered from the literal soul-sucking effects of wizard prison, and only a tiny CGI cameo in *Goblet of Fire*, Sirius is almost a different character. He is trying his best to be a good godfather and role model to Harry, even if he is still a little cracked, and was never a particularly responsible or sober type of character to begin with. Harry, never having had a real father figure before, can't get enough of it. Maybe it was a bit of Method acting, but Gary Oldman and Dan Radcliffe grew very close on set.

Gary gave Dan bass guitar lessons (As Dan told *Thrillist*: "Gary Oldman taught me the bass line to 'Come Together,' one day. I was learning bass at the time and he plays bass. I went in one morning—I was 14 and just looked up to him so much he had his bass in there and was teaching me the thing. That was amazing.") and acting lessons, as well.

While filming some of the more intense emotional sequences in *Order of the Phoenix,* Dan was having trouble mustering up tears. Oldman asked the younger actor if he would mind trying something "a little more physical." As he told Rotten Tomatoes, Dan agreed, thinking, "Maybe he's going to give me a hug, or something like that. And he grabbed me and shook me violently for 30 seconds while screaming at me. And then he sort of backed away slowly and you suddenly regress and I just started to cry. It was this really weird thing but he obviously knew it would work."

Oldman also served as a role model in Dan's personal life. By age 20, Dan had started drinking far too heavily. (The drinking age in England is 18.) Oldman himself had battled alcoholism in the 1990s, and Dan found himself talking to him about it. "I didn't say I had a problem—because I didn't think I did at that point—but I told him I shared that mentality he had for actively seeking out chaos," Dan told Shortlist. "He just said, 'You can't keep doing this. You've got too much to lose'. And that really went in."

Evanna Lynch as Luna Lovegood

Evanna Lynch was a huge fan of Harry Potter—so huge that while she battled anorexia from age 11 to 13 her main escape was reading the books. She eventually wrote to J.K. Rowling, who wrote back. "We stayed penpals," Lynch told *The Irish Times*. The author then told her she could get her into the films as an extra. Evanna had her heart set on the role of Luna, though, the character that she was so very much like. So she went to an open casting call without telling Jo first, and won the role through a series of call-backs.

She so completely inhabited her character that she even made her own radish earrings to wear to her audition. Jany Temime, the costume designer on the film, liked them so much, she thought Evanna should wear them on screen; so she did. The costume department had already prepared something but "[Evanna's] were better! More artsy-crafty, more like what a creative young girl would do. So we used hers."

Natalie Tena as Tonks

Unlike some of the younger cast members, 22-year-old Natalie Tena wasn't plugged in to the Potter phenomenon when she auditioned. "I hadn't seen any of the films," she told Pottermore. "I hadn't read any of the books. I didn't know what a Muggle was. I walked into the room and tripped over a chair, and for some reason, I was quite loud." The producers must have thought she was just channeling the notoriously clumsy Auror and called her back for a second audition. By then she had read the books and got even more interested in the character. She felt in the end the filmmakers didn't make Tonks "punk" enough, and that her hair should have been pink. "They didn't want to do that because pink would be associated with Umbridge, who is evil." So they settled for purple instead.

What to Look For

Big Balls

There's a cheeky joke hidden in the newspaper that Harry is reading in the opening scene of *Order of the Phoenix*. This isn't a real paper, but a prop created for the film. This film in particular has a lot of printed material props, including *The Quibbler* and Ministry-approved study pamphlets. The back page of this Muggle newspaper, which is the sports section, has a photo of tennis balls and a headline: "Balls Judged Too Big."

Latest New Forms of Wizarding Transportation

In this installment, the new form of magical transport Harry learns about is called Apparition (sometimes spelled Apparation, in some older editions of the books because J.K. Rowling's publishers were inconsistent). With Apparition, a wizard or witch can magically appear anywhere they've been before. But one must be seventeen to get a license to Apparate. If done improperly, one can end up Splinched—literally leaving body parts behind, which can be fatal. Fred and George have just gotten their licenses and are Apparating everywhere inside the house, instead of just walking. Harry himself won't start learning Apparition until sixth year, when he and his classmates will have to take a special course: the magical equivalent of driver's ed.

Then there's flying on thestrals, but that's not really a standard form of transportation so much as improvised out of necessity.

* * *

Order of the Phoenix Drinking Game:

Drink every time Dolores Umbridge gets her way.
Bonus drinks: every time Harry's scar or head hurts.

* * *

Book Lore

Mrs. Figg is a Squib

A crucial witness is called to the Ministry on Harry's behalf during his trial to appeal his expulsion from Hogwarts: Ms. Arabella Figg. She witnessed the two Dementors attack Harry and his cousin Dudley. Her testimony may come off as confusing, though subtly comedic, when she is asked "What did they look like?" and she replies "One was very large and one was rather skinny."

"Not the boys, the Dementors!"

The thing that isn't explained in the movie is that Mrs. Figg, being a Squib, cannot see the Dementors. (A Squib is someone with wizarding blood, but who inherited no magical ability. Argus Filch, the caretaker at Hogwarts, is also a Squib.) Since Mrs. Figg didn't actually see the Dementors, she must have been coached by Dumbledore on what to say to exonerate Harry. This is made more obvious in the book than in the film.

The other thing that isn't explained is that Mrs. Figg has been watching over Harry his entire life. In *Sorcerer's Stone* it's written that Harry "stayed at Mrs. Figg's house every year on Dudley's birthday, where he was forced to look at pictures of every cat she'd every owned." Harry thinks she's just a "cat lady" neighbor who babysits him sometimes, but she was actually placed there by Dumbledore to keep an eye on Harry. Even her cats have been helping keep watch over him.

No. 12 Grimmauld Place: Unplottable

When the Order rescues Harry from the Dursleys, they take him to a townhouse in London that magically appears between number 11 and number 13. It's never explained in the film, but the house is not only invisible to Muggles, but to magical people as well if they haven't been told the secret of where it is. An "unplottable location" is one that wouldn't even appear on a wizarding map. However, anyone who's been told the secret by the secret keeper can then find it. Harry's parents were hiding out in an unplottable location in Godric's Hollow with baby Harry when they were betrayed by their secret keeper—Peter Pettigrew.

The Prophecy

Harry finally gets to hear the prophecy that marked him as The Chosen One. The version given in the film is a shortened version of the one in the book. The full prophecy specifies that the one who has the power to Vanquish the Dark Lord was born at the end of July. Voldemort decided that must have meant Harry, and that's why James and Lily went into hiding (and why once he found out where they were, Voldemort went to kill Harry). Interestingly enough, there was another child born at the end of that July that could have fit the bill as well: Neville Longbottom.

And have you ever wondered why Professor Trelawney, who seems to be a pretty inadequate teacher, has been at Hogwarts all this time? We learn in the film that when Umbridge fires her, Dumbledore makes sure that Sybil stays at the castle. He's also the one who hired her. Could it be that he was protecting her all this time since if You Know Who found out who made the prophecy in the first place, he might go after her?

She did, after all, make a second prophecy that related to the Dark Lord: in *Prisoner of Azkaban* she predicts the return of Peter Pettigrew. In the book it happens during the Divination exam, while in the film Harry alone hears it.

Plot Recap

"The world isn't split into good people and Death Eaters. We've all got both light and dark inside us."

A monochrome WB logo and stormy title card are barely enough preparation for the grim opening sequence of this film. Things are serious, and the horrors of (magical) war and government corruption are hovering over our hero, ready to swoop down like a Dementor... and it's time to get ready to face CAPSLOCK! Harry.

Harry has a thousand-yard stare when his bully of a cousin taunts him about how Harry cries in his sleep about his dead mother and Cedric. Oh, wait, those are *actual* Dementors, attacking Harry and said bully, right there in Little Whinging. Harry saves Dudley's life (and his own) by conjuring a Patronus, but when he gets Dudley back to No. 4 Privet Drive—with some help from the cat-lady down the street, Mrs. Figg—he receives an owl from the Ministry informing him that for breaking the law against underage wizards performing magic he has been expelled from Hogwarts. Vernon locks him in his room, presumably forever.

This time it isn't the Weasley boys flying to his rescue in a Ford Anglia, it's the titular Order of the Phoenix, an underground group of freedom fighters that includes some Aurors who fought Voldemort previously (like the real Mad-Eye Moody), and other trusted folk like Molly and Arthur Weasley. You probably won't be surprised to learn—given the group's name—that Dumbledore organized it, or that the last time they fought You Know Who the membership included the Potters, the Longbottoms, Sirius Black and Remus Lupin. In the rescue party for Harry are Mad-Eye, Kingsley Shacklebolt and Nymphadora Tonks (who prefers to be called just Tonks), and two other characters who never get named (but who we know from the book to be Elphias Doge and Emmeline Vance).

They come bearing not only the good news that they're busting Harry out of there, but that Dumbledore has convinced the Ministry to give him a hearing to appeal his expulsion. Off they go via broomstick to the Order's "headquarters," a townhouse in London that is magically hidden between number 11 and number 13 Grimmauld Place, and a grim old place number 12 certainly is. Formerly the Black family home, where Sirius grew up, it's been in some disrepair while he's been in Azkaban. Harry is excited to see Sirius and other members of the Order plotting insurrection at the dining room table and wants very much to join them, but Molly shoos him upstairs with the rest of the kids.

Harry's a bit peeved to find out Ron and Hermione have been in the know about the Order of the Phoenix all summer, but Dumbledore made them swear not to tell him anything. Before he can really work himself into a lather, though, Fred and George magically appear in the room (they're old enough to be licensed to Apparate), and suggest if Harry really wants to know what's going on, they have a way of spying on the meeting. They've invented a thing called Extendable Ears.

Of course, the Order are talking about... Harry. "If anyone's got a right to know, it's Harry," says Sirius. "We wouldn't even know Voldemort was back without him."

"He's not an adult," Molly insists. She's *such* a mom.

"Harry is not your son," Sirius points out.

"He's as good as," she retorts. Wow, are the adults really arguing about who gets to claim Harry as their own? Being orphaned by an evil wizard sure is weird.

Oh yeah, and Snape is a member of the Order, too. Remember how he tried to give Sirius to the Dementors last movie? And how they've hated each other since they were 11 years old? They still hate each other now. Snape doesn't stay for dinner when the meeting breaks up.

Over dinner, Mr. Weasley tells Harry that, oddly, his expulsion hearing is to be in front of the entire Wizengamot (the wizarding equivalent of parliament or the United States Congress). "What's the Ministry got against me?" Harry wants to know. Well, it turns out all summer they've been running a smear campaign on him and Dumbledore, claiming that Harry is lying about Voldemort's return. Fudge thinks Dumbledore orchestrated the whole Cedric incident because he wants to seize power for himself.

When you think about it: doesn't the fact that Dumbledore set up a secret society that operates totally outside the rules and laws of the wizarding world kind of mean that the Ministry is right?

But never mind about that. Sirius and co. are concerned that not only is Voldemort trying to build up an army of followers and dark creatures like last time, he's trying to get something that he didn't have last time. Something that concerns Harry very much.

However they're not going to tell him what it is, because Molly thinks he's too young. From Molly's point of view, the very fact that Harry wants to jump into the fray just like his dad only proves to her he's too immature. So once again the adults around him keep Harry in the dark.

The next morning Mr. Weasley and Harry go to the Ministry (via the visitor's entrance, which is a red phone box, somewhat evocative of Dr. Who's use of the blue police box as the Tardis...) for the expulsion hearing. When they arrive they find out the time has been changed unexpectedly to... five minutes from when they set foot in the building. How fortunate, then, that Dumbledore just happened to be three hours early! He produces Mrs. Figg as a witness that Harry is not lying about the Dementors and his real need to cast the Patronus charm.

Of course that leaves only two possibilities for why the Dementors were in Little Whinging to begin with: either the Ministry ordered the attack on Harry or Voldemort did. Dumbledore implores the Minister for Magic to see reason. But Fudge refuses to believe Voldemort is back. Harry, however, is cleared of all charges by a vote of a wide margin. Elated, Harry tries to talk to Dumbledore after the hearing but is given the cold shoulder.

What the hell, my dude?

The next day of course it's time to catch the Hogwarts Express. Sirius, in dog form, comes to see Harry off and have a godfather/godson bonding moment somewhere out of sight. (Sirius can't go out in public because he risks being sent back to Azkaban.)

As he's getting on the train, Harry trips out and thinks he sees Voldemort dressed in an all-black business suit on the train platform. It's just a weird hallucination but... when they get to Hogsmeade, he has a run-in with Draco Malfoy who is... in an all-black suit. The only thing that cheers him up ever so slightly is that Cho Chang smiles at him.

When the next carriage to the castle pulls up for Harry and his friends, Harry wonders if he's having another hallucination. He sees what looks like a goth Pegasus, all black and skeletal, pulling the carriage. Hermione assures him nothing's there, the carriages pull themselves "like always." But in the carriage is a wispy blond girl who assures Harry what he sees is real, "you're just as sane as I am." Of course when she tells them her necklace is a charm that keeps nargles away... and none of them have ever heard of nargles... Harry's still not sure. This is Luna (Hermione accidentally calls her Loony) Lovegood.

At the Opening Feast, Dumbledore announces that Hagrid is off this year (he's off trying to recruit the giants to fight against, rather than with, Voldemort, but Dumbledore can't come out and say that), and as always, they have a new Defense Against the Dark Arts teacher. Dressed all in pink, Dolores Umbridge is an undersecretary for the Ministry for Magic and Harry remembers her speaking against him at his hearing. It can't be a good sign that she interrupts Dumbledore.

Worse, it's to give an insipid speech about how "Progress for the sake of progress must be discouraged and... [we must] prune practices that ought to be *prohibited*." The one person who applauds this enthusiastically is Filch. The one who understands it perfectly is Hermione: "It means the Ministry is interfering at Hogwarts." She looks ripshit. No one gets in the way of Hermione's education!

Back at the Gryffindor common room after the feast, everyone's giving Harry the hairy eyeball. (Again. I know—when will they learn? This is what, the fourth year out of five where everyone thinks Harry did something nefarious...? But common sense is not in the curriculum at Hogwarts.) Seamus gets into it with Harry right away, says his mother didn't want him to come back this year because of what the *Prophet* has been saying about Harry and Dumbledore. Do you believe the rubbish Harry's been spouting about You Know Who? Ron stands up for Harry, "Yeah, I do."

But when they get upstairs to their dorm room, Harry snaps at Ron. What's got Harry's knickers in such a twist? Alienation, pish-tosh, he's used to *that*. Could it be these freaky nightmares he's been having all summer? Like the one where he's moving along the floor of a dark corridor and then suddenly Voldemort is reaching out a hand that really needs a manicure?

Even Ron doesn't sleep through whatever Harry was crying out during that one. Which means they're both irritable the next day when Professor Umbridge informs them that this year in Defense Against the

166

Dark Arts all they'll be learning is theory, no actual practice necessary, because *there's no dark evil wizard waiting to attack anyone out there.* As you can imagine, Harry can't stand that and insists, *yes there is.* Umbridge tells the class it's a lie, and assigns Harry detention.

* * *

"Because if it's just you alone, you're not that much of a threat."

* * *

In case anyone ever thought that J.K. Rowling actually endorses the boarding school system, what follows is one of the most sadistic scenes ever committed to film. When Harry arrives at her office (now decorated entirely in pink, kitschy china plates with kittens painted on them mewing on the walls) Umbridge gives Harry a quill and says he'll be doing a traditional boarding school punishment: lines. Like when Bart Simpson has to write on the blackboard "There is no such month as Rocktober." Harry points out that she hasn't given him any ink.

That's because he'll be using his own blood. As he moves the quill across the parchment, the words are cut into the back of his own hand, over and over, until they leave a scar that reads "I will not tell lies."

It's brutal. But rather than complain to Dumbledore or let anyone else who would put a stop to the abuse know, or try to pretend he's learned his lesson and he's sorry, or any other thing other than plow right through as if it isn't bothering him never enters Harry's mind. Because he knows right from that moment he is in a power struggle with this woman, and doing anything else would mean she won.

Of course, willingly carving up his own hand for over an hour... that's really her winning, too, but let's not burst Harry's illusion that deciding to take his punishment is agency on his part. Ron and Hermione both urge him to tell someone he's been tortured but he refuses, only alienating himself from both of them, too. He writes to Sirius telling him how alone he feels. He goes down to Hagrid's hut, but of course Hagrid's gone, and lonely, alienated Harry ends up following a flying goth Pegasus into the woods.

There he runs into Luna who tells him they're called thestrals and only people who have seen death can see them. (They really *are* goth

Pegasus!) She can see them because she saw her mother die when she was young. Harry can see them now because of witnessing Cedric's death. Luna also tells him that she and her dad believe Harry about everything. "You're just about the only ones," Harry replies. Luna rather wisely replies that's probably exactly how You Know Who wants Harry to feel: cut off from everyone. "Because if it's just you alone, you're not that much of a threat." This makes Harry feel a little better, like, hey, maybe people aren't being dicks to him merely because they're dicks. Being able to blame things on an evil wizard sure is handy.

Next morning, at breakfast, there's a great shot of Ron stuffing his face while reading a pamphlet on studying for the OWLs (the wizarding equivalent of the SAT exam, only it may affect your job placement for life...). Harry has a moment where he's unsure if he's welcome to sit with him and Hermione, but before he can join them at the table, everyone's attention is drawn to an argument between Professor McGonagall and Professor Umbridge. McGonagall is chastising Umbridge for her "medieval" methods of discipline (perhaps Harry wasn't the only one she tortured?) and the Ministry-appointed Umbridge retorts that to challenge her is to be disloyal to the Ministry of Magic itself.

Next thing you know, Fudge has appointed Umbridge to be High Inquisitor of Hogwarts. A montage follows in which she interviews various members of the faculty and goes around using her wand to tighten students' ties, tuck in their shirts and ruin their fun in every way possible. When Professor Trelawney is unable to produce even "one teensy prophecy" for her, she has her sacked and ejected from the castle. Trelawney is in tears with her bags packed in the courtyard, when Dumbledore emerges. He is furious and sends Trelawney back inside, telling Umbridge that while the Ministry may have given her the power to sack his teachers, she holds no power to banish them from the castle. "For now," she agrees.

Harry once again tries to talk to Dumbledore as the scene breaks up, and Dumbledore once again turns a deaf ear and leaves without even a glance back.

That night in the common room, the Trio are griping about Umbridge when they hear on the wizarding wireless (magical radio) that there have been disappearances that are being blamed on Famed Murder Sirius Black. Who pops his head into the fireplace right then. They tell him what Umbridge is up to and that she's not letting them use magic in defense at all. Sirius says of course not, Fudge is afraid that Dumbledore is raising a fighting force of his own. (Um, hello, what's the Order of the Phoenix again? Never mind...) Sirius has to run off before he's discovered, and tells the kids things aren't going well for the Order either, and for now, they're on their own. Hermione is about equally upset that they're not learning what they need to pass their OWLs and they're not learning defense, right when they are going to really need it. "If Umbridge won't teach us defense, we need someone who will."

Guess who she has in mind? It's one of the two boys she drags to a secret meeting at the Hogs Head Pub in Hogsmeade, and it isn't the one with red hair. Harry's skeptical. After all, everyone thinks he's a nutball, right? Well, more than 20 are curious enough to show up, including Fred, George, Neville, Dean, Luna, Ginny, the Patil twins and Nigel (the replacement character for Colin Creevy). And also Cho, who can't take her eyes off Harry.

A few of them are skeptical, too. But Luna asks if it's true Harry can produce a Patronus: yes. Dean and the group find this impressive. Neville puts in: And he killed the basilisk. Ron adds: Third year he fought about a hundred Dementors at once. And Hermione: Last year he fought off You-Know-Who in the flesh. Harry himself refuses to be impressed by his résumé, telling the others it was mostly luck and that he always had help. But the room is won over. One by one the students sign up on the sheet to be part of the club. At the top of the sheet Hermione has written "Dumbledore's Army."

Of course, the very next thing Umbridge does is issue an Educational Decree (nailed by Filch into the entrance way to the Great Hall) disbanding all student organizations, and threatening expulsion to anyone who takes part in one. Dumbledore's Army needs a secret place to meet, where they can't be discovered.

Neville is walking through the castle, trying to find such a place when a previously unseen doorway reveals itself. He's found the Room of Requirement, also known as the Come and Go Room, which Hermione helpfully exposits just shows up when someone really needs it, equipped for the seeker's needs. (In the books, the Room's appearance is foreshadowed in passing mentions, like Dumbledore saying he once drank too much and discovered a room entirely full of chamber pots.) For Dumbledore's Army, it provides a wide-open practice space with target practice dummies and mirrors.

Cue martial-arts-style training montage, with Harry giving inspirational words and teaching them Expelliarmus, Stupefy, Levicorpus, etc. while Filch and Umbridge try unsuccessfully to catch them. Over time, Neville struggles with Expelliarmus, and Ginny develops a rather powerful Reducto. Neville finally nails Expelliarmus on the last D.A. meeting before the winter holiday break.

And Harry finally has his first kiss with Cho. After the rest of the students leave, they have a little bonding moment over how they both are kinda broken up about Cedric still, Cho since she was dating him and Harry because, yeah, well...

And then the Room of Requirement sprouts mistletoe right over their heads and... pow, right on the kisser.

A little romance is nice, but it doesn't stop Harry from having those disturbing dreams: the corridor, a doorway, flashes of something that looks rather like a crystal ball... he keeps seeing them. This one is different, though, it goes on longer. Harry sees Arthur Weasley being attacked, like he's being struck by a massive snake that leaves him bleeding on the floor, and it's like Harry is looking from behind the eyes of the snake itself.

Next thing we see is McGonagall and all the Weasley siblings hurrying a freaked-out Harry to Dumbledore's office. As soon as Harry describes the dream, Dumbledore springs into action, sending one portrait off to the Ministry to get help to Arthur, another to Grimmauld Place to tell them the Weasley children will be arriving by Portkey... he is still ignoring Harry utterly. The portrait sent to the Ministry pops back to say the Dark Lord did not acquire "it" (whatever it was Arthur Weasley was guarding) and that they reached him in time.

Harry finally stops Dumbledore in his tracks: "LOOK AT ME!" This is peak capslock Harry. He's nearly in tears. "What's happening to me?" he demands.

This is the moment when Snape enters. Dumbledore never speaks to Harry directly. He tells Snape they can't wait any longer, not even until morning, or they will be "vulnerable." So... poor, freaked-out Harry finds himself being dragged to the dungeons with his least favorite person in the world (well, maybe by this point Snape has slipped to number two, given that Voldemort is back, perhaps tied with Dolores Umbridge).

Snape finally gives him something like an explanation. "It

appears there is a connection between the Dark Lord's mind and your own." What's not clear is whether Voldemort knows about the connection or not. Snape tells him one of You Know Who's fave things to do is apparently fill someone's mind with such dark visions that they go mad, and that would be Very Bad. (Especially since Harry feels kind of like that's what's happening.)

Bottom line: Harry needs to learn to close his thoughts to the Dark Lord's probing—something Snape must excel at or he wouldn't be such a successful double agent, eh? The art of mind-reading is Legilimency, and the art of blocking mind-reading is called Occlumency. Snape must teach Harry to Occlude.

Of course Snape being Snape—filled with loathing for Harry from the first moment he set eyes on him back in the first film—his technique is just to hammer on Harry with mind-reading spell after mind-reading spell, "penetrating" him over and over. (Snape's word, not mine, I swear.) I wonder, is it more or less grueling than detention with Professor Umbridge?

At least Harry gets to take Christmas break at No. 12 Grimmauld Place with the Weasleys, Hermione and Sirius. This is when Harry learns that No. 12 is where Sirius grew up and sees the Black Family Tree tapestry that has the "blood traitors"—those like Sirius who consort with Muggleborns—blasted off it.

* * *

Easter Egg: As Sirius comes into the room with the tapestry, look to the lower left. You'll see the Starbucks logo done in the style of the rest of the tapestry. Think the art department drank a lot of coffee while working on the tapestry, eh?

* * *

Sirius shows Harry the burned spot where his face once was. His mother in her "pureblood mania" did that when he was 16 and ran away from home. To James Potter's. "You are so very much like him," Sirius says. But Harry's having that worry, again, that he's too much like Voldemort deep down. He explains about how he *was* the snake in the vision he had of Mr. Weasley being attacked. "What if I'm becoming more like him?" Harry asks, meaning Voldemort. "I just feel so angry all the time!"

Same, Harry, same. That just proves you're a warrior for justice, and you don't even have Twitter or Tumblr to enrage you all the time.

Sirius reminds Harry the world isn't split into good people and Death Eaters. We've all got some light and dark inside us. "You're a good person whom bad things have happened to," he says, which is the closest the films ever come to acknowledging the PTSD that an abused child would be suffering from. They hug, and Sirius promises him that when it's all over, they'll be "a proper family." Harry wants that more than anything in the world.

Except maybe to know the thing they *still* aren't telling him. Even Sirius didn't crack and tell him whatever it is Molly didn't want him to know. There's something at the Ministry that Arthur was guarding. It concerns Harry somehow and the Dark Lord wants it, but Harry still has no clue what it is.

Perhaps that's just as well, since he can't seem to Occlude. Voldemort is growing stronger. There's a breakout from Azkaban, among them renowned Death Eater Bellatrix Lestrange (Sirius's cousin, and Draco's aunt). Hagrid's back from trying to recruit the giants, but Voldemort is trying to recruit them as well.

Also back for another semester is Seamus, this time with an apology. He's had a hard look at the rubbish being published by the *Daily Prophet* and he chooses to believe Harry. He joins Dumbledore's Army. Neville's back with new determination too, with Bellatrix being one of the Death Eaters who tortured his parents into madness. "I'm quite proud to be their son," he tells Harry, "but I'm not sure I'm ready for everyone to know it yet." On the mirrors in the Room of Requirement they paste the news headlines and pictures of those (like Cedric) who are dead or disappeared. Harry teaches everyone the Patronus charm. (Hermione's is an otter... which is a kind of weasel, you know.)

Just when most of the group have started to get it, though, Umbridge and her Inquisitorial Squad break through the wall into the Room of Requirement. They've got Cho in their clutches, and they've caught them all red-handed. Umbridge summons Fudge to confront Dumbledore with charges of conspiracy against the Ministry: after all, the paper even says "Dumbledore's Army" on it. Harry tries to claim Dumbledore had nothing to do with it (which is true) but

Dumbledore shields him, taking full responsibility for the formation of the group. Before the Ministry can seize him and send him off to Azkaban to await trial, though, Dumbledore winks at Harry (Winks! It's the one moment when he looks at Harry all year!) and then takes hold of Fawkes' tail and disappears in a fiery whoosh.

Thus begins Dolores Umbridge's true reign of terror as she is now Headmaster of Hogwarts. All the portraits are removed from the walls and the whole school is in lockdown. The entirety of Dumbledore's Army are subjected to the bloody quill detention... all except Cho. She waits outside the hall to catch Harry as they leave, but he gives her the Dumbledore treatment. (I mean brushing her off by pretending not to see or hear her, not disappearing in a fireball.) Harry tells Hermione immediately after that maybe it's better not to care too much, because you only get hurt. Ouch. So much for that budding romance.

Before Harry can mope too much, though, Hagrid needs help. Seems he came back from his parley with the giants with a big surprise. A really big surprise: his half-brother Grawp. Hagrid's been keeping Grawp hidden in the forest, but he wants someone to know he's there since he suspects Umbridge will give him the sack quite soon. (Grawp likes Hermione. A lot.)

Plus there are still Occlumency lessons with Professor Snape to deal with. Harry's still crap at Occluding, and he's already been an emotional punching bag between Cho, Umbridge and everything, so he's a bit sensitive. The thing is, to Occlude successfully, Harry needs to control his emotions, otherwise Snape slips right through to see all kinds of private things Harry doesn't want him to see. But of course this year is the worst Harry's ever been at controlling his emotions, and it really doesn't help that what Snape does at every turn is goad him, telling him he's as lazy and arrogant as his father, that he's weak. ("I'm not weak!" "Then prove it!") After they've "been at it for hours," when Snape tries one more time to read his mind, Harry snaps, casting Protego (the Shield Charm) and causing the spell to rebound onto Snape himself.

Harry is suddenly thrust into seeing one of Snape's most private memories, in which he's a lonely Hogwarts student bullied mercilessly by... guess who? James Potter. Disarmed, levitated, and de-trousered in front of a taunting group of fellow students.

Harry's stunned and maybe even a bit mortified. He's speechless. Snape is not. "Your lessons are at an end. Get. Out." Harry does.

This is a film, so there isn't any time for Harry to reflect on the fact that maybe this is why Snape hates his father, and by extension Harry himself. It's time for O.W.L. Examinations. Umbridge is overseeing the entire fifth year class taking their exams in the Great Hall (where the giant pendulum has mysteriously reappeared), but the examination is interrupted. By fireworks and mayhem: the Weasley twins have decided to make a break for it and they're going out with a bang! Mounted on brooms, they toss fireworks around the Great Hall while flying back and forth before heading for the skies. The fireworks not only chase Umbridge around, they destroy all the Educational Decrees hung in the Entrance Hall, and all the students run into the courtyard to cheer them on their way.

But the happiness is short-lived. While the students around him are still cheering, another vision comes to Harry (who definitely still cannot do Occlumency) and in this one he sees not Mr. Weasley, but Sirius being threatened in the same spot. Voldemort is telling Sirius he will kill him if Sirius doesn't fetch him the prophecy he wants from the Ministry's archive. Harry now remembers where he saw the doorway and the corridor, not in his dreams, but when he went to the Ministry for his hearing! It's the Department of Mysteries. With Hogwarts in lockdown again after the Weasley twins' stunt, he has no way to get an urgent message to the Order. An owl would be too slow.

Harry decides the only thing to do is go to the Ministry himself. Hermione tries to talk him out of it. What if Voldemort is using Sirius as bait to get to Harry? Harry says, so what? Sirius is "the only family I've got left" and Harry will do anything to save him. The only Floo that isn't blocked or "tapped" by the Ministry is the one in Umbridge's office. Harry breaks in, Ron and Hermione on his heels, trying to convince him they're "in this together." They certainly are, since Umbridge catches them there, and the rest of the Inquisitorial Squad bring in Neville, Luna and Ginny. Umbridge interrogates Harry, and calls for Snape to bring her some Veritaserum. Snape informs her (and incidentally, Harry and the rest) that he can't do that because she used it up on Cho Chang. As Snape turns to go, Harry calls out to him: "He's got Padfoot in the place that it's hidden!" It's Harry's last ditch attempt to alert the Order, of which Snape is a member.

Once Snape is gone, Umbridge decides that she has no choice but to use the Cruciatus Curse on Harry, a curse so evil that using it is supposed to mean a one-way trip to Azkaban. As she's about to cast it, though, Hermione screams, "Tell her, Harry!" Tell her... what? To save Harry, Hermione then "confesses" to knowing where "Dumbledore's secret weapon" is. She and Harry then lead Umbridge into the dark forest, to the spot where Grawp... was. There's only the severed rope. However just as Umbridge figures out it's all a trick, the centaurs show up. She tries to assert her dominance as a representative of the Ministry over the "filthy half-breeds" which does not endear her to them one bit. She stands her ground, casting an Incarcerous spell on one of them (rope binding) who Hermione tries to help get free.

Grawp picks up the silly lady in pink though, who drops her wand, and then he tosses her to the centaurs, who still remember and respect Harry Potter. "Tell them I mean no harm!" Umbridge cries to Harry.

But Harry can't. After all, "Professor, I must not tell lies." As Snape would say, revenge is sweet. The centaurs drag her off into the forest, freeing Harry to return to his original mission, which was to save Sirius from certain death. He still wants to go it alone, but Luna, Neville, Ginny, Ron and Hermione, convince him they should all go, and Luna has the brilliant idea that they fly on thestrals.

Next thing you know they're stepping out of the elevator at the (apparently completely unguarded) Ministry of Magic, as the elevator voice intones "Department of Mysteries." Harry's scar appears particularly red as they head toward the giant room where shelf upon shelf of captured prophecies are held in crystal balls.

Sirius is not there, though. What is there, Neville finds, is a prophecy labeled with Harry's name. Harry picks it up, sees the face of Sybil Trelawney in the swirling mist in the crystal, and hears her voice recite:

The one with the power to vanquish the Dark Lord approaches
And the Dark Lord shall mark him as an equal
But he shall have a power the Dark Lord knows not
For neither can live while the other survives

No sooner has Harry absorbed that this must be the thing the Dark Lord was looking for than a Death Eater appears. It's Lucius Malfoy, who taunts our hero after Harry demands to know where Sirius is. He reveals that Harry saw only what the Dark Lord wanted him to see. In other words, Hermione was right. Cue your best Admiral Ackbar voice: it's a trap.

But Lucius acts like he doesn't want Harry. He just wants that prophecy, which only Harry could retrieve, since they can only be removed from the shelf by the person they are about. Harry threatens to smash the prophecy if Lucius doesn't stay back.

Lucius is the picture of placid calm. "Didn't you always wonder what was the reason for the connection between you?... I can show you *everything*," Lucius intones, trying to talk Harry into handing it over before Bellatrix snaps and decides to do to Neville what she did to his parents—or Neville tries to rashly avenge them. Other Death Eaters are moving in to flank the group of students.

And Harry's not about to listen to Lucius Malfoy. On Harry's command, the students all cast Stupefy—knocking back the encroaching Death Eaters—and run for the exit. But the Death Eaters can do something they can't: Apparate. The kids must keep attacking the Death Eaters with every spell they learned under Harry's tutelage. It's actually going quite well until Ginny lets loose a particularly powerful "Reducto!"

Have you ever seen those YouTube videos where some small mishap in a warehouse—a forklift hitting the end of a shelf, for example—sets off a chain reaction of collapses that ends with the entire place in a shambles? This is like that, but with thousands of glass-incased prophecies toppling from 50 foot high shelves. The students run for the nearest door and barely escape, but instead of leading to the corridor where they entered, this one drops them into a huge well-like chasm. At the bottom is a dais of ancient stone and an equally ancient archway, in which shimmers a mysterious Veil. Harry thinks he can hear voices from beyond the Veil, but only he and Luna can hear them.

"Department of Mysteries," Ron says. "Got that right."

Harry feels strangely drawn to the Veil. Hermione urges him to leave it, but before they can make their escape, the Death Eaters catch up. In a swirl of menacing Apparition, they swoop in, and Harry—still clutching the glowing ball of the prophecy in one hand—finds himself the only one of his group not held at wandpoint by a Death Eater. Bellatrix has Neville. (While filming this scene, Helena Bonham Carter got a little too into character and accidentally punctured Matthew Lewis's eardrum with the tip of her wand.)

Harry has no choice but to hand the prophecy over, or watch his friends die. He puts the glass into Lucius Malfoy's leather-gloved hand, but Lucius's success is short-lived. Sirius Apparates in and strikes him: Lucius falls, and so does the prophecy, which smashes on the stone. Whoopsie.

The rest of the Order isn't far behind, and soon Tonks, Mad-Eye, Kingsley and Lupin are fiercely engaged in battle with the Death Eaters. Sirius tells Harry to take the others and escape. Harry being Harry wants to stay and fight. He doesn't really have a choice, though. Lucius and another Death Eater are upon them, then, and Harry and Sirius duel side-by-side, forcing their opponents back across the stone dais. Sirius, caught up in the furious exchange of spells with Lucius, exults "Nice one, James!" to Harry as Harry disarms Lucius. Sirius dispatches Lucius with one final flourish of his wand.

But before they have even a moment to enjoy that victory, Bellatrix Lestrange casts the Killing Curse at her cousin. Sirius falls—drifts, almost—back into the Veil, and disappears from the world of the living, forever.

Harry nearly dives through the Veil himself, as if he could save Sirius from death itself, but Lupin holds him back. Harry only changes his objective when he realizes Bellatrix is still there, and that she's slipping away. He chases her into the Ministry atrium where she sing-songs "I killed Sirius Black!"

Harry, incensed and bent on revenge, casts a quick Crucio at her, which knocks her down but she barely feels it. Voldemort's voice comes into Harry's head, telling him he's got to *mean* it. She *killed* Sirius. Doesn't he want to hurt her? Voldemort Apparates in right behind him and urges: "Do it."

All Harry does is turn to curse the Dark Lord instead, but finds his wand easily swatted away. "So weak," Voldemort says, as if disappointed.

Not to worry, a stronger adversary appears out of the green fire of the Floo: Dumbledore.

Harry wisely gets out of the way as a spectacular duel between the two most powerful wizards in Britain takes place, light versus dark, fire versus water, shards of glass versus conjured shields. Perhaps sensing stalemate, the Dark Lord then disappears—or does he? Harry suddenly falls to the floor, writhing in pain. His eyes cloud as he is possessed by the Dark Lord and a strange voice issues from his mouth, Voldemort's: "You've lost, old man."

Every bad flashback Harry has ever had flashes through his mind at once—the deaths of his mother, Cedric, Sirius—and the words of Voldemort fill his mind. Dumbledore can only watch, helpless to defend Harry in the battle going on inside Harry's head. Harry sees his friends come into the Atrium, free from the Death Eaters' clutches, but they cannot help either.

Or can they? Harry's mind begins to fill with memories of love and laughter, even the loving images of his parents provided in the Mirror of Erised, and he finds the strength to speak to the evil soul possessing him: "*You're* the weak one. And you'll never know love or friendship. And I feel sorry for you."

Voldemort admits no defeat but he does reappear in his own body. "You are a fool, Harry Potter. And you will lose everything." It sounds like the beginning of a grand speech by a villain. But he is interrupted by the fire in many Floos as Cornelius Fudge and scores of other Ministry officials begin to pour into the Atrium. The Dark Lord knows now is not the time and he Disapparates.

Fudge looks like he was roused out of bed, his topcoat/robe thrown on haphazardly. He stares at the spot where Voldemort stood before his very eyes and gasps, "He's back!"

He's back. *The Daily Prophet* headline reads "DUMBLEDORE, POTTER, VINDICATED." Also Umbridge suspended, Minister to resign, Dumbledore reinstated, etc. etc. All well and good, but it is not a "happy" ending. Not for Harry, who just lost the only family he had—again. The wound is deep.

Dumbledore tries to console him. "I know how you feel, Harry."

"No, you don't."

Well, if he can't console, at least Dumbledore could explain why he gave Harry the cold shoulder all year, right? Seems he knew Voldemort would eventually make the connection to Harry's mind and he thought, "if I stayed away from you, he'd be less tempted. Therefore you might be more protected."

That doesn't look like it makes much sense to Harry, and it doesn't make much sense to me, but Dumbledore thought it up, so it must have been a good idea, right? Well, no, this is ol' Albus admitting that he was wrong.

Harry doesn't actually care by this point. He's much more concerned with bigger things, like the fact the prophecy says, "One of us is going to have to kill the other in the end. Why didn't you tell me?"

"I didn't want to cause you any more pain," Dumbledore says. "I cared too much about you." Do you get the feeling maybe Dumbledore is brilliant at magic but crap at relationships?

The person who actually helps Harry's heart feel lighter turns out to be the one who's helped him all year: Luna. He finds her putting up signs asking people to give back her shoes and things that they've been hiding from her throughout the school year.

She leaves Harry with a bit of wisdom from her own dead mother: things we lose have ways of coming back to us in the end, even if not in ways we expect.

She and Harry don't know it, but Luna has just prophesied something that'll happen, oh, three movies from now.

6: Harry Potter and the Half-Blood Prince

Film Data

    Title: Harry Potter and the Half-Blood Prince
    Release Date: July 15, 2009
    Director: David Yates
    Screenplay: Steve Kloves
    Producers: David Heyman and David Barron
    USA Opening Weekend: $77,835,727
    Running Time: 2:23

By the time the *Half-Blood Prince* movie was released, the world had read the conclusion of the Harry Potter books, and the film's own release was pushed back from a planned Christmas 2008 date into summer 2009. Neither the delay nor knowing Harry's ultimate fate dampened enthusiasm for the film franchise one bit, if the box office is any indication. *Half-Blood Prince* broke the record for the biggest single-day worldwide gross and over its first five days in theaters it took in $394 million, breaking the record for highest five-day worldwide gross. According to *The Hollywood Reporter,* the total gross of $934 million made it the eighth-highest-grossing film to date and 2009's second-highest-grossing film. (*Avatar* came in first.) The only "problem," if it can be called that, is that it was the most expensive of all the Potter films to make, reported to have a $250 million budget—twice what the early installments cost. I don't think the extra hundred-or-so million bothered the studio one bit. (Besides, *Avatar* cost about the same: estimated at $237 to $280 million.)

Roger Ebert, whose love of the early films had waned by *Order of the Phoenix*, came back on board the Hogwarts Express with his three-star review of *Half-Blood Prince*, writing, "I admired this Harry Potter. It opens and closes well, and has wondrous art design and cinematography as always, only more so," though he admitted that some scenes seemed to be in there only to please "devoted students of the Potter saga. They may also be the only ones who fully understand them; ordinary viewers may be excused for feeling baffled some of the time."

A few critics in the traditional press felt there was too much "marking time" (*Empire*) waiting for the final showdown between Harry and his ultimate enemy: I guess they wanted the filmmakers to just skip the sixth chapter somehow...? The *New York Times* opened their review with a petulant "Are we there yet?" And *The Guardian* summed up the UK reviews thus: "The consensus seems to be that these films are never going to be remarkable standalone cinematic experiences... but that the Potter phenomenon is so unstoppable that they remain enjoyable experiences nonetheless." But most critics recognized that there needs to be a build-up to a big showdown. The *Miami Herald*'s Rene Rodriguez nailed it: "*Half-Blood Prince* is the franchise's 'Empire Strikes Back'—the episode in which the pace slows down a bit, the characters deepen and mature, the good guys take a big hit, and all hell is gearing up to break loose." *Entertainment Weekly* concurred: "[T]he story is, still and all, only a pause, deferring an intensely anticipated conclusion. And it's in that exquisite place of action and waiting that this elegantly balanced production emerges as a model adaptation."

Among the online media raves, Collider called it "a masterpiece six films in the making." They deemed *Half-Blood Prince* to be nothing less than "the culmination of six books, four directors, scores of actors who have devoted the last decade of their lives to playing a single character, and teams of artisans bringing J.K. Rowling's beloved series to life... [T]he latest film in the series is easily its best yet and one of the best movies of the year." The *Salon* review is breathless throughout about "how subtle a spectacle Yates has given us" in both emotional depth in the small scenes and menacing grandeur in the big ones.

The emotional canvas of *Half-Blood Prince* covers a wider range of extremes than any previous installment, as well, with the stakes raised on all the romances and rivalries as well as the life-and-death situations. As noted by *Variety:* "Dazzlingly well made and perhaps deliberately less fanciful than the previous entries, this one is played in a mode closer to palpable life-or-death drama than any of the others and is quite effective as such." And the *Baltimore Sun:* "It flows like fast-moving lava to a climax filled with pyrotechnics. And for once in a summer blockbuster, the fireworks are both emotional and physical. The movie leaves you sated, yet wanting more—just what you want from a series with two entries left to go." (By then it had been announced that *Deathly Hallows* would be split into two installments.)

Most critics felt the cast handled the transition to greater emotional material well. "[H]aving grown up on screen, from pipsqueaks back in 2001's inaugural to the almost-adults they are today, Radcliffe, Watson and Grint evince a rapport and chemistry that feels authentic," writes Steven Rea in the *Philadelphia Inquirer.*

The *Washington Post*: "The three leads... give their most charming performances to date." *The Oregonian*: "The teen stars have all sprouted into hormonal little proto-adults, and they all turn in their calmest, most nuanced performances yet."

This includes Tom Felton as Draco who, up until now in both the books and films, has been largely a cartoonish bully, just the wizarding stand-in for Harry's Muggle cousin Dudley. In *Half-Blood Prince* we finally start to see the anguish Draco's living with (even if Harry still doesn't). Various reviews took note of this. Again from *The Oregonian*: "Tom Felton in particular dredges up a surprising (for him) amount of anguish as Draco Malfoy, who may not be quite as evil as he imagines himself to be. It's a major breakthrough." *Rolling Stone*, which panned the early movies, reveled in this new complexity: "[I]t's a pleasure to watch the mesmerizing Felton take the role to the next level, discovering a vulnerable humanity in Draco."

In the world of online media, which had grown drastically in reach and influence between the release of the first film in 2001 and 2009, there were also plot breakdowns point by point, comparing book and film, and there is no doubt that *Half-Blood Prince* deviates more sharply from the book than any previous film. (Stop reading this section now if you want to watch the film without spoilers.) Steve Kloves returned as screenwriter after taking one movie off, but was less faithful to the source material (possibly at the urging of director David Yates, then on his second of his four Potter films). The two most obvious of the changes are the insertion of a completely new action scene (Death Eater "drive by" arson at the Burrow), supposedly for "pace," and the handling of Ginny's emergence as Harry's latest love interest, and their eventual kiss in the Room of Requirement.

Love them or hate them, these scenes were largely praised by film critics, while panned by fans of the books. My take is that the attack on the Burrow is nonsensical for numerous reasons—Why are the Death Eaters attacking then and there? And if so, why do they just fly off without actually capturing or murdering anyone? What was the point? How does creating a ring of fire on the ground actually stop anyone from doing anything when in the films we have seen that wizards can levitate, conjure water from their wands, fly on brooms, etc.? And doesn't burning down the Burrow just leave everyone scratching their heads when the next movie opens with a scene there and it appears completely restored? If the entire building can just be completely restored by magic... then what's the emotional impact of burning it down in the first place? There isn't one. The scene neither advances the plot (this attack changes nothing) nor makes sense in the continuity of what we know about magic and future plot events. But critics praised the "crackling menace."

By contrast, the romance between Harry and Ginny is presented in the film far more sensibly than in the book. In the early books, which are more child-focused, Rowling presents romance as something funny, to poke fun at. Even later, as the emotions grow more heightened, the books still treat love with a satirical eye. Think of the black humor of Cho and Harry on the world's most uncomfortable date to Madam Puddifoot's, where Harry haplessly tries to woo her while she's crying into her hot chocolate over Cedric. In *Order of the Phoenix,* the filmmakers dropped the satire in favor of a true bonding moment between the two over their shared grief for Cedric.

They handle Ginny and Harry similarly in *Half-Blood Prince.* Ginny has been waiting in the wings for a shot at Harry since her very first moment on-screen in movie two, where as an 11-year-old she is shocked to see Harry sitting at her mum's kitchen table one morning. The crush only intensifies when Harry saves her from Tom Riddle and the Basilisk. There's a blink-and-you-miss-it moment in *Order of the Phoenix* when they're returning to the castle after the secret Dumbledore's Army meeting in Hogsmeade; when Hermione tells Harry that Cho couldn't take her eyes off him, Ginny shoots him such a look. One thing we are missing from the books is that Harry's reciprocal interest in her has been foreshadowed for a while now, so the filmmakers have to play a bit of catch-up. But from there the actual first kiss between the two of them makes much more emotional sense than the set up in the book.

In the book of *Half-Blood Prince,* Harry comes back from detention with Snape—which he's serving because he literally almost killed Draco with a spell, but rather than feeling guilty about it, he's just immeasurably pissed off—to find the Gryffindor common room aswirl with celebration because Ginny, who played Seeker in the big Quidditch match *because* Harry was in detention, has caught the Snitch and so *huzzah!* They're caught up in the moment and *pow,* smooch city.

To me, it read on the page like Rowling just couldn't figure out how to bridge the gap between the near-psychopathic funk she'd written Harry into and the inevitable relationship she'd been presaging consistently for the entire series. In fact, once the kiss happens, Rowling is so eager to get the romance off the page, now that it's been checked off the To Do List, that the entirety of the Harry/Ginny relationship happens in a single paragraph. "The kiss" ends one chapter, a paragraph of summary about "walks by the lake" opens the next, before Harry quickly flies off with Dumbledore on an urgent mission. The next time he speaks to Ginny in the book, he breaks up with her (so he can go marching off to war).

Wait, wait, you just spent six entire books leading up to this relationship so it could essentially happen off the page between chapters? Apparently.

The films, having not laid the inevitability of Harry/Ginny on quite so thick, end up feeling better balanced in this regard. When Ginny takes the initiative to kiss Harry, it's in a more believable emotional context. Harry, having just traumatized not only Draco but himself with the savagery of his spell, is still reluctant to give up the dangerously seductive book he learned the spell from. But Ginny takes charge, and helps him to get rid of it, in the Room of Requirement—the same room where Harry had his first kiss with Cho—only this time instead of being in its battle-practice configuration, the room is in its most cluttered "everyone has hidden something here" state. It's both foreshadowing for what's to come plot-wise and a visual representation of the emotional baggage Harry's carrying that no matter how high it's piled around him, still can't keep love from finding him.

Casting Notes

Jim Broadbent as Horace Slughorn

Another thespian with a long résumé who'll forever be known in headlines as "Harry Potter actor Jim Broadbent" from now on. If Broadbent seems familiar when you first see him in *Half-Blood Prince* it's because you've undoubtedly seen some of his previous work: *Brazil, The Borrowers, Bridget Jones Diary, Moulin Rouge, Cloud Atlas, Gangs of New York,* and now even *Indiana Jones* IV and *Game of Thrones,* to name only a few. Maybe it's also that his Slughorn exudes a kind of homey charm. "I'm always on the lookout for oddities and quirky characters, things that are surprising," he told *Screen Crush*, but perhaps the oddest thing about Slughorn is that compared to the rest of the Hogwarts faculty he barely warrants the "quirky" tag. He doesn't turn into a cat, wear a crooked hat or glide around in sepulchral regalia. His quirks are all internal. He's the inverse of Gilderoy Lockhart. He looks like nothing special and keeps to himself, and rather than taking credit for the accomplishments of others, he prefers to bask vicariously in his former students' successes. Broadbent captures this timid and ultimately gentle soul quite perfectly.

Helen McCrory as Narcissa Malfoy

Originally cast as Bellatrix Lestrange, McCrory had to step out of the role when she became pregnant, making way for Helena Bonham Carter to take the part. The producers decided it made sense, then, to bring her back to play Bellatrix's sister. "It was lovely that they invited me back and wanted me to be a part of it somehow," McCrory told *Parade* in 2011. One thing that was odd about the character design was the two-tone hairdo that the film gave to Narcissa, instead of the trademark Malfoy blond. Hair designer on the films, Lisa Tomblin, is quoted on WizardingWorld.com as saying, "We tried different types of blonde hair, and different configurations, and finally, we came up with this" in order to give her a bit more of a family resemblance with the dark-haired Bellatrix.

What to Look For

Jason Isaacs Cameo

Since Lucius spends *Half-Blood Prince* locked up in Azkaban, Jason Isaacs told MTV he only did one day of filming: for a cameo role as a moving portrait. I was unable to find confirmation of which scene—or even which portrait—so keep your eyes peeled and maybe you'll be the one to tell me! A photo of Lucius does appear in the opening sequence of Harry reading *The Daily Prophet* but none of the photos move, unlike most we've been shown in the magical newspaper in past films. (When that same paper is shown later in the film, the same shot of Draco and Narcissa *does* move.)

J.K. Rowling Cameo

Although she resisted being put into the movies for the first several years—even refusing the part of Harry's mother Lily as seen in the Mirror of Erised in *Sorcerer's Stone*—J.K. Rowling was finally talked into this one. She is seen on the cover of the knitting magazine that Dumbledore borrows from Horace Slughorn after Harry and he first meet.

* * *

Half-Blood Prince Drinking Game:

Drink any time a character eats or drinks anything, including a potion.
Bonus drinks: anytime Snape says something ominous.

* * *

Book Lore

Borgin and Burkes

This is the antiques and curios shop that Harry emerged into when he accidentally missed Diagon Alley by Floo back in *Chamber of Secrets*. In that book, Harry hides in a "large black cabinet" when Draco and his father come in to conduct business, while in the film he simply leaves. Later in the same book, Filch describes a "large black-and-gold cabinet" at Hogwarts as a Vanishing Cabinet when Peeves knocks it over. This Hogwarts cabinet shows up rather humorously in the *Order of the Phoenix* book, as well, when Fred and George shut Montague—a Slytherin Quidditch player and member of the Inquisitorial Squad—into it to Vanish him before he can dock house points from them. He eventually Apparates out, despite not being properly licensed to do so, and lands in a toilet. In the book of *Half-Blood Prince,* we learn that Tom Riddle, upon graduation from Hogwarts, actually worked at Borgin and Burkes, and that this was where he scouted out several objects he would later use as Horcruxes.

The Battle of the Astronomy Tower

The night Draco lets the Death Eaters into Hogwarts goes very differently in the book than it does in the film. In the film it's a small, elite squad who were sent to basically make sure Draco finishes off Dumbledore. In the books it's a full-on invasion, and by the time Harry and Dumbledore arrive back at Hogwarts, the Order of the Phoenix are battling the Death Eaters all over the school. (In the book it's the Order who guard the school all year long, not Aurors sent by the Ministry, as in the film.) It's during this battle that Bill Weasley gets attacked and scarred by Fenrir Greyback. Bill doesn't appear in the films until the next installment.

What the Heck Happened to Tonks?

A subplot from the books that was cut from the films involved Tonks spending a lot of time moping about with her hair no longer colorful, but instead a mousy brown. Harry's kind of wrapped up in his own issues so he doesn't really focus on it much, but in the end it's revealed that the reason Tonks is so mopey and lifeless is that she's fallen in love with Remus Lupin—and he's fallen for her, too, but he believes he's bad for her, that he doesn't deserve love, et cetera. The film skips right to "they're together" with no explanation, so you can be forgiven for wondering if you missed that they were even the slightest bit interested in each other.

Not-So-Secret Meaning of the Patronus

We know Harry's patronus is a stag, like his father's, and we assume this is some sort of outer expression of a person's innermost soul. But sometimes the patronus takes a form associated with a person the caster loves very much. Among the signs given in the book that Tonks' love for Remus is true is the fact that her patronus changes to a wolf after she falls for him. That makes Hermione's otter (a form of weasel) patronus a giveaway on her feelings for Ron, and the form of the patronus of some other characters will indicate some other important relationships in the final film(s).

The Courtship of Bill and Fleur

One element that is developed over several books but not revealed in the films until *Deathly Hallows 1,* is the relationship between Bill and Fleur. They're already engaged by the end of *Half-Blood Prince,* and when Bill gets scarred by Greyback, Fleur stands by him when others (Mrs. Weasley in particular) think she would be the type to call the wedding off. Fleur delivers a rousing speech about how the scars aren't ugly, they're a mark of how brave Bill is. Tonks then takes Remus to task, basically saying if Fleur can love Bill, I can love you, you stupid git. Remus comes around, and by the beginning of *DH1,* they're married.

Plot Recap

"Years ago, I knew a boy who made all the wrong choices."

Half-Blood Prince is the second of the Yates-directed installments, and in many ways the final four films all slot together as one continuous construction. In this one, the deviations from the books that began in slight ways in *Phoenix,* begin to magnify as the momentum of 5-6-7-8 sure-handedly builds. Never is this more evident than in the opening shot. Before the title has even risen, we are transported back to Harry near the end of the previous film, face still bloody from his fight with the Death Eaters, eyes still dead from having just seen his godfather killed right in front of him, facing a phalanx of photographers at the Ministry. Dumbledore's arm pulls him close as if to shield him, but there is no way to shield him from the pain inside him.

Yes, the films are growing progressively darker, like a glorious sunset that sinks into a deep, inscrutable night.

Our next scene is of three Death Eaters carrying out terrorist attacks, one on Diagon Alley, where they kidnap the wand maker Ollivander and leave his shop a shambles, and one on the Millennium Bridge in the Muggle part of London. When we focus in on Harry, he's reading about the attacks in *The Daily Prophet* while sitting in a Muggle transit station. Which seems a bit odd, given the whole Statute of Secrecy thing, you know, where the wizarding world is supposed to be kept secret from Muggles? Maybe the rules don't apply when the Muggles are as cute as the waitress (played by Elarica Johnson) who asks, "Who's Harry Potter?" (Harry: "Oh, no one. Bit of a tosser really.")

When Dumbledore mysteriously appears on the train platform, though, Harry's pretty sure he's not going to get a chance for any more flirtation. One of Dumbledore's hands is ashy and burned-looking, but the old wizard brushes that off and says they have something more important to worry about. Dumbledore Apparates them both (Side-Along Apparition, with one person hanging onto the arm of the one doing the spell, is a thing) to a house in a quiet neighborhood, saying, "Harry, you must be wondering why I've brought you here."

Harry doesn't miss a beat. "Actually, sir, after all these years, I just kind of go with it."

Inside, the house is a scene of wreckage and devastation. "Horace?" Dumbledore calls, as he and Harry pick through broken glass and splintered furniture by wand-light. He pokes his wand into the one armchair in the room that seems undisturbed and lo, it turns out to be Horace Slughorn, the former potions master at Hogwarts. But why was a potions expert masquerading as a chair?

Slughorn explains the Death Eaters keep trying to recruit him, so he never stays anywhere more than a week. The house isn't even his: it belongs to some vacationing Muggles. He and Dumbledore restore the room to order with just a few seconds of wand-work and then Dumbledore kips off to the loo, leaving Harry to make awkward conversation. Turns out ol' Horace taught both Harry's parents, and liked Lily especially: he has a photo of her in a collection of framed portraits of former students, most of them famous or influential in some way. When Dumbledore returns he says a quick goodbye and "I know a lost cause when I see one." He won't try to talk Slughorn into returning to Hogwarts. "You, like my friend Harry here, are one of a kind."

Of course as he and Harry make their way up the front walk, Slughorn bursts out the door and says he'll do it. But he wants a better office and a raise! Dumbledore nods and off he and Harry go.

Now Harry finally asks what that was all about. Turns out Slughorn had a thing for "collecting" famous students, and Dumbledore knew Harry would be too good to resist. Dumbledore drops Harry off at the Burrow. Hedwig and his trunk are already there from Privet Drive, and Harry gets caught up with Hermione and Ron. The homey, warm Burrow is the perfect setting for their reunion laughter.

What a contrast to the next shot, of dismal brick row houses in the pouring rain. Two women hurry through a narrow alley. "The Dark Lord trusts him," one says. "The Dark Lord's mistaken!" hisses the other.

They are sisters: Narcissa Malfoy neé Black and the Azkaban-deranged Bellatrix Lestrange neé Black. Narcissa has come to beg

Snape for help protecting Draco, her only child. The Dark Lord has given Draco some mission to fulfill at Hogwarts. But Bellatrix doesn't trust Snape at all. "I've played my role [as Dumbledore's man] too well," Snape suggests. She suggests in return that if Snape is truly committed to helping Draco and upholding the Dark Lord's agenda, he won't mind taking the Unbreakable Vow. Snape has no real choice but to go through with it, bonding himself to Narcissa and vowing to protect Draco as well as to finish Draco's deed if Draco should fail. (The film doesn't reveal what the consequences for breaking an Unbreakable Vow would be—the book specifies death.)

Okay, back to something happy for a while: the Weasley Twins, despite the terrorist Death Eater attacks on Diagon Alley, have gone ahead and opened a joke emporium. Love potions! Puking Pastilles! Peruvian Darkness Powder! It's a bubbling cauldron of fun and pranks... and teenage hormones. The twins rib Ginny about dating Dean Thomas while she's looking at the love potions display with Hermione, who quickly puts a bottle back on the shelf when she sees Cormac McLaggen looking at her. And Lavender Brown says a very pointed "hello" to Ron before he and Harry can leave the shop.

They go into the wreckage that was Ollivanders: it's empty. (If you think about it, since the wand can be used like a gun, by destroying Ollivanders, the Death Eaters deprive the wizarding populace of weapons.) Ron catches sight of Narcissa and Draco hurrying down into Knockturn Alley.

Harry hasn't been down there since his Floo accident back in *Chamber of Secrets.* And what do you know, they go into the selfsame curio shop that Harry emerged in years earlier: Borgin and Burkes. Snooping through a skylight, the Trio see Draco, Narcissa, and several Death Eaters—we recognize Fenrir Greyback from a Wanted poster. Draco runs his hands along a large cabinet that was seen in the earlier movie.

Next day on the train, Harry's still talking about Draco, the "weird looking cabinet," and "all those people." Harry's decided they witnessed the prelude to Draco's initiation ceremony as a Death Eater. Hermione thinks that's nuts; Ron agrees. Not finding a sympathetic ear among them, and just a bit obsessed with finding out whether Draco got a new magical tattoo recently, Harry goes to "get some air," rather obviously taking his cloak (*that* cloak) with him.

* * *

"He's covered in blood again. Why is he always covered in blood?"

* * *

Most of the Slytherins are gathered in a car at the other end of the train and *someone* sets off a cloud of Peruvian Darkness Powder. When the darkness clears, Pansy Parkinson urges Draco to sit down with her and Blaise. Draco seems rather on edge and he keeps glancing up at the luggage rack, while hinting that he won't be at school for the full two years they have left. When the train pulls into Hogsmeade, Draco hangs back after the other students leave, closes the blinds, and announces to the seemingly empty car: "Didn't your mum teach you it's rude to eavesdrop, Potter?"

He tosses a Petrification Hex at the luggage rack above where he'd been sitting and *thump*, Harry falls to the floor. Draco proceeds to stamp on his nose. "That's for my father. Enjoy your ride back to London." He covers Harry with the invisibility cloak and leaves.

Fortunately, Luna comes along wearing a trippy magical set of glasses that allow her to see wrackspurts. "Your head's full of them," she tells Harry, after un-hexing him. She even fixes his nose with a charm. "How do I look?" Harry asks, apprehensively, afterward. "Exceptionally ordinary," she assures him.

Luna and Harry witness Aurors checking through the baggage and giving Draco a hard time about his "walking stick" (Lucius', we presume?) and Snape vouching for him. We also see a sort of force-field barrier go up on the gates once they have entered the Hogwarts grounds. Security is tight this year.

In the Great Hall, Ron is chowing down, much to Hermione's dismay, since apparently she finds this unseemly, what with Harry now missing. "Turn around, you lunatic," Ron urges, as Harry and Luna, now in their proper school robes, are just coming in.

"He's covered in blood again," Ginny laments. "Why is he always covered in blood?"

Although the latter films have left off the obligatory opening chapter with Harry in the clutches of the Dursleys, there is still always the introduction of the newest Defense Against the Dark Arts teacher. No, not Horace Slughorn: he'll be teaching his old subject, Potions. Which frees up Severus Snape to finally take on the Dark Arts post. *Ooooooh.*

The first day of classes arrives. Ron and Harry survey the chaotic scene of first years trying to find their classrooms before they're late. They've got a free period since neither of them signed up to take Potions this year: Snape required sixth-years to have top marks in their O.W.L.s and the two of them came short of that. Professor McGonagall bursts their bubble. Professor Slughorn is happy to have second-rate students. They hurry down to the dungeon to catch up, but neither of them has the textbook for the class. He tells them to each take one of the secondhand volumes out of the cupboard. Two copies of *Advanced Potion Making* are sitting there: one nearly new, one a worn-out wreck. They wrestle, but Ron comes away with the newer book.

Harry opens the worn-out book to find the inscription: *This book is the property of the Half-Blood Prince.* Whoa. You know the book, or whoever owned it, must be really important since it's mentioned in the title of the film. That the book is a text in Harry's least favorite subject, Potions, is also notable, as potions and brewed concoctions of all kinds become something of a running theme throughout the entire movie, starting here.

Professor Slughorn shows the class several potions, including Amortentia—a love potion that of course doesn't cause "true" love, but only powerful infatuation—and Felix Felicis, also known as Liquid Luck, "one sip of this and you will find that all of your endeavors succeed... at least until it wears off!" He offers the tiny vial of Felix Felicis as a prize to whichever student can brew a Draught of Living Death in one hour.

Harry quickly discovers the "Half-Blood Prince" inscription isn't the only thing written in the book. It's full of handwritten notes, up and down the margins of every page, many of which are improvements on the recipes and instructions. All the students are struggling with the potion, even Hermione, who seems peeved that Harry's is going better than hers, when she is sticking strictly to the instructions given. Seamus blows up another cauldron in a reprise of his character's running gag.

Harry's potion turns out perfect. The only perfect one in the bunch, so the Felix Felicis is his. Harry's definitely keeping that old book!

Now on to more serious matters. Harry's been summoned to a chat with Dumbledore, who is looking at the old Tom Riddle diary and a ring. He shuts them into a drawer when Harry arrives, and goes off on a bit of a solicitously personal, father-figure kind of tangent, asking how Harry's life is going outside of classes, like... are he and Hermione developing a thing?

Harry quashes that idea immediately ("she's just a friend") but seems to feel it's a bit odd to be asked. This may be because Harry's been totally lacking in adequate father figures in his life so doesn't have any idea how to handle having one, or maybe it's just that after being given the cold shoulder the entire previous year, this just seems like whiplash. Maybe Dumbledore's trying to make it up to him.

Anyway, enough chit-chat, back to the mission at hand, which is figuring out something crucial about Voldemort's plans. Dumbledore has been collecting memories (in vials—a wizard's thoughts and memories can be extruded like juice from a sopophorous bean) about young Tom Riddle trying to figure it out. The memory can be poured out into the basin known as the Pensieve and any other witch or wizard can then immerse themselves in it, re-experiencing and re-examining it. (We've seen Dumbledore do this before, when Harry fell into his memory about the hearing of Igor Karkaroff at the Ministry back in *Goblet of Fire*.) This time it's a memory of the first meeting between Dumbledore and a 10-year-old orphan named Tom Riddle that Harry will see.

Tom has been in a Muggle orphanage for much of his life. As Dumbledore is led to him, the caretaker warns him there have been "nasty" incidents between Tom and other children and he's never had a visitor before. In Tom's spartan room we see flashes of the only things he has, seven rocks aligned on the windowsill, a postcard or photo of a craggy cliff by the sea, and a book with some torn pages in it.

"You can do things, can't you, Tom?" Dumbledore asks. "Things other children can't do?"

Tom replies he can move objects without touching them, control animals and make "bad things happen to people who are mean to me," all said with the flat affect of a sociopath. The only hint of a smile comes when Dumbledore, to prove he's magical, sets a wardrobe on fire.

"Did I know I'd just met the most dangerous dark wizard of all time?" Dumbledore says when Harry pulls out of the memory. "No." He then tells Harry that Tom Riddle grew close to Horace Slughorn when he was a student at Hogwarts. Dumbledore wants Harry to get close to him, too, to aid their cause of understanding what Voldemort is up to.

One thing Voldemort clearly wants is access to the school. We see the dark streaks that represent three Death Eaters in mid-Apparition bounce harmlessly off the shield that prevents anyone from Apparating in or out of Hogwarts.

But what about the Dark Lord's inside man? A tapestry now hangs over the section of wall where the entrance to the Room of Requirement was blasted out the year before, but the room is still there for Draco. He enters the room in its default state: heaped high with endless junk that the residents of Hogwarts have been tossing stuff into for centuries. He carries an apple in one hand and uncovers a large, angular piece of furniture, staring up at it meaningfully.

Harry, meanwhile, is holding Gryffindor Quidditch tryouts. He's now Quidditch captain and Ginny seems to be his co-captain or second in command. Ron, meanwhile, is trying out for the part of Keeper. So is Cormac McLaggen, the preppy dude who was giving Hermione the eye back at the joke shop. In fact, Cormac asks Ron if he "wouldn't mind introducing me to your friend Granger" because he'd like to get "on a first name basis, know what I mean?"

A couple dozen students are there to watch the tryouts, including Hermione, Luna, and Lavender Brown. Cormac appears to be putting on a clinic out there, blocking shots on the goal hoops with grace and panache. Ron meanwhile looks a bit green around the gills and nearly falls off his broom, though no shots get by him. At the last round, Hermione whispers "Confundus" into her sleeve and Cormac misses a shot completely, while Ron turns an awkward flip onto the wrong side of his broom into a block.

Having survived the tryout, Ron later humblebrags, "Thought I was going to miss that last one" and "Hope Cormac's not taking it too hard." While noticing that Lavender Brown is making cow eyes at him from across the room, he also tells Hermione that Cormac has a thing for her. ("He's vile," Hermione replies.)

But Harry's nose is buried in his potions textbook. "Have you ever heard of this spell?" he asks Hermione. "Sectumsempra?" She hasn't, and she doesn't approve of Harry using the notes in that book. She wants to know who the "Half-Blood Prince" really is. Harry is content not knowing.

They are still harping on him about the book ("you practically sleep with it!") as winter descends. They make their way into Hogsmeade. Harry catches sight of Slughorn going to the Three Broomsticks... this seems like a good time for a butterbeer and a shot at getting to know the professor. They sit where Slughorn will be able to see them. Fortunately or not, this gives them a view of Draco going into a private room upstairs, and of Ginny snogging her boyfriend, Dean Thomas.

But the bait works. Slughorn, well into his cups, comes over to greet Harry and smarmily invite him to a "little supper party." Hermione—who has somehow managed to suck down half a butterbeer within the past five minutes—gets the nod, too. Ron does not. Already resentful of Ginny growing up without his permission (how dare she!) and then snubbed by Slughorn, Ron demands to know what's going on. "Dumbledore's asked me to get to know him," Harry explains.

Hermione meanwhile has finished her entire butterbeer, and as they walk back to the castle, she is tipsy, hanging happily on Ron and Harry's shoulders as they make their way through the snow. Ahead two other students are walking, Katie Bell and Leanne (last name unknown). We hear Leanne say, "Katie, you don't know what it could be." Hermione's warm coziness is shattered by a scream. Katie falls and is suddenly dragged along the ground as if in need of an exorcist, then flung into the air. Her companion shouts in horror, "I warned her not to touch it!"

On the ground in the snow is a necklace, halfway out of its wrappings. Hagrid appears out of nowhere and carries Katie's now limp body back to the castle. Professor McGonagall questions the students about what happened. Leanne tells her Katie went to the loo at the Three Broomsticks. She came back with the package and said it was important she deliver it to Dumbledore.

Snape levitates the cursed necklace to study it and concludes that Katie is lucky to be alive. Harry insists Katie "wouldn't hurt a fly" so if she was delivering it to Dumbledore to cause him harm, she was probably under the Imperius Curse. Harry lays the blame on Draco.

Snape, who is, after all, now irrevocably sworn to protect Draco and his mission, asks Harry for his evidence. Harry, for his part, doesn't make a very convincing case when he says, "I just know."

That night, when they're lying in their beds, Harry watches Draco on the Marauders Map, and Ron mulls over his sister's relationship. He asks Harry what Dean could possibly see in her. Harry comes right back with, "What do you suppose she sees in him?" Ron says Dean's "brilliant" but that when a guy puts his hands all over your sister "you've got to hate him on principle." Harry tries not to react to that, but then Ron presses the question, what does Dean see in her? Harry's like, look, it's a no-brainer: "She's smart, funny, attractive... she's got nice skin."

Ron's never considered this before, which leads him to conclude you know who else has nice skin? Hermione.

Harry's had enough of this awkward conversation and he puts himself to bed... which means he misses seeing Draco disappear right off the map.

Speaking of awkward conversations, it's soon time for Slughorn's dinner party. We join them during what looks like dessert: ice cream and cream puffs in tall dishes. One of the students, Marcus Belby, is a nephew of the inventor of the Wolfsbane potion. He reminds us of the potions and concoctions theme: "The only potion worth having is a stiff one at the end of the day." Cormac is there, too, along with Blaise Zabini, Neville Longbottom and a few others. Ginny comes in late (Hermione whispers that she and Dean have been fighting "again") and Harry finds himself standing as she takes her seat. (He's the only one who does.)

After Slughorn sees the rest of the students out—some of whom will be invited back, some who'll be relegated to handing out towels in the loo at Slughorn's next party—Harry lingers, peppering Slughorn with questions about Tom Riddle. As Slughorn pours himself a nightcap, all he'll tell Harry is that Tom was a quiet, bright student "not unlike yourself" and "if there was a monster, it was buried deep within."

Next morning, it's time for Quidditch! Ron's ill with nerves, can't eat a bite, and sullenly jealous over Harry and Hermione getting invited to Slughorn's Christmas party. "We're meant to bring someone," Hermione says. Ron pops off: "I expect you'll bring

McLaggen." "Actually, I was going to ask *you,*" she replies in a huff. Harry's got to get his Keeper's head back in the game. He hands Ron a cup of pumpkin juice.

Luna, who often states the obvious, says, "You look awful" to Ron, and to Harry, "is that why you put something in his cup? Is it a tonic?" Harry plays innocent but Hermione sees him put the vial of Liquid Luck back into his pocket. "You could be expelled for that!"

"For what?" Ron drinks heartily and off they go to play the match.

His chest swelled with confidence, Ron excels as Keeper. After the game, a raucous crowd in the common room chants his name, while Hermione looks on, still mildly disgusted. "You shouldn't have done it," she says to Harry. "I know," he answers. "Maybe I should've used a Confundus charm." Take that, Little Miss Goody Two Shoes. Harry then shows her the vial: still full. "Ron only *thought* you put it in!" Harry is all smiles and nods. Meanwhile, in the revelry, Lavender Brown has made her move, snogging Ron for all he's worth to the cheering encouragement of the entire house.

Well, not the entire house. Hermione slips away and the only one who notices is Harry. He finds her at the bottom of a little-used stairwell, crying, conjuring canaries that fly and sing. She knows Harry has been attracted to Ginny for a couple of years now (even if that hasn't been shown much in the films). And we saw Ginny had a crush on Harry when she was younger... but has she outgrown that? She comes right out and asks him, "How does it feel when you see Ginny with Dean?" Before Harry can answer, Ron and Lavender come stumbling in, looking for an out-of-the-way place to snog. Whoops. Hermione sends the canaries to attack Ron, and after he flees with his new paramour, she dissolves into tears. Harry answers: "It feels like this."

Harry tries to patch things up between his two best friends, but Ron is all about "what Lav and I have" while Hermione has settled into vehement denial: "He can snog whoever he likes." Meanwhile, Slughorn's Christmas party looms. Hermione warns Harry that various girls like Romilda Vane are trying to slip him a love potion so he better find a date quickly. He asks Luna.

While Harry and Luna get dressed up in their finery, Draco is back at work in the Room of Requirement. He places an apple in the cabinet and shuts the door, whispering an incantation. When he opens the door again, the apple is gone. This seems to be progress. He shuts the door and intones the spell again. The apple comes back... with a bite missing.

At Slughorn's party, Harry finds Hermione hiding behind a curtain, her hair disheveled. Apparently she *did* take Cormac as a date (only because it would "annoy Ron the most") but he's grabbier than an obscure many-tentacled thing only she knows about. Harry is in turn found by Snape who brings a message from Dumbledore: he's traveling for the holidays and won't return until classes resume.

The flow of the party grinds to a halt when Filch drags Draco in, caught skulking around in a corridor. Draco admits/claims he was trying to "crash the party." Snape takes charge of his student and escorts him out, each of them glaring at the other. When they reach a deserted corridor their unspoken conflict bursts forth: Snape accuses him of hexing Katie, Draco admits nothing. Snape tells him of the Unbreakable Vow, but in an anguished voice Draco insists he doesn't need protection and refuses Snape's assistance.

Harry overhears all this, and tells Ron about it on the train back to London for the holidays. Tonks and Remus come to Christmas at the Burrow and Harry tells them what he heard, too. (Tonks looks mysteriously normal compared to her previously punky, technicolor appearance, but the movie never gets around to explaining why she's changed.) Harry thinks Snape is working for You Know Who for real now—maybe because of the vow—and Draco is, too. Remus is having none of it. Either you trust Dumbledore who trusts Snape, or you don't.

Harry and Ginny get a moment when she sits down beside him and Mr. Weasley quickly leaves the room to give them some time together, but a few seconds later Ron comes and pointedly sits right between them, the hypocritical git. Harry eventually ends up out in Mr. Weasley's workshop where he tinkers with Muggle devices that fascinate him. (You may or may not remember he works at the Ministry in the Misuse of Muggle Artifacts office.) He tells Harry he knows a bit more about Draco's situation than Remus does. He sent an agent into Borgin and Burkes after what Harry saw there in the summer, and he's certain that the object Draco was so interested in is a Vanishing Cabinet. "They were all the rage when Voldemort first rose to power," he explains. Very handy if the Death Eaters came calling, just "slip inside and disappear for an hour or two. Very tricky contraptions, though. Very temperamental." But Draco and Narcissa didn't buy the cabinet. It's still there on Knockturn Alley.

Tonks and Remus soon make ready to leave and it's clear they're a couple (she calls him "sweetheart"). Remus seems to sense something out there in the dark fields of reeds all around the house. Harry and Ginny are literally upstairs about to kiss when a fireball flies out of the sky and next thing you know, Bellatrix Lestrange and Fenrir Greyback have Apparated in. A ring of fire isolates everyone at the Burrow except Harry, who tears off into the swamp, chasing Bellatrix, who repeats her taunts of last year: "I killed Sirius Black!" Ginny also is allowed to run past the fire to chase Harry. There are scary moments of stalking through the reeds. Then the two Death Eaters set the Burrow on fire and Apparate away. (It was apparently just a mad feint on the part of Bellatrix who didn't feel like killing anyone that day but was too bored to leave them alone? The movie never really explains why this attack takes place.)

Back at Hogwarts, Hermione is frankly incensed about what a close call it was, almost as incensed as she is about Lavender calling Ron "Won Won" and riding him piggyback through the hallways.

Dumbledore has returned, and he has more memories for Harry to sift through in the Pensieve. Harry descends into a memory of Slughorn's in which the young Tom Riddle asks him about a kind of Dark magic. But the memory is damaged—tampered with—and parts of it are not clear. Harry's new mission is to get Slughorn to divulge the true memory.

Harry being Harry, charges right in, confronting the Professor rather ham-handedly in the potions classroom after a class, and speaking the same words that Tom had used, asking about rare, Dark magic. Slughorn sees right through it. "Dumbledore put you up to this, didn't he!" He flees from Harry and begins avoiding him entirely, refusing to speak to him again.

Harry returns from another unsuccessful attempt to get Slughorn to talk one night to find Ron staring glassy-eyed at the moon, a trippy smile on his face. He begins to profess his intense love for Romilda Vane. "Have you actually met her?" Harry asks. "No, could you introduce me?" Ron asks in return. Ron has apparently eaten the candy that was in a heart-shaped box on Harry's bed, and it's turned him loopy.

Harry brings Ron straight to Slughorn. While the professor whips up an antidote for the love potion, Harry apologizes for all his Riddle questions. Once Ron comes back to Earth, Slughorn opens a bottle of mead for the three of them to settle their nerves with and celebrate the successful reversal of the potion. No sooner does Ron have a sip, though, than he keels over, foaming at the mouth. He's been poisoned. The professor seems paralyzed by the shocking turn of events, but Harry grabs a bezoar out of the potion-making kit and jams it into Ron's mouth.

The bezoar saves Ron's life, but the aftereffects of the poison necessitate a stay in the hospital wing. Unconscious Ron is flanked by his sister and Hermione, while they wait for him to regain consciousness. Dumbledore, Snape, Slughorn and McGonagall discuss the incident with Harry at Ron's bedside. The poisoned mead was originally intended as a gift... for Dumbledore. Lavender rushes in demanding to know if Won-Won's been asking for her and why Hermione is there when Lav-Lav is his girlfriend...? Ron groggily begins to come to, trying to say something, what is he saying...?

Oh. Hermione's name. He's calling for Hermione. Well. Lavender flees, Snape rolls his eyes, Dumbledore says something pithy, and the professors take their leave.

On his way back to Gryffindor tower, Harry catches sight of Draco and follows him, but he finds only an empty corridor. Inside the Room of Requirement, Draco takes a songbird from a cage and places it inside the Cabinet. When he closes the door, this time the camera pans to the Cabinet inside Borgin and Burkes. We can hear the bird fluttering and singing inside it. But when Draco opens the Cabinet again at Hogwarts, the bird is dead.

Draco is the bird, and he knows it. But there's no one who can hear his tears as he breaks down.

At breakfast the next morning, Lavender is staring daggers at Ron and Hermione, and Harry is reading the marginalia in his potions book again, when Katie Bell returns. Harry asks her if she remembers who cursed her, but she can't remember anything. On the other hand, the second Draco catches sight of her, he looks stricken, and hurries out.

Harry follows.

Draco takes refuge in one of the places no one goes at Hogwarts, Moaning Myrtle's disused lavatory. He breaks down in tears again. In the mirror he can see he's cracking. (In the book version, he cries to Myrtle he's so desperate.) Harry bursts in with an accusation. Draco throws a hex in answer. Soon they're ducking behind exploding ceramic and bursting pipes. When Harry finally gets a clear shot, it's not his trademark Expelliarmus or—as he called it when he taught it to Dumbledore's Army, your "bread and butter" fighting spell Stupefy—that he casts. He uses the spell the Half-Blood Prince had labeled "For Enemies":"Sectumsempra!"

Draco falls back, out of sight, but when Harry comes around the corner, Draco is lying in a deepening puddle of water, and he's bleeding out. Blood is seeping through his shirt like his chest's been torn to ribbons underneath the intact cloth. Harry's stunned.

Thank goodness, Snape is there. As Snape begins to chant the counter-curse, Harry flees.

Shaken, almost unable to speak, Harry sits in Gryffindor tower looking at the book that has been his constant companion all year. Ron, Hermione and Ginny are there, and it's Ginny—who knows what it's like to be sucked into a book and to believe the person who wrote it is your secret friend—who tells Harry, "You have to get rid of it. Today." She leads him to the Room of Requirement.

In there, they are intrigued by a noise they hear. Harry opens the door to a cabinet (yes, that cabinet) and out flies a bird! Ginny makes him close his eyes while she hides the book somewhere he won't find it. And then she comes back and kisses him before he can open his eyes. It's a true tender moment between two people who have been through a lot together.

Still in a bit of a daze from the kiss, in the hallway Harry runs into Slughorn, who promptly runs the other way. Harry knows he needs to make progress on getting that memory for Dumbledore: they're running out of school year. He decides now is the perfect time to drink that Felix Felicis that's been hanging around in his pocket all year.

So begins one of the best comic sequences of Dan Radcliffe's acting career. Harry when "under the influence" is almost as giddy as Ron was on the love potion. No, maybe *more* giddy. Harry's always been more about improvising with his instincts than following a logical plan, and the potion works like a charm. He feels good about going to Hagrid's for no apparent reason, but on his way down there he runs into Professor Slughorn clandestinely snipping tentacula leaves from some of Professor Sprout's plants. He tells the professor he's on his way to Hagrid's. Slughorn warns Harry he can't leave him wandering the grounds at nightfall alone so Harry insists the professor come along. They arrive just as Hagrid is crying over the death of his oldest friend, the giant acromantula (spider) Aragog. This leads to a full-on Irish wake with Hagrid and the professor drinking heartily and singing songs, and drunkenly rhapsodizing on the meaning of life and death. Harry, still quite bright-eyed with Felix, is enchanted by it all.

After Hagrid passes out, Slughorn tells Harry a tale of a thing of incredible beauty and wonder—a magical fish in a bowl, that Harry's own mother Lily had created for him, and which disappeared when she died. This is Harry's chance to get through to him. Harry tells Slughorn it was Lily's love that protected him, in death her love was stronger than Voldemort, and that if her sacrifice meant anything, then Harry needs to know what Tom Riddle learned all those years ago. "Be brave, professor. Be brave like my mother."

Slughorn relents.

Harry takes the memory straight to Dumbledore and they dive in. The complete conversation has Tom asking the professor about a thing called a Horcrux. Slughorn tells him it's an object in which someone has hidden part of their soul. But Tom presses him for more. Slughorn explains this would mean if your body was destroyed, your soul would live on, and you would not die. And Tom's already guessed the rest: to split your soul takes a murder. He asks about whether it would be possible to split the soul into seven pieces? A purely academic inquiry, of course.

Dumbledore is shaken by what they've learned. "This is beyond anything I imagined." He'd already suspected something like this was at work: he shows Harry Tom's old diary and a ring. The ring is what cursed Dumbledore's hand, which is looking much worse than it did back in September.

Harry is seized with the sense of purpose, though. If you can destroy all the Horcruxes, you can destroy the Dark Lord! But how can you find them all? Dumbledore explains that such Dark magic always leaves traces. Not only that, he thinks he has found one more, while he was traveling during the holidays... and he wants Harry's help tracking it down. "Once again, I must ask too much of you, Harry."

Cut to the Astronomy Tower at sunset the next day. Snape is there, demanding of Dumbledore "Have you ever considered that you ask too much?" But he's not talking about Harry; he's referring to the sacrifices he himself is making at Dumbledore's behest. (In the book, Snape's words are "And my soul, Dumbledore?" implying that Dumbledore is requiring him to do something deeply wrong.) "You agreed," Dumbledore says coldly. "There is nothing more to discuss." Snape departs, brushing past Harry on his way out.

Dumbledore has apparently extracted some promise from Snape, and now he extracts one from Harry. Harry must give his word to do exactly as Dumbledore tells him, whether that's run, hide, or even leave Dumbledore to die. He has to be pressed on that last point, but Harry gives his word.

Dumbledore, it turns out, is the one person with the power to Apparate in or out of Hogwarts. Harry takes his arm and finds himself transported to a craggy cliffside by the sea. After making a payment in blood, Dumbledore leads him into a cave by wand-light, and they cross an underground lake to a mysterious crystalline island that holds a basin full of a mysterious liquid. The potions and concoctions theme runs heavy, my friends. "It has to be drunk," Dumbledore says. "All of it. This potion may paralyze me, might make me forget why I am here, might cause me so much pain that I beg for relief. You are not to indulge these requests. It is your job, Harry, to make sure that I keep drinking even if you have to force it down my throat."

Thus ensues the most grueling montage since Harry's detention with Professor Umbridge.

When it is done, Harry picks up a locket that he finds at the bottom of the basin, as Dumbledore, weakened and ravaged by the effects of the potion, begs for water. Harry tries to conjure some, but the cursed scoop won't hold it. He finds himself trying to scoop water up from the lake instead.

This, of course, is when the Inferi (basically zombies) attack. Harry tries fending them off one at a time with his many defensive spells, as usual forgetting that someone else might be able to help. If only Dumbledore could reach his wand...

Harry is pulled into the lake by one of the animated corpses, but above him he sees a great glow. Fireballs seem to shoot down into the water: Inferi that have been beaten by Dumbledore's magic. When

Harry gains the surface again, he finds the great wizard controlling a whirlwind of fire. As Kingsley might say: Dumbledore's got style.

But I bet you're wondering what's happening back at Hogwarts. Ominous music can't mean anything good. Draco pulls the cover off the Vanishing Cabinet in the Room of Requirement for the last time, looking rather stricken as he does. He looks younger than we've seen him in a long time, round-eyed and apprehensive. This time he doesn't open the cabinet. It opens from within, and Bellatrix, Fenrir and two masked Death Eaters emerge.

Up on the Astronomy Tower, Dumbledore and Harry return, Dumbledore leaning heavily on Harry, who wants to get him to the hospital wing. But Dumbledore sits where he is, and insists only Snape must be summoned, no one else. Harry turns to go, but they hear someone else entering the tower. Dumbledore orders Harry to hide on the level below, not to act, not to speak, saying, "Trust me." Harry figures he's still under the promise to do as he's told, so he does.

And who should be coming up the stairs of the tower but Draco Malfoy. Dumbledore greets him mildly, and tells him, "Draco, you are no assassin." Giving Katie Bell a cursed necklace and sending her to Dumbledore? Poisoning a bottle of mead meant for Dumbledore? These attempts were "so weak your heart can't really have been in them." Draco shows Dumbledore his Dark Mark, saying, anguished, "I was chosen!" The wording of the script is deliberate: Draco is the dark side of the "chosen one" coin. The dark side, too, puts their faith in a boy, but it is bad faith, indeed.

Dumbledore seems to think he still has a chance to talk Draco down and fix everything—maybe even gain an ally—as he must have once done with a young, equally anguished Severus Snape back in the day. But Draco disarms him with a quick Expelliarmus, and then Dumbledore realizes that others are coming. Others on the Dark side.

"How?"

Draco explains he mended the Vanishing Cabinet: it forms a passage to Borgin and Burkes.

"Ingenious!" praises Dumbledore, and then tries to tell the story of Snape: "Years ago, I knew a boy who made all the wrong choices. Let me help you."

"You don't understand!" Draco cries, eyes red with fear. "I have to kill you, or he's going to kill me." (In the book, the line is, "I've got to do it! He'll kill me! He'll kill my whole family!")

And then it's too late to bargain. Bellatrix, Fenrir and some others emerge onto the observation platform, praising Draco and then exhorting him to finish the job. Harry draws his wand below—Dumbledore's orders be damned—but then Snape sidles up. He holds a finger to his lips for silence. Harry trusts Dumbledore and Dumbledore trusts Snape, so... Harry lets him pass.

Bellatrix is screaming at Draco, telling him to do it, but Snape silences her with a word. "No."

Dumbledore meets his gaze. "Severus," he says. "Please."

And Snape casts the Killing Curse, a flash of green light, and Dumbledore's body tumbles backward off the tower. Draco looks is if he's about to vomit, but Bellatrix fires the Dark Mark into the sky and then herds him away, the party of Death Eaters and Snape hurrying down the stairs. Harry emerges from his hiding place and follows them.

Bellatrix can't help herself. On their way out she vandalizes the Great Hall, and Draco can't keep the distress off his face. They exit, heading down the hill, and she sets Hagrid's house on fire as Harry stumbles after them, calling out Snape. "He trusted you!"

Bellatrix knocks Harry down with a spell, but Snape stops her. "No, he belongs to the Dark Lord!" Snape sends her and the others on ahead, as Harry tries again to attack. Snape flicks Harry's hexes away with ease, even Sectumsempra. "You dare use my own spells against me?" Snape says in a voice low with threat. Because yes, *he* is the Half-Blood Prince. Snape has been the key to the entire book. He leaves Harry lying helpless in the grass. By the time Harry gains his feet again, the Death Eaters are long gone, and a crowd is gathering at the foot of the Astronomy Tower.

Harry is the only one who will approach the body. He kneels, taking up the locket, and putting his hand over Dumbledore's still heart. Eventually Ginny goes to Harry, embracing him, and he cries on her shoulder.

Every wand is raised in silent tribute to the wizard, the man, who has left them, and their collected wand-light disperses the evil mark overhead.

Final day at school. The Great Hall, previously the site of so many triumphant last feasts, is empty, the windows smashed, the torches cold. Harry enters Dumbledore's office, which is also empty, but it almost seems as if Albus might be back any minute, a half-finished zarf of tea at his desk, his glasses in a book as if he might be back to pick up where he left off reading. Above the desk, though, a new portrait has appeared, joining the other headmasters in the gallery. Dumbledore's portrait: asleep.

The Trio go to the Astronomy Tower, where Hermione wants to know if Harry thinks Draco would have done the deed. "No," Harry says. "He was lowering his wand. In the end it was Snape. It was always Snape." Harry feels guilty that he didn't stop Snape. Not only that, the locket is a fake. He hands it to Hermione.

Inside is a message, intended for the Dark Lord: "I have stolen the real Horcrux and intend to destroy it as soon as I can," wrote the mysterious R.A.B. As she ponders this new mystery, Hermione's mind decides it's a good time to fill Harry in on something else, too: Ron's decided that it's okay for Harry to like Ginny. "But keep the snogging to a minimum." Harry must think she's nuts. He explains he's not coming back to Hogwarts *at all*. He's off to finish what Dumbledore started, to track down the Horcruxes, and then rid the world of Voldemort for good.

Hermione doesn't see any reason why a person can't multitask, and besides, it's Harry who's being "thick." After all, he's not going to find those Horcruxes by himself. "You need us, Harry."

Yes, he does. The mission is finally known, and there is one final chapter in the saga of He Who Must Not Be Named versus The Boy Who Lived yet to come. (Well, technically, two, but you know what I mean.)

7: Harry Potter and the Deathly Hallows, Part One

Film Data

Title: Harry Potter and the Deathly Hallows: Part 1
Release Date: November 19, 2010
Director: David Yates
Screenplay: Steve Kloves
Producers: David Heyman, David Barron, and J.K. Rowling
USA Opening Weekend: $125,017,372
Running Time: 2:26

In March 2008, Warner Brothers made the announcement that the film adaptation of *Harry Potter and the Deathly Hallows* would be split into two installments. This word came after screenwriter Steve Kloves and director David Yates had been wrestling with the final book, which had been released in July 2007, for many months. "We feel that the best way to do the book, and its many fans, justice is to expand the screen adaptation of *Harry Potter and the Deathly Hallows* and release the film in two parts," said Jeff Robinov, president of Warner Bros. Pictures Group, in a statement. It wouldn't hurt, of course, that each of the films would be a guaranteed galleon-maker, making the decision a no-brainer. J.K. Rowling agreed with the approach because there would be so much plot and so many loose ends to tie-up.

As David Yates told the *L.A. Times,* the decision "was born out of purely creative reasons. Unlike every other book, you cannot remove elements of this book. You can remove scenes of Ron playing quidditch from the fifth book, and you can remove [other] subplots... but with the seventh, that can't be done." Producer David Heyman, the progenitor of the film project back in 1997, told Reuters, the book "is so rich, the story so dense, and there is so much that is resolved that after discussing it with Jo, we came to the conclusion that the two parts were needed to do it justice."

As with many things, the Potter films pioneered new techniques and trends, but "one book, two movies" becoming a trend wasn't expected. But in short order, *Twilight* jumped on the bandwagon, then the *Hunger Games,* and then Veronica Roth's *Divergent* series. Each of these YA series had vocal critics of how the books ended, so maybe it shouldn't be too huge a surprise that the double-shot finales for those film series' weren't particularly successful with critics, either. One didn't need a crystal ball or tea leaves to correctly predict that both the final Potter films would be box office juggernauts. They were. But how did the critics find them as movies?

Metacritic rates the reviews for *Deathly Hallows, Part 1* as "generally favorable," with 31 favorable, eight mixed and only three negative reviews among the 42 major review outlets they compiled. The main criticism voiced multiple times was that anyone who hasn't seen the previous six movies "will be hopelessly lost," as *USA Today* wrote, though the film is "arguably the best installment... of the film franchise." The *Chicago Sun-Times* agreed: "A handsome and sometimes harrowing film... will be completely unintelligible for anyone coming to the series for the first time."

This worry that a newcomer might be baffled if they hopped on the Hogwarts Express 75% of the way through the journey seems like concern trolling to me. *Now,* of course, is different: new generations of fans are always growing up into fandom—one reason why this book exists. But in 2010? After the previous films had racked up over $4 billion at box offices worldwide, was there anyone left on the planet who hadn't seen at least some of them by then? (Not to mention the fact that the *Deathly Hallows* book sold 2.65 million copies in the UK alone on just its first day in stores—one for every 24 Brits in *just one day*. By the time the book had been out for a year, 44 million copies had been sold worldwide in English alone.) It seems a little strange that critics were troubling themselves over the fact there might be a Rip Van Winkle out there who had slept through the entire phenomenon, when it had been so dominant in the landscape of pop culture for the entire decade. By the time *Deathly Hallows, Part 1* was released, the ubiquity of Harry Potter was such that the first Wizarding World theme park at Universal Orlando had been open for nearly half a year, causing the attendance at Islands of Adventure to jump 36% in 2010.

Overall, critics very much enjoyed the continuing "maturity" of the stories, themes and the performances that went with them. "The movie belongs solidly to Mr. Radcliffe, Mr. Grint, and Ms. Watson, who have grown into nimble actors, capable of nuances of feeling that would do their elders proud," writes *The New York Times*. *Slate* writes, "The three young leads—especially Emma Watson, who can do more with a still face than any actress her age—are all terrific."

Slate wasn't the only publication to call Emma Watson's performance as a standout in DH1. Hermione's character gets to really shine as times get tough, and screenwriter Steve Kloves had told J.K. Rowling at their very first meeting that she was his favorite character in the books. (Remember that if you ever wonder why Hermione in the films seems to "steal" some of Ron's best lines.) "Watson's so good," enthuses the *Philadelphia Inquirer,* "that one wishes Rowling had built her septology around Hermione Potter."

The other common criticism in the reviews is one that mirrored criticisms of the book: our heroes seem to spend an awfully long time wandering aimlessly in the woods. "The first third is brisk, the middle third gloomy, and the finale of Part 1 not so much a cliffhanger as a grim, inspiring, tease," writes the *Orlando Sentinel.* "Slower and stranger than the previous films," concludes the *St. Louis Post-Dispatch,* largely based on the slow middle spent in the woods. The *Charlotte Observer* called it "nearly devoid of plot twists and marked by long patches where Harry, Ron, and Hermione camp in the woods or by the sea or near a frozen lake and ponder What It All Means." They don't spend quite as long as Sam and Frodo spend traipsing across Mordor in the book of *The Return of the King,* but it definitely feels too long.

On the other hand, that's the time when the most character nuance and maturity come through. If the Harry Potter books are truly literature (they are!) then it's to be expected that there will be parts that are not merely bang-zoom action thrills, but most expect those to be the first parts of a book cut when adapted to film. Kloves's nearly 10-year-long relationship with J.K. Rowling herself and as the longtime screenwriter of these characters gave him the stones to keep much of the "camping scenes" intact, and even to invent new ones. The scene where Harry and Hermione alleviate their loneliness and dread by (innocently) dancing to a Muggle radio station was a Kloves invention given full support by Rowling.

It's one of the best scenes in the film, but I still felt there was too much camping. In my view, the parts where the Trio are wandering the woods trying to figure out their next move was Rowling's subconscious wandering around doing the same. Once they escape the woods, in both book and films the plot speeds up to breakneck pace right through to the very end. If I were the editor (and we weren't behind deadline), I would have suggested some trimming. But the truth is the camping scenes don't really hurt the success of either book or film. If we've been with Harry, Ron, and Hermione this far, we're going to stick with them, just as they've stuck with each other.

Casting Notes

Bill Nighy as Rufus Scrimgeour

"Until I was in Harry Potter—and I only got in under the wire—I was trying to find some distinction in being the only British actor who hadn't been in Harry Potter," Bill Nighy told Buzzfeed in 2014. "I was trying to invent that as a kind of a performer's status. So I was relieved, finally, to be invited." He decided to play Scrimgeour with a Welsh accent. "I just thought it might be, you know, interesting. I went to the director [David Yates] and said, 'You know what, I think he might be Welsh.' Much to my amazement, [he] said, 'Yeah, well, why not? Try that!'" In an interview with SciFiWire, Nighy revealed he considered Scrimgeour to be "a rather tragic figure. ... So that's a very moving thing to play." Ultimately he doesn't get much screen time, but like most of the top shelf Brits in the series, he makes the most of his appearance. From Buzzfeed: "I had a very, very impressive wig, which I thought made me look kind of cool. It made me incredibly notable in the world of 9 to 15 year-olds. To a whole generation, I am simply Rufus Scrimgeour."

Domnhall Gleeson as Bill Weasley

Domnhall Gleeson is the son of Brendan Gleeson, who played Mad-Eye Moody. The family connection certainly didn't hurt, although until he landed the role of Bill Weasley, Domnhall was relatively unknown. "I was a massive [Harry Potter] fan. When they asked my dad to play Mad-Eye I was so incredibly excited. I said, 'Listen, if one of the other brothers' parts comes up, you need to get me in for an audition,'" he told *Entertainment Weekly* in 2018. But what clinched the role was probably something simple: "I got that role because I'm a ginger! Red hair was my only qualification," he told *The Telegraph* in 2013. "I was a Weasley waiting for a role."

He's been very prolific since playing a Weasley, spanning indie art films, plays, a live-action Peter Rabbit, and also the part of General Hux in the recent *Star Wars* films, and his Potter role may have helped with that launch trajectory. "There was about a year between shooting and the movie's release where I was going into meetings and people didn't know I only had two lines in [Deathly Hallows], so I probably got auditions for things that I may not have otherwise."

Rhys Ifans as Xenophilius Lovegood

Luna apparently gets her hippie-dippy vibe from her dad, who's the one to provide the Trio with the most information about the titular Hallows themselves. Rhys Ifans is a BAFTA and Empire award winning veteran character actor (*Notting Hill, Elementary, The Amazing Spider Man*) who admitted he hadn't read the books or seen the previous films, but later compared being cast in the Potter franchise with being knighted. "You just sit with all these actors you've starved with in the theater... sitting there dressed as wizards [and] having wand-offs. So it's very pleasantly surreal," he told MTV, sounding rather Lovegoodian. "When you're an English actor and you get the 'Harry Potter' call—it's like Batman, you know? You have a normal phone, and then you have one that is made out of wood. That's the 'Potter' people. They call you up [and] you get your wand out, you put your cloak on and off you go. It's a real honor. It's like getting knighted or something."

What to Look For

Shell Cottage

"A cottage has appeared, as if by magic, on a remote beach in Pembrokeshire, Wales," reported *The Telegraph* in spring 2009. The exterior shots of Shell Cottage were done on location and required the building of the three-story cottage that appears to be covered entirely by shells. The scallop-shell roof and exterior were actually done with molded plastic, and the interior, which wasn't used for filming, was filled entirely with containers of water to ensure the house wouldn't move.

Back at The Burrow

Plot continuity issues aside, it's great to be back at the homey jumble that is The Burrow again. In various scenes leading up to the wedding you get a sense of the ramshackle, haphazard way it's decorated. Bonnie Wright, who played Ginny Weasley, spent some time during the filming of *Half-Blood Prince* working in the art department at Leavesden studios between stints where she was needed for filming. "I spent about a week in the art department," she says on the DVD extras. "Some of the things I was doing were to help decorate the Weasley house [where] everything is meant to be homemade, and I was actually making [the props] which was quite weird because in scene I'd be looking around thinking 'Oh, I did that.'"

Deathly Deleted Scenes

There are several deleted scenes on the *Deathly Hallows* DVDs that are worth watching. These would really have deepened the film(s) considerably, but were cut for time constraints. Two involve Harry saying goodbye to the Dursleys. They're fleeing Privet Drive because it's too likely that Death Eaters may show up to possibly kidnap, torture or just kill them, thanks to their connection with

Harry. One has Aunt Petunia reminding Harry that although he lost his mother, she also lost a sister that night. The other has Dudley stopping to say goodbye to Harry and that he doesn't think Harry is "a waste of space."

* * *

Deathly Hallows, Part 1 Drinking Game

Drink every time anyone gets anything out of
Hermione's beaded string bag
(or any time the bag is mentioned, really).
Bonus drinks: anytime the Deluminator is clicked.

* * *

Book Lore

Despite the breaking of *Deathly Hallows* into two films, there are still elements from the books that didn't make it onto the screen.

The Power of the Dursleys

So, you may have wondered why, if the Dursleys abused Harry so badly, did Dumbledore insist on him going back to live with them every summer? Why couldn't he have lived at The Burrow with Ron's family, who even offered to take him in, or later at Number 12 Grimmauld Place, where he would even be magically hidden from Voldemort? (In fact, after Sirius' death, technically No. 12 might have passed to Harry, if his godfather left him everything...?) The film doesn't have time to go into it, but Dumbledore eventually explains in the books that the "bond of blood" between Lily and her sister Marge would mean that while Harry was a minor, as long as he stayed under Marge's roof, it would extend the charm of protection that Lily Potter's sacrifice bestowed on baby Harry. However the moment Harry turns 17, which is the age of majority in the wizarding world, it'll be open season on Harry once again.

Dumbledore's Legacy

You might be wondering why the Minister for Magic, Rufus Scrimgeour, shows up at The Burrow to hand over the things left in Dumbledore's will to Harry, Ron and Hermione. In the book there's a more complicated set-up (of course there is...) in which the Ministry held onto the items for a full month after Dumbledore's death to examine and investigate them, trying to figure out what Dumbledore was up to. When Scrimgeour shows up to pass the objects on, it's not only that he can no longer legally hang on to them after the month is up: if that were so, he could have just owled them over. He wants to use the opportunity to interrogate Harry, Ron and Hermione about Dumbledore's plots. (They of course play innocent, as if they aren't about to go looking for Horcruxes, a plan Dumbledore had urged them to keep secret from the Ministry.) The text of the will and the reasons why each item are given are changed in the movie, though they are just as cryptic. In the book, Harry and the Minister get into such a heated argument that the Minister burns a hole in Harry's shirt. In the film he merely warns, "I don't know what you're up to Mr. Potter, but you can't fight this war on your own. He's too strong."

Teddy (Edward) Lupin

Although an actor was cast to play Teddy—the son of Tonks and Remus—in the epilogue, he was cut from the film, and almost all mention of young Teddy—or even of Tonks being pregnant with him—is cut, as well. Among the deleted scenes there is one where Remus asks Harry to be his child's godfather. As it is, the only scene that made it into the films where he's mentioned at all is when Harry goes into the forest and the Resurrection Stone brings the spirits of his guardians visible to him. Harry says to Remus, "But [what about] your son?" and Remus replies, "Other people will tell him what his mother and father died for." I get the feeling if there had been any other dialogue between Harry and Remus in that scene, they would have gone with that instead, which would have erased Teddy from the film canon completely. As it is, he goes without a name.

Plot Recap

"Really, my boy, are you sure you knew him at all?"

The films left behind the literary formula of always showing us Harry stuck with the Dursleys for the summer long ago, but we'll get a glimpse of them soon enough. This film opens with a montage, establishing the threat all are under now. Brand new Minister for Magic Rufus Scrimgeour looking very phlegmatic as he proclaims the Ministry's "strength." But that strength doesn't help the Muggle families being killed, now, does it? Cut to Hermione in her bedroom at home looking at a *Daily Prophet* headline about Muggle murders, and then to the Dursleys, who are hightailing it into hiding—much like they did back in *Sorcerer's Stone*, except this time they leave Harry behind. The Weasleys are at Shell Cottage (presumably because in the previous movie, Bellatrix's attack showed that The Burrow wasn't safe?). An emotional Hermione erases herself from the memory of her parents with a spell.

This is serious business. Cue the darkest title card yet.

The streaky, dark CGI cloud that represents Apparition lands at the gates of Malfoy Manor and resolves into the equally dark figure of Severus Snape. He strides through the wards and up to the formal dining room. The long banquet table is full of Death Eaters, but suspended in the air above them, bloody and beaten-looking, is someone he knows quite well. In fact since Snape is Hogwarts headmaster now, she is one of his employees: Charity Burbage, Professor of Muggle Studies.

Voldemort wants to know when Potter will be vulnerable. Harry is, for some unstated reason (see Book Lore), safe until he leaves Privet Drive. Snape has conflicting information from their sources within the Ministry itself about when Harry will be moved to "a safe house" where it will be difficult to attack him again. ("Inconvenient" is the word Snape wryly uses.) Who will the Dark Lord believe? Meanwhile, Voldemort has another quandary: he knows now that he must be the one to kill Harry, but when he last tried that (at the end of *Goblet of Fire*) his wand and Harry's connected. He can't risk that happening again. Whose wand will he take?

How about Lucius Malfoy, rescued from Azkaban, but looking very much like a prisoner in his own home, which the Dark Lord has taken as his base of operations? Voldemort snaps the fancy metal handle from Lucius' wand and proceeds to see how well it works, casting the Killing Curse on Professor Burbage and feeding her corpse to his giant snake, Nagini.

Back at Privet Drive, Harry has packed his things and is taking one last look into the cupboard under the stairs where he spent most of the first 10 years of his life. In short order, the Order arrive, with a plan to get Harry out of there safely: by flying, with six others impersonating him using Polyjuice. In quick order we re-meet Mad-Eye Moody, Kingsley Shacklebolt, and Fleur Delacourt who gives a werewolf-scarred Bill Weasley a kiss on the cheek—ooh la la—and another couple is re-established: Tonks calls Remus her "husband" and tries to give another "bit of news" but Mad-Eye cuts her off to get the operation underway. (Spoiler: the "news" is that she's pregnant, but it never gets mentioned again until rather late next movie...)

They have to fly instead of Apparate or Floo because with Harry still underage, he's subject to a spell called The Trace, which lets the Ministry monitor him. So brooms, thestrals and flying motorcycles it is. Of course the real Harry goes with Hagrid in the motorcycle, a fitting bookend to his arrival there when he was 15 months old. (There will be a lot of bookends and things coming full circle in these last two films.) The Weasley Twins, Fleur, Hermione, Ron and a new character named Mundungus Fletcher—who came from Central Casting when they asked for a sketchy scam artist/thief type, complete with Cockney accent—will be impersonating Harry. It's serious, but it's highly entertaining to watch Dan play the parts of people playing him ("Bill, look away! I'm hideous!", "Harry, your eyesight really is awful."). Also, who knew Harry Potter had so much chest hair?

Of course, wouldn't it make sense to have Harry Polyjuice into someone else, also...? Mad-Eye doesn't seem to have thought of that.

Things turn serious soon enough. They're ambushed almost as soon as they take off. If the murder of a Hogwarts professor in the first 10 minutes didn't clue you in that no one is safe, the killing of Hedwig surely will. Isn't there a rule against killing the main character's beloved animal companion? Not in the UK, apparently. The ruse doesn't work: Voldemort follows Hagrid and Harry, but when he attacks, Lucius' wand does not withstand Harry's counterattack and is destroyed.

Hagrid and Harry make it to The Burrow first. (Wait. The Burrow? The same Burrow that was *destroyed* last film? This is the "safe house" where it will be difficult to attack Harry? The *same place they attacked him* last film? WTF? Cast a Hand-wave Spell—maybe there are better protections in place now...?) The others start to arrive: George has been hit, an ear sheared clear off. Lupin challenges everyone, trying to ensure there is no impostor among them, since it's obvious they were ambushed. Someone ratted them out. (We know it to be Snape... but how did Snape know when presumably the Order are no longer sharing information with him since he is Dumbledore's killer...?)

One pair is left unaccounted for: Mundungus, who was flying with Mad-Eye, Disapparated as soon as the ambush hit. And now Mad-Eye's dead. It's a blow.

That night, Harry dreams of Voldemort and sees him holding Ollivander prisoner. Determined that "no one else is going to die... not for me," Harry packs his things and tries to leave the Burrow before dawn. Ron is right on his heels. "You think Mad-Eye died for you? You think George took that curse for you? ... This is a whole lot bigger than that."

Besides, what's Harry think he's doing leaving Hermione behind? Ron sagely points out, "We wouldn't last two days without her." Also, Harry's still got the Trace on him. So he's got to *at least* stay through Bill and Fleur's wedding.

Ginny asks Harry for help zipping up her party dress, which is how you know they're still an item, because otherwise she would have just asked her Mum... Also, nice kiss, even if George is sneaking around behind them.

While everyone's raising the wedding tent outside with levitation charms, who should come along but the Minister of Magic himself? He's come to personally present Harry, Ron and Hermione with the items left to them in Dumbledore's will. (See "Book Lore" if you're wondering why the heck the actual leader of the wizarding world would bother with this errand other than to get actor Bill Nighy more screen time.) Ron gets Dumbledore's Deluminator—a thing that looks like a cigarette lighter except it captures the light from any lamp or lantern. When you're done doing whatever you were doing in the dark, you can send the lights back from whence they came. Dumbledore wrote that it should be Ron's "in the hope that when things seem most dark, it will show him the light."

Hermione is given a book of wizarding children's stories, *The Tales of Beedle the Bard.*

The will bequeaths to Harry the first snitch he ever caught as Gryffindor Seeker. Scrimegeour seems disappointed that nothing happens when he hands it over, but says nothing. Dumbledore also left a second bequest for Harry: the Sword of Gryffindor (!) but "the sword was not Dumbledore's to give away." Plus there's the fact it can present itself to "any worthy Gryffindor." And besides, Scrimgeour admits, the current whereabouts of the sword are unknown. Welp.

Cut to a night exterior of the Burrow and the wedding party tent all lit up. Irish folk music plays, but as the camera draws close to the revelry, we can see Aurors standing guard all around the tent. Inside, Harry meets Luna and her father, Xenophilius. He's got the same hippy trippy style as his daughter, and Harry can't help but notice the triangular pendant hanging around his neck. As the editor of *The Quibbler*, Xenophilius expresses his support for Harry—"unlike those toadies at the *Daily Prophet.*"

The wedding guest Harry really wants to speak to, though, is Elphias Doge, who wrote an elegy to Dumbledore in the *Prophet.* He finds Elphias, who was Dumbledore's oldest friend, drinking alone and happy to talk. From him Harry finds out Dumbledore had a brother—Aberforth—and we find out Harry's really forgetful because we actually have already seen Aberforth (and his goats) two movies back. He's the bartender at the Hog's Head, where Hermione organized the first secret meeting of Dumbledore's Army.

Harry learns something even more shocking about the Dumbledores from a third wedding guest, a gossipy witch who horns into their conversation. She tells Harry that Rita Skeeter has just written an 800-page biography on the notoriously private Dumbledore, with

Bathilda Bagshot spilling the beans. Ms. Bagshot is the author of *A History of Magic* (a text used at Hogwarts) and a longtime associate of the Dumbledore family. They all lived in Godric's Hollow together after Dumbledore's father killed three Muggle boys. "Honestly, my boy," she said. "Are you sure you knew him a'tall?"

Before Harry can reflect much on the fact that perhaps his hero has feet of clay, a silvery Patronus shoots into the tent, proclaiming in Kingsley's voice that the Ministry has fallen. Mere seconds later, Death Eaters swoop into the tent. Guests begin Disapparating as quickly as they can, but not before someone is killed with a curse. Harry runs through the chaos calling Ginny's name, but Remus grabs him, screaming "Go! Go!" Hermione and Ron take hold of Harry and a moment later they appear in Piccadilly Circus, a crowded, busy area of London. Hermione Apparated them to "the first place that popped into my head," because her parents used to take her to the theater there.

In a back alley she pulls street clothes for Ron and Harry out of her beaded string bag. Apparently she's been packed and ready to flee at a moment's notice all along. She's used an Undetectable Extension Charm to make the bag much, much bigger on the inside. (You can hear a large pile of books fall over.) They retreat to a cafe to plan their next move. Harry wants to go back to the wedding to help, but Ron points out it's Harry the Death Eaters are after. There is no going back.

* * *

Easter Egg: The area Hermione has taken them to has many theaters. On the wall in the cafe is a poster for the 2007 West End revival of *Equus,* which starred Daniel Radcliffe and Richard Griffiths (Vernon Dursley). The play caused quite a stir since the role required Dan to appear in the nude. In the run-up to *Order of the Phoenix,* Warner Brothers had built a marketing campaign around Harry having his first kiss, and meanwhile the actor who played him was on stage baring it all. The role of disturbed Alan Strang in the infamous play was certainly one way Dan established that he wasn't going to allow himself to be typecast as Harry Potter for his whole life. He later reprised the role on Broadway.

* * *

The Trio can't go to the Leaky Cauldron or any of the usual places. Before they can decide what to do, or even get their cappuccinos, they're attacked by two Death Eaters. They fight them and win (half-destroying the cafe in the process). Harry recognizes Rowle ("he was on the Astronomy tower the night Dumbledore was killed") and Ron knows Dolohov from his Wanted posters. Ron wants to kill them, but Harry says no, just wipe their memories and let's get out of here.

They hit the streets, trying to figure out how they were found. It can't be the Trace, which broke when Harry turned 17 (on some unspecified moment between the wedding and now). They decide their next best bet is to try hiding out at No. 12 Grimmauld Place.

They spend the night, and Harry wakes up from another one of those dreams of Voldemort interrogating Ollivander. "I believed another wand would work! I swear!" the wand-maker tells him. Harry doesn't know what that means, but as long as he's awake, he may as well snoop around his godfather's old bedroom. Look, Sirius even had an old copy of Bathilda Bagshot's *A History of Magic*.

Ron's the one who stumbles on a more interesting clue. The other bedroom, the one that belonged to Sirius' brother, has his name on the door: Regulus Arcturus Black—aka R.A.B.

So it was Sirius' brother who stole the Horcrux from the cave and intended to destroy it. The Trio soon run across Kreacher, the old house elf, who tells them (after much browbeating) that Regulus had given it to Kreacher to destroy, but no matter how he tried, Kreacher could not. But Kreacher doesn't have it anymore, because Mundungus made off with many things, the locket among them. Harry sends Kreacher to find Mundungus.

Meanwhile, the whole of Voldemort's efforts are thrown into finding Harry. The Ministry declares him Undesirable No. 1, printing Wanted posters and filling the *Daily Prophet*. Death Eaters stop the train to Hogwarts but find only other students. (Neville tells them, "hey, losers. He isn't here.") The new Minister is a skinny, goateed fellow we last saw seated at Voldemort's table in Malfoy Manor—Pius Thicknesse—and he announces all Ministry employees will be "evaluated." Meanwhile we see some rough-looking wizards ("Snatchers") dragging a beaten, bloody figure through the Ministry atrium. Sure doesn't look good.

Back at No. 12, Harry's staring at the Snitch, trying to divine what message he was supposed to receive from Dumbledore through it. Hermione points out that Snitches have flesh memories, so one can always prove which Seeker caught it, so she "thought it might open at your touch. That Dumbledore might have hidden something inside it." But no such luck.

Kreacher arrives, forcing Mundungus back to No. 12 with some help from an old friend: Dobby. Mundungus confesses he tried to sell the locket on Diagon Alley, and ended up giving it as a bribe to a Ministry witch wearing a "bleeding bow"—Dolores Umbridge.

Next stop: the Ministry.

Our heroes kidnap three Ministry employees on their way to work the next morning and with the help of Polyjuice, take their ID badges, clothes and their places. The employee entrance is through a set of not-metaphorical-at-all public toilets. After flushing themselves in, Ron is accosted by Yaxley, the head of Magical Law Enforcement, who thinks he is a chap named Reginald. Yaxley wants something done about the fact it's been raining inside his office for two days, especially if Reginald wants his wife to survive her Blood Status hearing, which is about to start down in the courtrooms.

No sooner do they leave Ron off to deal with the rain than Umbridge herself steps into their elevator. Apparently Hermione is Mafalda Hopkirk (the same official who sent Harry's expulsion letter at the start of fifth year). Umbridge expects Mafalda to accompany her to the Blood Status hearing.

Harry, in the guise of Albert Runcorn—who appears to be something of a heavy—leaves them to it and finds himself at the door to Umbridge's office, which overlooks a propaganda factory where a few dozen employees are churning out pamphlets: "Mudbloods And The Dangers They Pose To A Perfect Pureblood Society." Harry surreptitiously drops a Decoy Detonator (a Weasley twins invention) and as the pamphleteers panic, he slips into the office. "Accio locket!" produces nothing, and as he rifles through Umbridge's desk he finds nothing...

Well, nothing relating to the locket. He does find dossiers on Arthur Weasley, Hermione, Mad-Eye (a huge X through his photo now that he has been killed) and Dumbledore (similarly X'ed). Hermione's dossier is stamped TRACKED. (Presumably that's how they were found in the cafe on Shaftesbury Avenue, and also presumably Polyjuice foils the tracking somehow, or they'd know she was at the Ministry.) Harry gets out of there quickly after that, running into disguised Ron in the elevator again. They go down to the courtrooms to see what's happening with Hermione.

She's serving as a sort of stenographer for Umbridge who, as head of the Muggleborn Registration Commission, is interrogating a witch named Mary Cattermole—the wife of the chap Ron potioned into. Harry can instantly sense the locket in the courtroom. Umbridge, the foul creature, is *wearing* it. Not only that, she has the courtroom guarded by Dementors. Her patronus (a cat) sits next to her, keeping them at bay.

Mary sees Ron-as-Reg peering into the courtroom and calls out to him. Harry, as Runcorn, pushes him into the hearing area. Umbridge demands to know what witch or wizard Mary took her wand from. Mary cries as she says she got it at age 11 from Ollivander. "You're lying," Umbridge says.

But Harry has stepped close to her now. No, he says, as his Polyjuice is beginning to wear off, "You're lying, Dolores. And we must not tell lies!" He Stupefies her and Hermione grabs the locket. They run, with Mary and Ron-as-Reg, Dementors in cold pursuit. Harry has to blast them away from the elevator with a Patronus charm and then they ascend to the lobby atrium. Harry and Hermione look fully like themselves now and they walk as quickly as they can toward the exits. Ron grabs Mary and tells her "Leave now. Get the kids. We have to get out of the country." She grabs him and kisses him... just as he turns back into Ron Weasley.

The real Reg Cattermole shows up then, in just his underthings. Ron says "Long story," and they run for it. Yaxley comes up from the courtroom then, and chases them. Harry makes it into the Floo, but Yaxley has nearly caught up to Hermione and Ron when they leap into the flames. The disorientation of Apparition hits and when everything stops moving, Harry finds he's lying on a forest floor, the locket on the leaves a few feet from him. He picks it up, then realizes Hermione and Ron are across the clearing and Ron is clearly hurt. Yaxley had caught hold of the two of them when they tried to Apparate to Grimmauld Place, and although she shook him off and Apparated them all again—to this forest—Ron got Splinched in the process. He's got a gash through his chest and shoulder like his arm was nearly torn off. Hermione seals the gash with a potion of dittany she had packed, but Ron won't be going anywhere for a while. Good thing that little string bag has a tent in it. (Gee, it looks a lot like the Weasley tent from the Quidditch World Cup.)

The next day they try every destructive spell they know, but nothing puts so much as a scratch on the locket. Ron seems angry at Dumbledore for not telling Harry how to destroy it, and Harry seems angry at Ron for being right. Later, Harry gets another vision from Voldemort: he wants something from Gregorovitch, another famous wand-maker. Voldemort reads the wand-maker's mind to see it was stolen years ago by a young, blond thief. Harry tells Hermione about it, but it's yet another lead they don't have enough information to follow. And Ron isn't ready to travel again yet, anyway. Harry bites Hermione's head off when she points it out.

She's too smart to take it personally. "Take it off," she insists, until Harry finally removes the locket. He's been wearing it to keep it safe. They'll rotate who wears it now, since it obviously makes whoever is wearing it feel like shit and act even worse.

That night, Harry hears reports on the wizarding wireless that with Snape as headmaster of Hogwarts, discipline is enacted by Death Eaters on the staff, and Hermione has a close call with the Snatchers. Tromping through the woods right near the tent, they can't see or hear her, or the tent, because of the many defensive spells she has layered around them, but they can smell her perfume. This spot is no longer safe.

Since Ron can't yet Apparate without potentially worsening his condition, they go on foot across the English countryside, while dark streaks of Death Eaters on the move cut across the sky. The Horcrux seems to darken Ron's mood the most, filling him with paranoia that Harry doesn't know what he's doing (well, he doesn't) and that Harry and Hermione are going to pair up romantically and leave him behind. Cue montage of traipsing across fields, under bridges, past burned out trailer parks (would Muggleborns have been living in trailer parks...?). One night, Hermione is cutting Harry's hair (now you know they're *really* bored) when she has a brainstorm. The Sword of Gryffindor. That's what they need to destroy the Horcrux. That must be why Dumbledore intended for them to have it.

But they *don't* have it. And Ron's had enough. He and Harry nearly come to blows when he says Harry doesn't know what it's like to worry that your family members might die because *his family's dead.* (Yeah, I would've gone after him for that, too, Harry.) Ron storms off.

Well, at least the other two can Apparate now. Except there's still the problem that they don't know where they're going. Neither does the audience which makes this whole section of the movie (and the book) feel interminable.

But at least it gives us a chance for Harry and Hermione to have a little scene together. Without Ron obsessively listening to the wizarding wireless broadcasts from the resistance, Hermione happens across a Muggle radio station. Harry holds out his hand, silently asking her to dance, and they do, just two friends who are desperately lonely and in need of comfort.

Are you ready for yet another lead that our heroes can't figure out? Sure you are. The next day, Harry has an idea. He's staring at that Snitch again and on a whim, he kisses it. Words appear on it—*by magic!*—that read "I open at the close." Harry remembers that he didn't catch the Snitch with his hand. He caught it in his *mouth*, so that was the secret to activating it... except that this message still doesn't mean anything to them.

Hermione's found something, too. In the book of stories Dumbledore gave her, there's a symbol drawn in by hand, a triangle around a circle around a vertical bar. Harry recognizes it as the shape of the pendant Luna's father was wearing at the wedding. But what does it mean? For now it's yet another clue they don't have a clue about.

Harry tells her his latest idea for where they should go, though: Godric's Hollow. It's where Harry was born, where his parents are buried (not to mention where the Dumbledores lived, and where Bathilda Bagshot lives now). And Voldemort himself almost died there, so doesn't that sound like the kind of place he'd hide a Horcrux? Hermione isn't so sure about that... but she thinks maybe if Dumbledore had hidden the sword so that Harry could find it later, wouldn't that be the logical place for it?

They arrive at a quaint village in the snow in the middle of the night. A church bell is ringing and they can hear a hymn being sung: it's Christmas Eve, that's how long they've been traipsing around. Bill and Fleur's wedding was at the end of August and now it's December! No wonder it feels like they've been getting nowhere fast!

They go into the church cemetery because Harry wants to look for his parents' graves. Hermione finds the tomb of Ignotus Peverell, which has the triangular glyph they're looking for engraved in the stone. But Harry only has tear-filled eyes for the double headstone of James and Lily Potter. He's only torn away when they realize a woman is staring at them: Bathilda Bagshot.

She knew Dumbledore, he thinks. Maybe she's got the sword. She leads them silently to her home, where Harry sees a photo of the thief who stole a wand from Gregorovitch...! But old Bathilda doesn't answers questions, just leads Harry silently upstairs. All that can be heard is the occasional fly buzzing around. Hermione stays downstairs and finds a copy of Rita Skeeter's book on Dumbledore with a "thank you" note from Rita attached to it. You probably can't read it because it goes by too quickly, but it looks to me like it says:

Dear Batty,

> *Thanking you for your help.*
> *You said everything, even if you don't remember.*

> *—Rita*

Upstairs, Bathilda finally speaks her first words to Harry... and they are in Parseltongue. (Harry can never tell when someone, human or snake, switches into Parseltongue and he's not aware when he speaks it in return.) She seems to be showing him a photo album that includes the young Dumbledores and the young man Harry was asking about. But this is just to distract Harry while she transforms from the old woman into a giant snake. The old woman wasn't alive, just an animated corpse, inside which Voldemort's snake Nagini was hiding. She emerges and attacks Harry, as giant snakes are wont to do. Hermione and he fight it. Harry loses his wand but Hermione is able to grab it. She casts one last curse at the snake and then Apparates them both the hell out of there.

This time they land in the Forest of Dean. Yep. Back to camping. Only now Hermione's got a new book to read, and Harry's got to recover from the snake attack. In the Skeeter book, she finds the guy Harry was wondering about and it's none other than Gellert Grindelwald who, before Voldemort came along, was the *previous* worst-ever evil wizard.

There's a new complication in their lives now, too. As they fled

Godric's Hollow, you know that last curse Hermione threw? It rebounded and, um, kind of destroyed Harry's wand. It's in pieces. Given how much damage Ron's wand did when they taped it back together in second year at Hogwarts, they know better than to try that now. So they'll have to share Hermione's.

While Harry's on watch that night, he sees a mysterious glow in the trees. It's a Patronus, a doe, and it leads him to a frozen pond. And what's in that frozen pond? The Sword of Gryffindor. Yes, there it is, right there! It can't be Summoned, and Harry isn't going to wait around for some Lady of the Lake to hand it to him, so quite logically he tries the direct approach. He takes off all his clothes and dives through a hole in the ice into the freezing cold water.

But the locket knows damn well that Sword is impregnated with basilisk blood and will destroy it, so it strangles Harry. Harry's trapped under the ice, being murdered by a piece of evil jewelry and Hermione's none the wiser.

Someone else is there, though. Someone dives into the water, gets the sword, and then pulls Harry out of the water.

It's Ron. Neither of them can figure out who cast the Patronus, but they'll worry about that later. They're not even going to pause to cast drying and warming charms. They've got both Horcrux and Sword and they're going to destroy it before anything else can go wrong. Harry urges Ron to do it, who hesitates at first. "I think it affects me more than you and Hermione." Then all the more reason it should be him.

A massive cloud of darkness emanates from the locket, creating masses of spiders (Ron is arachnophobic) and Voldemort's voice speaks all Ron's worst fears: that he's the least loved by his mother, that Hermione prefers Harry... the cloud forms into the shape of naked Harry and Hermione making out. But Ron is ready to literally slay his demons and he bashes the Horcrux to bits.

It works. It's over. The locket is destroyed, and a piece of Voldemort's soul with it.

"Just think," Ron says, sounding much more like his old self. "Only three to go."

Apparently then these two old school chums spend all night catching up, or something, because by the time they wake Hermione to tell her what's been going on, it's well into the morning.

And Hermione is ripshit. She's so angry at Ron, she could spit like a cat, and she wants her wand from Harry so she can hex him. You think destroying a Horcrux fixes everything? Well, not after you've had weeks to worry and build up resentment, it doesn't!

Ron explains: he wanted to come back as soon as he left, but once they Apparated away he had no way to find them. But on Christmas morning he heard Hermione's voice whisper his name coming from the Deluminator. And he clicked it, and a ball of light came out and went straight into his heart. He just trusted that feeling and Apparated wherever that feeling took him, and he landed right by them. And then he just had to wait for one of them to show themselves, and Harry did, when he followed the doe Patronus.

She's still mad, by the way, but at least she's not mad enough to hex him anymore, so Harry can give her wand back. (Ron's got an extra wand for Harry, by the way, that he got off a rather "dim-witted" Snatcher a few weeks back.) What Hermione wants to do next, though, is go see Xenophilius Lovegood. In the Dumbledore biography she has found that triangle symbol again and he's the only person they know who will know what it means.

Off they go to the Lovegoods' which—like the Burrow—is a weird, tall, magical structure out in the middle of nothing. Mr. Lovegood seems quite suspicious when they knock on his door—I guess you wouldn't get a lot of canvassers way out there—but Harry reminds him they met at the wedding and asks if they can come in. They sit down with mugs of tea in uncomfortable silence. Hermione asks after Luna. Mr. Lovegood says she'll be along and they lapse into silence again. Harry finally leaps into the breach, asking about the pendant and what the symbol means.

"It's the symbol of the Deathly Hallows, of course," Lovegood says, asking if they're all familiar with the "Tale of the Three Brothers." Harry definitely isn't, but Hermione's read it in the book of tales Dumbledore left for her. She reads the fairy tale aloud—while fanciful animations play out the story on the screen—of three brothers who tricked Death into giving them each a boon. One asked for the most powerful wand ever, one asked for the power to see people who'd died again, and one asked for a way to leave that place without Death following him, and death gave him his own cloak of invisibility.

The first brother went directly to a village and killed a wizard he quarreled with, then bragged about how powerful his wand was. Someone killed him that night for the wand, of course, so Death had the last laugh on him.

The second brother went home and brought the girl he had wanted to marry back from the dead. But she didn't belong in the mortal world and was unhappy, and in his misery and unfulfilled longing, the second brother killed himself. Score 2 for Death, brothers 0.

The third brother, though, Death was unable to find, until the brother had reached a great age. The brother passed the cloak to his son and then "greeted Death like an old friend and went with him gladly."

Yeah, so...? Xeno draws the symbol for them. The line is the Elder Wand, the circle is the Resurrection Stone and the triangle is the Cloak of Invisibility. "Together, they make one master of Death." When Hermione asks why the symbol was on Ignotus Peverell's grave, he tells them the Peverell brothers were thought to be the original three.

But he's growing more and more agitated. When they try to leave, Lovegood tells them they can't go. He's turned them in, you see, in exchange for getting his daughter back. Luna's been held hostage to keep him from publishing the truth about Voldemort in *The Quibbler*.

Death Eaters attack and our heroes barely escape before the house comes down around them. They land in yet another forest Hermione knows about.

But this time their luck has run out. They land right in the midst of a band of Snatchers, Fenrir Greyback among them. And try as they might to get away, there are too many of them. When Hermione realizes they have no choice, she hits Harry with a Stinging Jinx that balloons his face so much that he's unrecognizable. Harry, knocked back by her spell, finds himself in Voldemort's head again. This time he's visiting an elderly Grindelwald in a prison cell, and Grindelwald is telling him who has the Elder Wand now. Of course: it's been buried with Albus Dumbledore, who has had it for decades!

The Snatchers aren't really sure who they have in their clutches, so instead of taking them to the Ministry, they take them to Malfoy Manor, where mayhem quickly ensues. If this is Harry Potter, after all, they want to call the Dark Lord right away, but if it isn't, as Bellatrix says: "[Voldemort] will kill us all. We have to be sure." She and Lucius press Draco to identify Harry, yes or no?

Draco (barely looking at him): "I can't be sure."

Bellatrix checks Hermione's wand and sees her last spell was a Stinging Jinx, which makes her more certain this could be Harry. But she also catches sight of the Sword of Gryffindor on the belt of a Snatcher. "Where did you get that?" He says he took it from Hermione. Bellatrix freaks. She hexes him immediately, takes back the sword, hexes a few of the others, and then tells them all to get the hell out. The Snatchers—even Fenrir—flee before she decides to just kill them all. Bellatrix then orders the boys imprisoned while she has a little chat "girl to girl" with Hermione.

Harry and Ron find themselves locked in the Manor cellar (it's not "really" a dungeon), and they find they're not alone. Luna is there, along with Ollivander, and a goblin. Upstairs, Bellatrix is torturing Hermione because that sword was supposedly in her vault at Gringotts. Wormtail (Peter Pettigrew) retrieves the goblin from the cellar to join the questioning.

And then Dobby shows up, because Dobby, using elf magic, can pop in and out of the cellar even though wizards and witches can't. Now, you're probably wondering why or how Dobby knew to show up then. To explain this I have to explain a continuity glitch that goes back to *Order of the Phoenix*. In the book, Sirius gives Harry one of a pair of mirrors that he and James had used to talk to each other when they were in separate detentions as schoolboys. Sirius keeps the other. After Sirius' death, an angry Harry smashes the mirror (which he never used, and if he'd used it to contact Sirius the night Voldemort sent the vision that lured Harry to the Ministry, Sirius wouldn't have died in the first place). But in the movies, the mirrors are never shown or spoken of. So where does Harry get this shard of a mirror from? He's been carrying it around for the whole movie with no explanation. The movie never says where it came from or why he's carrying it. All we know is every now and then Harry thinks he catches a glimpse of someone in it who looks a little like Dumbledore.

So while in the cellar at Malfoy Manor, Harry pulls the shard of glass out of his sock (his sock?!), sees the eye of someone looking back, and says "send help." That's it. He doesn't say where they are, but Dobby shows up. Maybe Dobby has ways of knowing either where Harry is or what's going on at Malfoy Manor since he used to be the house elf there.

Tl;dr—Harry has this shard of a mirror, through which he summons help in the form of a house elf, who just so happens to be able to go right through the enchantments that prevent Disapparition. They send Luna and Ollivander with Dobby to Shell Cottage, and then Dobby will come back for the Trio.

And then Harry and Ron start collecting wands, apparently. They ambush Wormtail at the cellar door, and take his. Then they get into a fight with Bellatrix and the Malfoys, Expelliarmus is liberally used, and Harry grabs at least two, but possibly three wands from Draco (in the book, it's three), and Dobby ends up with Narcissa's wand. "How dare you take a witch's wand!" Bellatrix bellows. "How dare you betray your masters!"

Dobby, of course, has to deliver his tag line before he can disappear with the entire party of good guys: "Dobby is a free elf!" Bellatrix, bloodthirsty as always, throws her dagger at him in disgust as the group disappears. The blade disappears, too.

When they reappear, on the shoreline at Shell Cottage, the dagger has connected, lodged deep in Dobby's chest. Dobby dies in Harry's arms. If you're not crying in this scene, you should fire your cardiologist because you have no heart.

Harry decides to bury him, "properly, without magic," and he does, digging the grave himself, laying Dobby to rest in the dunes above Cornwall.

Speaking of graves, though, check out what's going on at the white stone tomb where Dumbledore was laid to rest. On the island in the lake beside Hogwarts, someone's levitating the stones away and cracking the coffin. Oh, look, it's Voldemort. Yeah, he's the type who would desecrate a tomb to get the most powerful wand in the world.

Which means that now Voldemort has the most powerful wand in the world.

But don't worry! There's still another whole movie to go.

8: Harry Potter and the Deathly Hallows, Part Two

Film Data
   Title: Harry Potter and the Deathly Hallows, Part 2
   Release Date: July 15, 2011
   Director: David Yates
   Screenplay: Steve Kloves
   Producers: David Heyman, David Barron, and J.K. Rowling
   USA Opening Weekend: $169,189,427
   Running Time: 2:10

It all comes down to this: 14 years in development, ten years since the release of the first film, $1.2 billion dollars spent, four directors, two Dumbledores and one movie to cap it all off. *Deathly Hallows, Part 2* was released on July 15, 2011, to what Metacritic rates as "Universal Acclaim" (41 positive reviews, none mixed, none negative). Could one expect better raves that this? *San Francisco Chronicle:* "The epic and impassioned close that the saga deserves." *Entertainment Weekly:* "The thrilling conclusion to a phenomenal cinematic story 10 years in the telling, [DH2] is proof that authentic movie excitement is its own form of magic." *New Orleans Times-Picayune:* "A dazzling stirring capper to a once in a generation movie franchise." Roger Ebert, *Rolling Stone, The New York Times*—even the *New York Post!*—all lined up to sing the praises of the film. *The Hollywood Reporter* even confessed that the film "fully justified the decision, once thought purely mercenary, of splitting J.K. Rowling's final book into two parts."

You get the feeling that many critics were just waiting to stand up and applaud once the final installment arrived, having already proved that what was once considered impossible had been achieved. The filmmakers managed to successfully bring—arguably—the most beloved book series of the latter twentieth century to the screen, without having to recast the lead actors, without having to "Hollywood-ize" the plot or ending, without dropping the ball or losing sight of the goal. "It is indeed impressive," writes Richard Corliss in TIME, "and we mean not just this [film] but the entirety of producer David Heyman's blockbuster franchise." Even the *Boston Globe*, which panned most of the earlier installments, admits, "[T]he series has come to represent the *ne plus ultra* of intelligent blockbuster filmmaking, with contributions from every corner of the lot: music, makeup, costume, sound."

"Amazingly, Daniel Radcliffe, Emma Watson and Rupert Grint, as Harry, Hermione and Ron, have remained plausible and captivating in their roles over the 10-plus years," enthuses *USA*

Today. Many felt Daniel Radcliffe graduated with full honors to a higher degree of actor. The film "above all others, supplies Radcliffe with the gravitas of not just an epic story come to completion, but some real dramatic heft," writes *Time Out.* "The burdens of the consummation lie squarely upon Harry's shoulders and lead one to appreciate Radcliffe's accomplishment here and throughout the series," concludes *The Hollywood Reporter.*

Much praise is lavished on both Steve Kloves as screenwriter and David Yates as director. "Yates, a sensitive director of actors, structures his movie like the final movement of a symphony. He reprises themes and characters from the previous films that swell in the epochal siege of Hogwarts and ends his films with an almost wordless coda that will wring tears even from Harry haters," writes the *Philadelphia Inquirer,* adding of Kloves, that he "sculpts J.K. Rowling's massive books into shapely scripts, finding the emotional through-line in the thickets of her prose, and bringing into relief her humor and humanism."

THR feels that after being workmanlike in earlier films, "Yates has finally come into his own in this last installment, orchestrating a massive chessboard of events with impressive finesse and a stronger sense of dramatic composition than he has previously displayed" and that "perhaps the key player all along has been screenwriter Steve Kloves, who made what must have been a vexing decision to put a promising directorial career on hold for more than a decade to write all but one of the Potter episodes."

The *Globe* framed its review in terms of not only the end of an era, but the end of childhood itself for an entire generation. "The Harry Potter series has come sighing and crashing to a close after a decade of movies and 14 years of page-turning, and a generation must now move on from its defining myth," writes Ty Burr. "The 'Potter' stories, books and movies alike, have been central tent poles of our popular culture, as critical to a young person navigating the first decade of the new millennium as post-9/11 anxiety and the rise of social media. (Think of all the novels, films, and TV shows that wouldn't exist without them. Yes, *Twilight,* I'm talking about you.)"

Burr's right about it being the end of an era, but he's wrong about having to "move on" from Harry Potter. Not when there will be multiple theme parks around the world, continual new editions of the books, and of course binge-watch parties and movie marathons of the films forever. Let's bring this marathon of film mania to an end ourselves now, with all the details from *Deathly Hallows, Part 2*.

Casting Notes

Wait, there are casting notes for this film? Haven't we long since met everyone? In many ways the final chapter in Harry's film journey seems designed to bring us cameos of every previous character. We have a reprise of John Hurt as the wand-maker Ollivander, giving Harry a crucial piece of information. As in several previous films, Harry's parents make their appearances. Harry's own youngest incarnation is even seen via flashback to bring things full circle. Through other forms of flashbacks, visitations and Pensieve memories we also see various other deceased characters, mentors and guardians of Harry's. There isn't a lot of room for new characters to show up, but there is one definitely worth a mention:

Griphook the Goblin

Another "full circle" character, Griphook appears back in the very first film/book as the goblin who takes Harry to his Gringotts vault—but at that time he was played by the late Verne Troyer, better known to filmgoers as "Mini Me." Except he was *voiced* by Warwick Davis, the Potter series' go-to actor for characters of minimal physical stature, also playing Professor Flitwick, the choirmaster (who they eventually decided was just an incarnation of Flitwick), another goblin bank teller and a random Ministry employee. Davis took over the role of the hard-bargaining, morally ambiguous Griphook for *Deathly Hallows.*

What to Look For

No Hedwig's Theme

This is the first and only of the films that doesn't feature "Hedwig's Theme" as the music when the title cards appear at the start of the film. Which makes sense given that Hedwig is no more and/or because this is really just the second half of one long film when combined with part one. A new musical piece, "Lily's Theme," appears for the first time, however. When it is heard is quite telling. (Spoiler alert!) Although the theme naturally plays when Harry speaks to Lily's spirit in the forest, the other two times both feature Snape: in the opening montage when he oversees Hogwarts, and during his final scene.

Full Circle Knight

In the Room of Requirement, among all the junk, the knight that Ron rides in the chess scene in *Sorcerer's Stone* can be seen. This is both a full circle moment and also a practical effect: to dress the "junk" set, the filmmakers liberally re-used old props.

Epilogue Casting

In the epilogue we get to see several characters "19 years later." One of them is Draco Malfoy and his wife and son. In the book version his wife is described as also very blonde, but in the film she has dark hair. Two possible reasons for the change: one is that Draco's mother Narcissa was also meant to be a blonde but in the films they went with a witchy black-and-white two-tone look and perhaps the character is meant to resemble her. The more likely reason is that the filmmakers decided to cast Tom Felton's real-life girlfriend, Jade, in the role. Tom and Jade met on set because she was the stunt coordinator's assistant. He told *Cosmopolitan* that one day she was playing a part as an extra in the Great Hall and he was struck with love at first sight.

Full Circle Frog

Remember that chocolate frog that escaped from Harry on his first trip on the Hogwarts Express with Ron? In the epilogue, where we see a 36-year-old Harry sending his 11-year-old son Albus off to Hogwarts, you'll see a chocolate frog hop across the train compartment window. Perhaps that frog has been on the train for over 20 years?

* * *

Deathly Hallows, Part 2 Drinking Game

Drink every time something comes full circle from an earlier film.
Bonus drinks: every time someone gets wet.

* * *

Book Lore

Harry's Visions from Voldemort

Remember back in *Order of the Phoenix,* when it was so vital for Harry to learn to block the connection between his mind and Voldemort's? He never did learn to Occlude, but for some reason in *Deathly Hallows* instead of seeing what Voldemort wants him to see, Harry sees what Voldemort would *not* want him to see. What's different? In the books, early in *Half-Blood Prince,* Dumbledore asks Harry if his scar hurts anymore, and Harry realizes that it doesn't. Dumbledore's theory is that after the incident at the Ministry, when Voldemort possessed Harry fully ("you've lost, old man") but Harry was able to fight back ("you'll never know love and I feel sorry for you"), that Voldemort doesn't dare invade Harry's mind again. In fact, the tables have turned: "Lord Voldemort has finally realized the dangerous access to his thoughts and feelings you have been enjoying," Dumbledore tells Harry. "It appears that he is now employing Occlumency against you."

This means that when Harry has visions from Voldemort in *Deathly Hallows,* they're from the times Voldemort is so emotional or out of control that he can't keep his thoughts from leaking over to Harry.

"Malfoy's gaunt, petrified face seemed branded on the inside of his eyes. Harry felt sickened by what he had seen, by the use to which Draco was now being put by Voldemort."

Harry's Visions of Draco

There are more book visions that we don't see in the movies, and the scenes are more detailed. Many of the visions involve Draco Malfoy being forced to serve the Dark Lord, and seem to imply a connection between Draco and Harry, as well—if not a literal connection like the one Harry has with Voldemort, at least in a literary sense. The constant presence of Draco in these visions gives weight to the theory that metaphorically Draco and Harry are two sides of the same coin. In many ways, Harry has been manipulated by Dumbledore ever since he was marked as The Chosen One. In fact, Dumbledore affected the fate of Harry's parents, as well, since they were members of the original Order of the Phoenix. On the other side Draco's parents were members of the original Death Eaters and groomed by Voldemort to do his bidding.

Now both sons are being asked as teenagers to shoulder tremendous hopes for their causes. Draco is tasked with breaching the Hogwarts defenses and with killing the headmaster. Harry is tasked with killing Voldemort by destroying the Horcruxes and ultimately confronting him, as well. And ultimately it will be the actions Draco's mother takes that save him—and all the wizarding world—just as it was Harry's mother's actions that saved Harry and the wizarding world on the night she died.

Plot Recap

"I open at the close."

The filmmakers took "I open at the close" literally here, starting us with a repeat of the closing scene of part one: Voldemort taking the Elder Wand from Dumbledore's dead hands and shooting a powerful spell into the sky. Grim Hogwarts montage follows: Snape, looking quite melancholy, overseeing the literal march of regimented lines of students through the courtyard, Dementors hovering around the castle.

Meanwhile, on the coast of Cornwall, Harry's kneeling at Dobby's gravestone and looking into the mysterious shard of mirror through which he may or may not have summoned Dobby's help. Neither he nor the audience is truly sure.

Another thing Harry's not sure about is one of their rescues: Griphook the Goblin. Full circle: he's the same fellow who showed Harry to his vault on his first trip to Gringotts when Harry was 11. Griphook is impressed that Harry not only rescued him, but that he buried Dobby. "You are a very unusual wizard."

Griphook tells the Trio that Bellatrix Lestrange has what she thinks is the sword in her vault, but it's fake—*Snape* gave her a fake—and there are *other items* of interest, as well. Harry suspects Horcrux. Not least of all because of Bellatrix's outsized reaction to thinking they'd been in her vault and constant asking what *else* they had stolen. (Although with Bellatrix, out-sized emotional outbursts seem to be the norm, so...?) Harry hatches a plan to get into the most well-guarded vault in Gringotts with Griphook's help.

Griphook's price for his cooperation is the Sword of Gryffindor, which he sees as Goblin property. Harry agrees, even though it's their only current method of destroying the Horcruxes. (It's likely Harry knows the sword has a mind of its own and might present itself back to him or other Gryffindors in need later—but it's likely Griphook knows this property of the sword, too.)

Harry talks next to their other famous rescue, Ollivander. Ollivander evaluates the wands Harry took from Malfoy Manor: Bellatrix's ("unyielding") and Draco's ("reasonably pliant"), but the wand is no longer Draco's, telling Harry "I sense its allegiance has changed." Turns out wands can change who they're attuned to. Ollivander also gives a quick recap of what the Deathly Hallows are, in case you went six months between films: the Elder Wand (most powerful wand in the world), the cloak of invisibility and the Resurrection Stone (brings people back from the dead, sorta). Together the three would make one master of Death. But Ollivander insists those are "old wives tales."

Harry, after seven movies of people speaking to him cryptically and the death of his ultra-cryptic mentor, is finally fed up and ready to call people on it. "You're lying," he says, flat out to Ollivander's face. "You told him about the Elder Wand." (Him being Voldemort.)

Ollivander is frank in return. If Voldemort really has found the Elder Wand, well, Harry, "you really don't stand a chance."

But they have to try. Oh, full circle, how we love thee: this time Hermione gets the correct hair for her Polyjuice Potion and instead of turning into part-cat, she becomes 100% psychobitch: Bellatrix Lestrange. The result is a hilarious scene in which Helena Bonham Carter gets to play Hermione-playing-Bellatrix. Ron just gets heavily glamoured, and Harry—with Griphook on his back—goes along under the Invisibility Cloak. I guess we're supposed to forgive our heroes for using the Imperius Curse to get them past the head bank goblin, who leads them down to the deepest high-security vaults in a ready-for-theme-park-adaptation trolley cart.

Unfortunately the cart leads them right through a waterfall that washes away all enchantments and their cart dumps them to fall to certain death—except that Hermione is ready with an Arresto Momentum to stop them right before they hit rock bottom. There's no other way out, but might as well forge on with the mission anyway, eh? Bellatrix's vault is in a cul de sac guarded by a chained, tortured dragon. They can safely pass the creature by shaking rattles at it because, Griphook explains, it has been trained to "expect pain when it hears the noise." As the giant, fire-breathing creature cowers away from them, Hermione calls it "barbaric."

Inside the vault there are heaps of gold. The heaps are about to get even bigger, though. Harry senses the Horcrux—it's a golden cup up on a high ledge—but everything they touch in the vault begins to multiply. Under the Gemino Curse, our heroes are in danger of dying like Han, Leia and Luke in the trash compactor, except in gold instead of garbage. Except they don't die, Harry gets the cup, then loses it as the still-growing pile of gold tosses him about. Griphook picks it up, and insists the cup for the sword: that's the deal. Harry throws him the sword, Griphook tosses Hermione the cup, and informs them, "I said I'd get you in. I didn't say anything about getting you out." He takes the sword and the still-Confunded older bank goblin and hightails it out of there, taking the dragon-rattles with him.

The executive goblin doesn't fare too well—he is quickly fried without a rattle to protect him—and the bank's guards are descending to the vault. Soon they have the Trio pinned down, as spells fly like gunfire. The only reason they haven't been overtaken already is the dragon is spitting fire at everyone, guards included.

Hermione has an idea. "But it's mad!" she worries. That's okay, Hermione, live a little!

She jumps onto the dragon's back, urging the guys to join her. As soon as they do, she severs the dragon's chains with a spell. The dragon, sensing freedom, begins to climb out, eventually breaking right through the bank's normally silent lobby. As the dragon emerges onto the roof, it pauses for several long moments and just breathes, savoring its freedom.

"That moment meant so much to me," J.K. Rowling told screenwriter Steve Kloves in a 2011 "DVD extra" conversation. She'd set that stage all the way back in 1993 when she was first writing *Harry Potter and the Philosopher's Stone,* in a passing line about how there are dragons guarding the high-security vaults. "And I, because I can't just write that and not think about it... I'm thinking, *God, that's a winged animal, you know, that's not right!*" So when the dragon breaks free in book seven/movie eight, "It's bringing to light literally but figuratively all the injustices in that [wizarding] world. Harry enters this beautiful world, glittering with jewels and gold in Gringotts, but it hides ugly stuff."

The dragon is another full circle thematic element, as well, after the saga of baby Norbert.

* * *

"When have our plans ever actually worked?
We plan, we get there, and all hell breaks loose."

* * *

The Trio stay on the dragon's back until they're far from London, and drop into a mountain lake. As Harry hits the cold water, he is also hit by more visions from Voldemort: a Gringotts guard, cursed and probably killed, the cup, the locket, as well as a woman and a Ravenclaw banner. "He knows!" Harry tells the others as they clamber to shore. Voldemort knows they're hunting down the Horcruxes. But Harry now knows that one of the Horcruxes is at Hogwarts. Hermione wants to make a plan.

"Hermione," Harry says. "When have our plans ever actually worked? We plan, we get there, and all hell breaks loose." The best they can come up with is to go to Hogsmeade and try to use the secret passage in the Honeydukes cellar to sneak in. (Full circle: Harry used that passage to sneak *out* back in *Prisoner of Azkaban*.)

Confirmation that Harry's vision is spot on comes from Voldemort himself. At Malfoy Manor, the Dark Lord speaks Parseltongue to his giant snake: "The boy has discovered our secret, Nagini. You must stay close," he tells her as he walks barefoot through spilled blood and goblin corpses. (As pointed out in *Puffs: The Play*... the Dark Lord has never bothered to put on shoes or a proper robe since his re-embodiment at the end of *Goblet of Fire*...). Poor Narcissa, she's clearly wondering if all this goblin blood is going to wreck her floors. Or does she have deeper thoughts in mind? She, Lucius and Draco look on in horror as You Know Who takes his gory stroll.

Griphook gets his comeuppance, by the way. He is among the dead lying on the floor, the sword of Gryffindor still in his hand. It disappears as the camera lingers.

When our heroes Apparate to snowy Hogsmeade, it's night. Alarms begin to screech the moment they appear and they run for cover, as dark-robed figures with their wands out begin searching for them. Another alarm sounds, though, across town, sending the guards that direction—someone is helping them. A voice urges them into a cellar and they get a quick glimpse of a guy who looks a bit like Dumbledore.

Down there, they find a portrait of a young girl, and when Hermione looks into a partly shattered mirror, she sees... Harry? Harry, looking into his shard, sees her. So *this* is who sent Dobby to rescue them. But who is he?

Remember back in the previous movie when Harry said he didn't even know Dumbledore had a brother? Now it's time to meet him. Aberforth isn't happy to see the Trio right in his backyard: it's too dangerous. He gives them butterbeer and bread (he is a tavern-keeper, after all) and tells them the Order of the Phoenix is finished. "You Know Who's won. Anyone who thinks otherwise is kidding themselves."

Well, Harry's been told for seven years already that he's delusional, so he's not about to listen. "I don't care what happened between you and your brother, and I don't care that you've given up. We need to get into the castle tonight."

Fine. Aberforth sends the portrait of his sister Ariana on an errand. When she returns, she's got Neville with her! And several other members of Dumbledore's Army. Behind Ariana's portrait is the only secret passage that still works to get into the castle. Neville fills them in: the school is crawling with Death Eaters and Dementors. They hardly ever see Snape. The harshest abuse comes from a brother and sister team, the Carrows, who are in charge of discipline.

The other end of the passageway comes out in the Room of Requirement, which has become a camp for Dumbledore's Army. Neville sends one student off to alert Remus and the Order, while the rest break into applause and greet Harry. Luna, Cho, Dean, Seamus, Nigel, the Patil sisters, Lavender, even McLaggen—at least 30 students are there, and they all want to help. Harry tells them there's something they need to find, something associated with Rowena Ravenclaw. Luna suggests the Lost Diadem of Ravenclaw; "It's quite famous!" But as Cho points out, "It's been lost for centuries. There isn't a person alive who's seen it." (Meanwhile Ron just wants to know what the bloody hell a *diadem* is. Just think tiara, Ron.)

Ginny rushes in with the news that Snape knows Harry was in Hogsmeade. The entire school is called to assemble in the Great Hall, marching in rows as straight as their uniform ties. Snape announces that Harry was spotted in the village and "Should anyone—student or staff—attempt to aid Mr. Potter, they will be punished in a manner consistent with the severity of their transgression." (That's curiously non-specific, Severus... are you leaving yourself an out?) Not only that, anyone who "has knowledge of these events who does not come forward will be treated as equally guilty." So, who's going to rat out Harry?

Only one Gryffindor is brave enough to stand up to Snape. He steps out of the queue and a gasp goes through all assembled: it's Harry Potter.

"You have a bit of a security problem, Headmaster," he says, and the doors to the Great Hall swing open to reveal the Order of the Phoenix (Kingsley, Remus, Fleur, Arthur, Molly, Fred, George and Bill Weasley) plus Neville, Dean, Ron, Hermione and a few others. Harry isn't about to hold back saying what he needs to say now: "How dare you stand where he stood. Tell them what happened on the tower that night. Tell them how you looked him in the eye, a man who trusted you, and killed him!"

Snape draws his wand, but Minerva McGonagall interposes herself between him and Harry. She, too, has had enough. She begins throwing spells at Snape, backing him toward the dais as he deflects the spells—incidentally right into the Carrows, taking both of them out of action. Snape is done for. He smashes through the window and escapes into the night, while the students break into cheers.

But the cheers are quickly snuffed, as the sky overhead, reflected as always in the enchanted ceiling of the Great Hall, darkens ominously, and everyone (not just Harry) hears the voice of Voldemort inside their heads: "Give me Harry Potter. Do this and none shall be harmed... and I shall leave Hogwarts untouched. You have one hour."

Pansy Parkinson, Draco's old girlfriend, points at Harry. "Well, what are you waiting for! Someone grab him!"

Yeah, right. Ginny steps between them, then Hermione takes Harry's other side, Cho, Parvati and Padma forming a protective ring around him. And then more and more students join the ranks around him.

McGonagall has Mr. Filch lead Pansy, and the whole of Slytherin House, to the dungeons. (This is different from the book, where she has them leave Hogwarts entirely.) While Harry runs off to look for the Ravenclaw Horcrux, Hermione and Ron go off to look for a basilisk fang to destroy it with, and Professor McGonagall sets about securing the castle.

She sends Neville to do one crucial piece: blowing up the footbridge. "You want us to blow it up? Boom?" "Boom," she confirms. "Why don't you confer with Mr. Finnigan. As I recall he has a certain proclivity for pyrotechnics." Full circle: Seamus is the one who blew up all those cauldrons throughout the years. McGonagall also animates the stone knights throughout the castle, activating them for defense, and the members of the staff and the Order who are there set about creating a protective shield around the school, forcing the Dementors back.

Luna gets Harry to see that if he wants to know about the diadem, he'll have to talk to someone much older: "The Gray Lady," the ghost of Helena Ravenclaw, daughter of Rowena. But the ghost is touchy and emotional. Can Harry get through to her before the hour is up? No. Voldemort has amassed an army on the cliffs near the castle, and they begin their bombardment of spells.

Helena tells Harry he's not the first to seek the diadem. Years ago there was a boy who also said he would destroy it, but he lied and "defiled it with dark magic." Helena is still quite ripshit over it, in fact. But Harry convinces her he can and will destroy it once and for all, if she'll tell him where it is. She answers: "It's in the place where everything is hidden. If you have to ask, then you'll never know. If you know, you need only ask."

Harry, who after seven years has gotten good at decoding cryptic wizarding crap like this, knows exactly what she means: the Room of Requirement. He dashes off to the third floor while various defenders take their places: The Weasley Twins, Remus and Kingsley and others. So far the defensive shield is holding. Neville taunts a horde of Snatchers. They had tried to charge the bridge and after the first few were completely incinerated by the protective shield spell, they are hanging back.

Meanwhile Ron and Hermione are down in the Chamber of Secrets with Hufflepuff's cup. Ron yanks a fang out of the basilisk's skeleton, but it's Hermione's turn to destroy a Horcrux now. When she stabs it, both Harry and Voldemort feel it. The release of evil energy causes the water in the Chamber to rise up and attack Hermione and Ron, but in the end, water is all it is. It washes away, leaving them soaked and exhilarated with success: and in each other's arms for a rather long-awaited kiss. (I think this means she's not mad at him anymore.)

Voldemort, on the other hand, is hella mad, and he strikes the defense shield with everything he's got, pushing the Elder Wand to its limit, and the shield fragments. Remus and Tonks reach for each other, waiting for the first attackers to come. Down at the bridge, the horde finds the boundary down, and they chase Neville onto the bridge. Neville sets off the charges as he runs for his life, barely making it to where Ginny, Seamus and the rest of the D.A. are waiting for him, while the bridge collapses behind him, taking out a few hundred Snatchers and others as it goes.

Giants are coming now, knocking aside the stone knights and soldiers, and Death Eaters are Apparating right into the castle—something no one but Dumbledore could do in the past. Harry runs into Neville and Ginny on a chaotic stairwell, as students run from place to place trying to find somewhere safe and/or trying to join the fighting. Neville, in quite high spirits, asks if Harry's seen Luna because "I'm mad for her. Figure it's about time I told her, since we'll probably both be dead by morning!" Off he runs. Harry and Ginny locks eyes. Then lips. And she tells him, "I know." She always knows, and she's always known. It's time for Harry to get going.

In the chaos, the Slytherin students have gotten free of the dungeon. Draco Apparates in and grabs two of his old cronies, Blaise Zabini and Gregory Goyle. (It would have been Crabbe instead of Zabini, except actor Jamie Waylett was cut from the production after getting into trouble with the law over drug possession.) Harry meanwhile makes it to the Room of Requirement. Hermione and Ron are trying to find him on the Marauders Map and they see him disappear, so they know that's where he's gone. But Draco is also headed there.

The Room is in its "full of junk" phase, and Harry has to use the Force... I mean, reach out with his feelings to sense it. He finds the diadem at last, but just as he does, Draco finds him. All Draco wants from Harry is his wand back. He's using his Mum's, and "it's just not the same." Harry, though, finds he wants something from Draco: an answer. "Why didn't you tell her?" In other words, *why didn't you betray me to Bellatrix and the Dark Lord?* "You knew it was me."

Goyle's had enough of the confusing talk. He doesn't know anything about Draco's moral ambiguity or "reasonable pliancy" or any of the other hints dropped throughout that maybe Draco's not doing exactly as the Dark Lord might wish. "Come on, Draco. Do him!" he goads. That's when Ron and Hermione show up and the spells start flying... and so does the diadem. It goes sailing into the air and lands atop a huge pile of furniture. We've seen in several previous scenes that Horcruxes apparently don't respond to Summoning Charms like Accio, so he and Hermione start climbing while Ron chases after the Slytherins. (Full circle: they come upon a bunch of pixies that have probably been there since the days of Gilderoy Lockhart.)

No sooner do they get the diadem and climb down than Ron comes sprinting back, screaming, "Goyle's set the bloody place on fire!"

Goyle is his spell's first casualty, when he can't escape the blaze that he can't control. Draco and Blaise climb a heap of junk, but they'll quickly be overwhelmed as well. Harry, Ron and Hermione find every path through the junk blocked by fire, but they're in luck. There are a handful of old brooms *right there,* and they mount and fly!

Harry, though, can't leave Draco and Blaise to die. I mean, come on, he's *Harry Potter.* Rescuing them is so on-brand. After a near miss, he gets Draco onto the back of his broom, Ron grabs Blaise, and they make for the exit. Just outside the door, Harry stabs the diadem with another basilisk fang and then Ron kicks it into the Fiendfyre, which explodes into giant likenesses of Voldemort just like the water did down in the Chamber. This time the door of the Room of Requirement slams shut, and Harry and Voldemort both stagger as that piece of Tom Riddle's soul dies.

Pius Thicknesse, the current Minister for Magic and also a Death Eater, has the nerve to ask You Know Who if he's all right, saying "My Lord?" He is killed instantly for this. Voldemort tells Nagini he needs to keep her safe, and he Disapparates with her.

Harry can see all this through his mind-connection to the Dark Lord. "The snake. She's the last one," he tells Hermione and Ron.

Every previous time Harry's seen through Voldemort's eyes, Hermione's warned him to cut it out, block him. (Hermione apparently didn't read Dumbledore's conclusion in *Half-Blood Prince* that Voldemort is no longer trying to invade Harry's mind, and that Harry can now invade his. See "Book Lore.") This time Ron urges him to use the connection to see where Voldemort is now. Harry feels anguish whenever his mind touches Voldemort's, but he pushes on, to see that he and the snake are at a nearby boathouse. Lucius is there, urging him to call off the attack on Hogwarts and "seek the boy yourself."

"Before the night is out he will come to me!" the Dark Lord insists, punctuating his argument with a slap across Lucius's face and an order to go fetch Snape.

As the Trio try to get from where they are to where Voldemort is, the attack on the castle continues, towers ablaze and ramparts crumbling. Acromantulas have come out of the forest and the giants are swinging giant-sized scythes. A werewolf kills Lavender and drinks her blood before Hermione can hex him into oblivion. As Harry, Ron and Hermione finally make it out of the castle, a swarm of Dementors come at Harry, but are driven back by a powerful Patronus from Aberforth. They hurry toward the boathouse.

Snape is already down there. Voldemort is telling him that the Elder Wand "resists" him. Our heroes arrive to overhear Snape replying that he has just witnessed the Dark Lord perform extraordinary feats with that wand and "when the boy comes, it will not fail you. I am sure of it. It answers to you. You and you only." But no, Voldemort says: "I am not its true master."

Unfortunately, you know who *is* the wand's true master? Voldemort believes it must be the guy who killed the wand's previous owner. And that's Snape. So only the guy who kills Snape will be able to master the Elder Wand. In other words: this guy.

Voldemort slits Snape's throat with a vicious slash of his wand and then lets Nagini finish off the job with a flurry of strikes to the neck. And then they Disapparate.

Harry and crew hurry into the boathouse but it's too late to save Snape. Snape is crying silver tears—no ordinary tears, but wizard memories. "Take them," Snape insists, "Take them to the Pensieve." And then he asks one last favor of Harry, who is trying to stanch the blood to no avail. "Look at me." Harry does. Snape says one last thing before he expires, something Harry has heard from others before, but never from Snape, who always compared him to his father. "You have your mother's eyes."

Before they can figure out how to get back up to the castle, Voldemort throws another twist. His voice reaches them all again, ordering his forces to withdraw and telling those defending Hogwarts to retrieve their dead and bury them with dignity. But to Harry he says, and I'm paraphrasing here: *you let all these people die for you, you dishonorable schmuck. Meet me in the Forbidden Forest or I'll make it even worse.* In other words, he'll kill every man, woman and child who shields Harry from him.

By the time the Trio get back to the castle, the Great Hall has been turned into a combination trauma center and morgue. There's Professor Slughorn treating Mr. Filch's wounds with dittany. Professor Trelawney and one of the Patil twins cover a body. Tonks and Remus' corpses are lying side by side, hands nearly touching.

And all the Weasleys are gathered around the body of one of their own. Fred's dead. Ron breaks down in tears, something Harry's never seen, and it only seems to drive home that Voldemort was right. Harry can't let anyone else die for him.

He goes to Dumbledore's office, which is now spartan and spare. Gone are the magical instruments, the clutter of curios, the dishes of sherbet lemons and pepper imps. But the Pensieve is still there. Harry pours Snape's memories into it and, as is his way, plunges right in.

Here comes the flashback to end all flashbacks, the montage to beat all montages. You thought in fifth year when Harry saw Snape getting bullied by James *that* was "Snape's worst memory?" You ain't seen nothing yet.

A beautiful young red-haired girl makes a flower open and float through the air. "Freak!" shouts her sister, batting it out of her hand. "I'll tell Mummy you're a freak, Lily!" The girl runs away, and finds a dark-eyed boy in ill-fitting clothes, who can make leaves fly like birds. This is young Severus Snape and young Lily Potter. They become fast friends.

But when they get to Hogwarts, Lily goes into Gryffindor and meets James, while Severus... well, one guess which House he goes to. Harry remembers Snape saying he was "just like your father" as he sees James knock Lily's books out of her hands and Severus helping her to pick them back up again. Of course we know how it turns out. Lily grows up to marry James. And we know there is a Prophecy made by Trelawney. (Although the Prophecy we see in this memory is the wrong one... it's the one about Pettigrew, not the one about Harry... but maybe Snape got confused. He was dying, after all.)

And then there is Snape, on his knees, begging "don't kill me." He's begging Dumbledore to protect Lily because the Dark Lord "thinks it's her son" that the prophecy is about. "He intends to hunt them down now, to kill them. Hide them, hide them all, I beg you."

"What will you give me in exchange?" Dumbledore wants to know.

"Anything," says Snape.

The house in Godric's Hollow is a shambles from the fight Lily and James put up when Voldemort came to kill their son. Baby Harry cries in his playpen, as Lily's voice whispers, "Mama loves you, Dada loves you."

Harry sees Peter Pettigrew, and then an anguished Snape confronting Dumbledore, "You said you would keep her safe!"

"Lily and James put their faith in the wrong person, Severus," Dumbledore replies. "Rather like you." Gee, way to rub it in, old man. In fact, Dumbledore is not done with Severus, no not at all. Dumbledore believes the Dark Lord will return, and then Harry will need protection. "If you truly loved her," he says, pouring more salt into the wound, *then you'll be the boy's protector, won't you?*

Severus has one condition: "No one can know."

Very well. Dumbledore promises to "never reveal the best of you, Severus."

Harry sees himself sorted into Gryffindor and hears Dumbledore say that Snape *risks his life every day to keep Harry safe.* He hears the arguments he had with Snape over the years: Snape calling his father *lazy* and *arrogant*, Harry calling him a *great man.* How different those arguments sound now that he knows...

The memories pour on. Dumbledore putting on the Horcrux ring, Snape treating Dumbledore's cursed hand, telling him the potion will keep the curse from spreading for now, but it is a temporary fix. "It will spread, Albus." Dumbledore has maybe a year to live, and he plans to use his death to the greatest advantage. "We both know Lord Voldemort has ordered the Malfoy boy to murder me." Dumbledore presumes that if Draco should fail, the duty will fall to Snape. "You *must* be the one to kill me, Severus. It is the only way. Only then will the Dark Lord trust you completely."

Harry sees that night on the Astronomy Tower, sees Snape cast the Killing Curse... How different it looks now that he knows it was actually Dumbledore's orders.

But killing Dumbledore was far from the only order Snape had to follow. Dumbledore also insists there is something that Snape must tell Harry, but "only when the Dark Lord is at his most vulnerable." As Dumbledore explains that the Killing Curse cast on baby Harry "rebounded," Snape's memories travel back to Godric's Hollow, to his own discovery of James and Lily's bodies, to cradling her while tears poured down his face.

When that curse rebounded, a piece of Voldemort's soul "latched itself onto the only living thing it could find, Harry himself," Dumbledore says. This is why Harry can speak Parseltongue and why he can see through Lord Voldemort's eyes. "A part of Lord Voldemort lives inside him."

Realization dawns for Snape: he's been protecting this boy... why? "You've kept him alive so that he can die *at the proper moment.* You've been raising him like a pig for slaughter!"

Is Dumbledore being sincere or sarcastic when he asks, "Don't tell me now that you have grown to care for the boy?"

Snape conjures his Patronus, a doe, representing his undying love for Lily. Dumbledore seems dumbfounded by this fact. "After all this time?"

"Always," Severus intones. Even though that love was both the carrot and the cudgel that Dumbledore used to keep Severus in line. Think about it. Dumbledore's words to Snape boil down to: *If you love Lily, you'll protect her son. And if you value her sacrifice, you'll be the one to tell him he has to die, anyway.* No wonder Snape's so damn bitter.

Harry remembers the wonder that met his eyes, seeing that doe in the forest, leading him to the Sword. It was Snape protecting him all along.

"He must die. And Voldemort himself must do it," Dumbledore is saying to Snape. "That is essential."

And that is the end of the memories. Harry finds himself alone in the headmaster's office, stunned by all he has learned. Yeah, it's a lot. Fate's a bitch.

He runs across Hermione and Ron huddled together on a rubble-strewn staircase. "We thought you'd gone to the forest," Ron says, catching sight of him.

"I'm going there now," Harry answers.

Hermione can tell right away that he knows something and Harry has no reason not to share the truth. He says: "There's a reason I can hear the Horcruxes. I think I've known for a while, and I think you have, too." Yep, you guessed it: our girl already guessed that Harry is a Horcrux, too.

"Kill the snake and then it's just him," Harry says. What he doesn't say is: *because I'll be dead by then.* And then he goes to what he knows is his doom.

Inside the forest, he takes the Snitch out of his pocket. Remember that? "I open at the close." Well, this is the close if there ever was one. "I'm ready to die," Harry says to the Snitch, and then touches it to his mouth. This time it opens, and inside is a small, octagonal stone. The Resurrection Stone! Do you realize what this means? Until he passed the Invisibility Cloak to Harry, Dumbledore had all three of the Deathly Hallows: the cloak, the Elder Wand and the Resurrection Stone. Dumbledore was the legendary Master of Death, but he chose to do all in his power to oppose Voldemort.

The stone is no bigger than a die to be rolled. As Harry holds it in the palm of his hand, the spirits of his four guardians appear before him: his mother and father, and Sirius and Remus.

"Why are you here?" Harry asks. "All of you?"

Time for Lily Potter to have her Mom Moment. "We never left," she tells him. Because these are the guardians he carries in his heart.

Harry speaks to each of his guardian spirits, to Sirius of dying ("does it hurt?") to Remus of having a son (a son who isn't mentioned at any other time in the film... whoops). His father encourages him: "You're nearly there, son."

"Stay close to me," he asks, and Lily replies, "Always."

Harry lets the stone fall into the bracken. He doesn't need it anymore.

And he doesn't need anything but his own unerring sense to lead him to Voldemort. The Dark Lord senses him nearing in the dark gloom of the forest.

The Death Eaters have Hagrid tied up, held prisoner, and he calls out, "No! Harry! What are you doing here!"

But Harry doesn't answer. He says nothing, not to Hagrid, not to Voldemort. Just closes his eyes as the Killing Curse hits him. A blinding white light fills the forest...

And when Harry opens his eyes, he's in a hushed realm of white on white. He's not wearing glasses. There's a sort of... bench there, like he's on a train platform, kind of like King's Cross. Under the bench is a sort of bloody, fetal-looking creature, starkly dark and red in this otherwise white world.

"You can't help it," says a rather angelic Dumbledore. "You wonderful boy. You brave, brave man." The flayed-looking thing is a part of Voldemort that has been sent to death, the part of him that had been in Harry, destroyed "mere moments ago by Voldemort himself," Dumbledore explains.

Harry, meanwhile, has a choice. He can go back, or he can board a metaphorical train into the afterlife. Harry thinks it over for a bit.

He can't stop thinking about the unfinished business back at Hogwarts, though. Voldemort still has the Elder Wand, and one Horcrux, Nagini, is still alive. "And I have nothing to kill it with," he laments.

"Help will always be given at Hogwarts to those who ask," Dumbledore says, quoting himself, and then amending his statement. "...To those who deserve it."

Harry has a million questions he wants to ask, but Dumbledore is already meandering away into the distance. He tosses one out, about Snape and his mother's Patronuses being the same, but Dumbledore doesn't give straight answers in death anymore than he did in life. Harry tries one last time: "Is this real? Or is it all in my head?"

"Of course it's in your head," Albus Dumbledore explains. "Why should that mean it's not real?"

And then he's gone.

Back in the forest, Voldemort is getting to his feet after having been flung back by the force of his own spell. Harry Potter's body lies slumped some distance away. As Bellatrix tries to help the Dark Lord up—and gets flung aside for it—Narcissa Malfoy goes to check if Harry is truly dead this time. It's time for Narcissa's Mom Moment.

She discerns immediately that Harry is alive, and she has one whispered question for him: "Draco? Is he alive?" Harry makes one tiny nod. This is the moment Narcissa has been waiting for, probably since long before the Dark Lord sullied her dining room floor with goblin blood.

She stands. "Dead," she pronounces.

Now let's check in with what's going on back at Hogwarts, shall we? As the sky lightens toward dawn, Neville, bloody and battered-looking, finds the Sorting Hat, equally bloody and battered-looking, among the rubble in the front courtyard. He sees a gleam within it, but... what's that coming across the stone bridge? It's a group of people. He limps toward them.

It's the Death Eaters, with Hagrid carrying Harry, and Voldemort leading the way. Nagini slithers along beside him and the Dark Lord can barely keep his emotions contained, his total victory is so close at hand.

The courtyard is beginning to fill with people. Ginny asks Neville, disbelieving, wanting it not to be true: "Who is that Hagrid's carrying?"

Voldemort announces it. "Harry Potter! Is! *Dead!*" He repeats it to the Death Eaters, assembled behind him, and they laugh.

Then he extends his welcome to the Hogwarts faithful, spread out in front of him, to come and join his side, or die. None move. Not even Draco, who stands with the other students.

That is, until Lucius calls to him—"Draco!"—in an embarrassing stage whisper, as if the entire assemblage can't obviously hear him. Draco looks like he's not going to budge, but then his mother adds her much-saner voice. "Come."

He walks like he's going to the gallows, as he accepts the wizarding world's most awkward hug from the Dark Lord, and then Narcissa leads him away.

Next to step forward is Neville, limping as he goes. Voldemort jokes at his expense. "Well, I hoped for better." The Death Eaters laugh. "And who might you be?"

When he says his name, they laugh even harder, but Voldemort is magnanimous. "I'm sure we can find a place for you in our ranks."

But Neville doesn't have joining the dark side on his mind. He has something to say. Voldemort looks like a vicious kneazle, unsure whether to just kill him on the spot or play with his prey a little longer. He opts to let Neville say his piece.

Neville gives a rousing speech. "Yeah, we lost Harry tonight.

But he's still with us. In here," he says, touching his heart. And so are all the rest of the people they've lost. "It's not over!" Neville draws the Sword of Gryffindor out of the hat.

That's Harry's cue to stop playing dead. He drops from Hagrid's arms, shoots one curse at Nagini—it misses—and then jumps behind a column as Voldemort starts his counterattack. For many Death Eaters, Harry coming back from the dead is the last straw: many Disapparate on the spot. (The Malfoys, on the other hand, choose to walk briskly away.)

Many others stay to fight. Down in the Great Hall, Bellatrix tries to curse Ginny and Molly Weasley has her Mom Moment. "Not my daughter, you bitch!" she cries, her spells powered by her outrage, and she rids the world of Bellatrix Lestrange with a one-two magical punch that pulverizes her to bits.

While the battle rages through the corridors of Hogwarts, Ron and Hermione try to kill Nagini. But they're running low on basilisk fangs and spells alone won't work. Harry and Voldemort fight each other up and down the staircases and into the rafters. The Dark Lord has spells Harry has never seen before, and he's taking quite a beating. But he puts doubt into Voldemort's mind. "You were right when you told Professor Snape that wand was failing you. It will *always* fail you." (After all, just a little while ago it failed to kill Harry, didn't it?)

"I killed Snape!" the Dark Lord insists.

"But what if the wand never belonged to Snape?" Harry asks, as Voldemort backs him to the edge of a precipice. "What if its allegiance was always to someone else?" Harry grabs Voldemort by the neck and throws them both off the edge into the chasm. They fly into the air, fighting and clawing at each other even as Voldemort tries to Apparate them elsewhere, until they crash land in the courtyard, several meters apart. Like they did that night in the graveyard when Voldemort was re-embodied, they cast simultaneous curses and their wands lock, beams of power meeting in the middle, Voldemort's green and Harry's red. They're not using those old wands with the twin cores, though— Harry's now using what was Draco's wand, remember? And Voldemort is using the Elder Wand. But still, here we go.

Nagini has almost caught up to Ron and Hermione, there in the courtyard. Isn't it a good thing Neville's still got that sword? He beheads the snake as it rears to strike, and the Horcrux formerly known as Nagini splinters into darkness. Voldemort falters and Harry sees his chance is now. They cast again, their spells interlock again, and this time Harry's spell forces Voldemort's Killing Curse back through the Elder Wand, into his hand, which begins to blacken just like Dumbledore's when he was cursed by the Horcrux ring. The Elder Wand flies out of his hand and into Harry's. It would appear Harry is the master of the Elder Wand after all. The curse spreads quickly up the Dark Lord's arm to his face, and within seconds, there is nothing left of the him at all but dark soot and ash, floating away on the wind.

It's over.

Well, "it" is over, but the movie is not—there are still 20 minutes to go, if you count the credits. In the Great Hall, folks are tending the wounded again and Poor Mr. Filch is pushing at a giant pile of rubble with one little push broom. Luna sits down next to Neville, who is still holding the sword. Remember that prophecy that predicted the one who would vanquish the Dark Lord was born at the end of July and it could have applied to either Harry or Neville? Guess in the end it applied to both of them.

Percy's there with the rest of the Weasleys—we'd caught glimpses of him before but now a nice clear shot. Cho's sitting with some of the other girls. Professor Slughorn and Professor Flitwick are comparing injuries.

Harry runs into Hagrid, who wants a hug. He gets one, of course.

But it's Ron and Hermione that Harry has to catch up with. They walk out onto the rubble-strewn stone bridge together.

Hermione, of course, just can't leave the big unanswered question alone. Why didn't the Elder Wand work for Voldemort? "It answered to somebody else," Harry explains. "It was Draco who disarmed Dumbledore that night on the Astronomy Tower." So the wand was really his... until Harry disarmed Draco during the escape from Malfoy Manor. When Draco's own wand switched allegiance to Harry, apparently the Elder Wand did, too.

So, yeah. Harry's the master of the Elder Wand. "With that," Ron says, Harry's "invincible!"

But this is Harry Potter we're talking about. HARRY. POTTER. It just wouldn't be like him to do anything other than to follow the impulsive good-heartedness that has served him so well his entire life, would it? He breaks the Elder Wand in two and pitches the pieces off the bridge. There. *Now* it's over.

Well, except for the epilogue.

As in the book, it's labeled "19 years later."

Some cute kids are pushing luggage trolleys through the train station. One boy goes at a bit of a run at the column between platforms 9 and 10 and disappears. The other boy hesitates. His father, 36-year-old Harry Potter, comes up behind him to help. 35-year-old Ginny Weasley follows with their young daughter, who isn't old enough to go to Hogwarts yet. On the platform we see Draco and his wife saying goodbye to their very blond son, and Hermione and Ron seeing their daughter off as well.

The boy hesitates again, and this time Harry hangs back with him, while Ginny goes to greet her brother and Hermione. "Dad," the boy asks nervously, "what if I am put in Slytherin?" Because (apparently) despite all the lessons learned during the Voldemort wars, people still think Slytherins are bad.

"Albus Severus Potter," Harry says, "you were named after two headmasters of Hogwarts. One of them was a Slytherin and he was the bravest man I've ever known."

Albus isn't interested in hearing a lesson about Dad's old chums. He's starved for approval: "But just say that I am...?"

Harry is happy to provide: "Then Slytherin House will have gained a wonderful young wizard." Harry also clues him in, though, that if it means that much to him, he can choose his house. Thus reassured, young Albus gets on the train and into a compartment with his brother, Hermione's daughter, and some other witches. They all wave heartily to their parents through the window.

And that's the last we see of our Trio, standing on platform 9 3/4 as the train pulls away.

If You Only Watch One Film

This chapter of every *Binge Watchers Guide* is meant to give you the heart and soul of the show or series in a nutshell. In the case of the cinematic Potter experience, I have to break it into two, depending on whether you've read the books or not.

If you've never read the books, the only installment it makes sense to choose is the first one. *Harry Potter and the Sorcerer's Stone* is Harry's introduction to the entire magical world, and it is the viewer's introduction, too. Most importantly, though, it is the introduction to the characters. Both screenwriter Steve Kloves and the author J.K. Rowling have said that character had to come first; if the characters weren't right, it didn't matter how compelling or intricate the plot was. In the literary universe, of course, the author creates the characters, but in a cinematic one, it is the collaboration between actor and script (and director) that brings the character to life.

Harry in particular is the key to everything. It's not just that he's new to magic and can be our eyes, our entry point into something new, but there's a deep innocence at the core of both our hero and the story, and before the series can descend into some of the dark places it eventually goes, I think it's important to be grounded in the basic good-heartedness that is Harry. Harry himself is grounded in a way that is immediately recognizable and yet difficult to explain, and one of the more remarkable things about 10-year-old Daniel Radcliffe's performance is that he absolutely nails that ineffable groundedness.

It's there when Hagrid shows up on Harry's 11th birthday to tell him he's a wizard, and the boy's response is "But I'm just Harry! Just Harry." When you see interviews of young Daniel, he may as well be saying "But I'm just Dan! Just Dan." There's something, well, *magical* about seeing this child using his own groundedness and his own wonder at the strange and interesting world of blockbuster filmmaking as the template for Harry's reactions.

But which came first, the Harry or the Dan? One of the clips that has surfaced on YouTube is of Dan's early screen tests, with the director Chris Columbus reading the part of Hagrid. Little Dan approaches his part with a wide-eyed joy, an edge of mischief, and a tinge of wisdom that is captivating and completely fitting for the character, but which comes across as largely him. Director Chris Columbus has said one of the reasons he wanted to go with relatively inexperienced child actors was that he would get a "pure" performance out of them, and it's hard to imagine anything more pure than that.

The interplay of how much Dan shaped Harry and how much Harry shaped Dan continues in the later films. For *Goblet of Fire*, Dan was asked to do some challenging stunts on his own, including extended filming under water and sliding/falling down the roofs of Hogwarts during the dragon chase scene. In the "making of" documentaries, crew members and the stunt team talked about how fearless Dan was, leaping into any situation without hesitation... just like Harry Potter would.

Not every child performer captivates this way. At the time the Potter films were being planned, *Star Wars: The Phantom Menace* hit screens in May 1999. Like Potter, the film was highly anticipated by legions of fans the world over, and also like Potter, the film would hinge on a fresh-faced child actor being propped up by veteran British thespians (Ewan MacGregor and Liam Neeson). Eight-year-old Jake Lloyd played nine-year-old Anakin Skywalker; many critics were not won over by his performance. "Designed as an alter-ego for millions of children wishing to project themselves into the Star Wars universe, the character is unlikely to interest anyone much older than 13, and the child actor, though cute, isn't up to the task of carrying so much of the film," wrote *The Hollywood Reporter*. And that's one of the nicer reviews.

Jake Lloyd would later say that Star Wars "ruined" his childhood and put him off acting forever. He would go on to have various brushes with the law, eventually landing in jail after a drug-fueled high speed chase with police, and then later undergo a diagnosis of schizophrenia and move from jail to a psych facility. Well, Anakin Skywalker was supposed to be mentally unstable enough to end up Darth Vader...

Maybe Dan was blessed to be playing a character like Harry instead.

Of course after the massive success of the Potter films, many other literary fantasy properties with child characters were adapted. *The Golden Compass* by Philip Pullman went into development in

2002 but after its 2007 release drew mixed reviews and disappointing US box office numbers, the rest of the books in the Pullman series were not adapted by New Line Cinema. (HBO is now doing an adaptation as a 16-episode TV series.) C.S. Lewis's *The Chronicles of Narnia* also had a go: three of the seven books were adapted, but the critical reception and box office draw for each film diminished, and a planned fourth film was never made. Now the Lewis estate is in talks with Netflix about a reboot. Looking back at the incredible success of the Potter films and just how much of it was resting on Daniel Radcliffe's shoulders, when compared with these other adaptations, it's clear that nothing was guaranteed.

So my recommendation is start at the first film. Go back to see that pure, captivating essence that is both the spirit of Harry Potter and the performance of a young Daniel Radcliffe, and experience a rare kind of movie magic.

Now, if you already have read the books, you can hop onto any of the eight cars on the Hogwarts Express—perhaps with whichever is your favorite. My poll of fans puts *Prisoner of Azkaban* squarely in the lead as the favorite of all the movies, with about a third of all votes. Both movie critics and fans love Cuarón's touch, Remus and Sirius' characters, and the maturing performances of all three young stars, Dan, Emma and Rupert. The main reason I can't recommend *Prisoner of Azkaban* as a first-watch for anyone who hasn't read the books is that the ending of the film simply won't make any sense at all.

Next in the voting with 18% is *Half-Blood Prince*. This one is my personal favorite both of the books and the movies. It was the book that finally made me realize that although Draco acts like he's spoiled rotten and is quite a bully, it's because he himself is bullied at home. His father is almost as insane as his aunt, and we finally see the ways his father's poisonous ideology victimizes Draco.

Tom Felton's performance surpasses anything he's been asked to do in the earlier films and it's thrilling to see him rise to the occasion. Meanwhile, the Trio get to stretch their wings in various ways in *Half-Blood Prince* that are pure entertainment to watch. Dan and Rupert each under the influence of mind-altering potions are nearly as much of a delight as their 11-year-old selves giddy from eating too many sweets on the train. And Emma puts in her most mature performance as well, broken-hearted over Ron's infatuation with another girl. But each of the films has qualities to recommend it. There's no wrong choice.

After You've Watched

So, you've watched the films, and now you're wondering, what can I watch next? Well, you could just start the magical journey over again, but you're in luck, there are more things to put on your screen! Some of them are official, licensed parts of "J.K. Rowling's Wizarding World™," and some of them are transformative works and fan creations worth digging into.

Harry Potter and the Cursed Child

This stage play is an official sequel to the Harry Potter books and films, co-written by John Tiffany and Jack Thorne, based on a short story by J.K. Rowling. It starts at "19 years later" and goes forward from there, following the adventures of Harry's middle child, the super low-pressure-named Albus Severus Potter, as he makes best friends with Hogwarts' worst misfit, Scorpius Malfoy. The action swaps between the trouble the boys get themselves into while trying to undo the damage done to the wizarding world by their parents, and the parents themselves coming to grips with a lot of stuff they didn't deal with or process back in the day. (You know what the wizarding world could use instead of time travel? *Therapists.*)

One can purchase the script in book form, but the play is much better appreciated in a theater, as a live theatrical event. It's, well, *magical.* When I read the script I thought it read like a lot of Albus/Scorpius fanfics I have read, but the staging and acting really elevate it to a truly emotional experience. As this book is being published in the summer of 2020, though, theatrical productions worldwide are at a standstill because of the global COVID-19 crisis. No one knows when live theater will be safe to resume, and right now there is no streaming or televised version of the *Cursed Child* production. Presumably when the health crisis ends, live productions will resume in London, on Broadway, and in San Francisco and Melbourne, Australia. Plans were in the works for productions to also open in Toronto, Hamburg (in German translation), and Tokyo (in Japanese).

Puffs: The Play

This hilarious play, billed as "Seven Increasingly Eventful Years at a Certain School of Magic and Magic," rocked Broadway and then moved to Australia. It has since been staged in Boston and elsewhere. Essentially a transformative work, the play retells a familiar story from an underrepresented point of view. "For seven years a certain boy wizard went to Wizard School. This, however, is not his story. This is the story of The Puffs who just happened to be there too. *PUFFS* gives you a new look at a familiar adventure from the perspective of three new heroes just trying to make it through wizard school." At this wizard school there are four houses, the Braves, the Smarts, the Snakes, and the Puffs. The play is absolutely packed with in-jokes, some of which make fun specifically of the Potter movies. I saw it with a group of Potter cosplayers in New York City and laughed so hard I literally cried. It's not "just" slapstick comedy, though—there's real emotional depth and thought-provoking questions asked of the beloved canon. You can see a video livestream of it via Amazon home video or Apple iTunes for $4.99 (or own the download for $12.99). Also of note: While the *Cursed Child* play is impractical for high school drama departments to stage (it takes two days!), *Puffs* is actually perfect for any Potter-loving drama club!

Fantastic Beasts and Where to Find Them

Announced at the same time as the *Cursed Child* play, the news hit in 2016 that J.K. Rowling was set to write the screenplay of a new movie starring Newt Scamander and taking its title from the Hogwarts textbook that Scamander wrote. The first movie in the series is generally a delight, giving us back some of the fun in the wizarding world (this time visiting the United States) while still clearly being a movie for adults. For those who felt J.K. Rowling's handling of the romances in Harry Potter were awkward at best and flat-out unbelievable at worst, this movie somewhat redeems her. It's a romcom, for goodness' sake, while also being a bit of a whodunit. Although, as in the early Potter installments, there is darkness lurking and there are themes of children suffering in deprivation, there is also a truly sweet, heart of gold at the center of it all. Despite some flaws, this film was quite enjoyable, though I don't count it as an achievement on the scale of the Potter films.

Fantastic Beasts: The Crimes of Grindelwald

I'll come right out and say it: this film is a wreck. Everything that made the first installment of *Fantastic Beasts* a delight—namely Newt's gentle and patient manner winning the day, the quirky and fun characters, and their deepening emotional connections to each other—is gone. Instead we have a raft of new characters with angsty backstories we don't really care about, anachronistic appearances of old ones that break the canon timeline (Minerva McGonagall can't be teaching at Hogwarts in 1927 if she wasn't born until 1935?? Dumbledore is scheming against Grindelwald even though he doesn't duel and defeat him until 1945? Nagini is a woman with a curse that means she'll eventually be trapped forever in the form of a snake, guaranteeing a tragic end?), and the rise of wizarding fascism. Don't get me wrong: we could use some strong anti-fascist films right now in this world. But this is not one. This is supposedly the set-up for three more films in the FB series. Perhaps the trainwreck will make sense later in context if the set-ups pay off. But I think the problem with writing a screenplay instead of a book is that Rowling hasn't done all the deep work necessary to get all the ducks in a row. Go back to writing them as novels, Jo, and let Steve Kloves mine them for which gems to include in the films!

Fan Films on YouTube

We have official entered the era of the transformative work. Not only are there literally millions of Harry Potter fanfics written every year, but there's a whole genre of music (Wizard rock, aka Wrock), Muggles play a rugby-like version of Quidditch (on non-flying brooms), and of course it's easier than ever to turn out a professional-looking film or video using tools available to the consumer. So fan films have proliferated. Warner Brothers, which holds the film rights to Harry Potter and related Wizarding WorldTM properties, has even given the official OK to some fan films out there so long as they aren't done as a commercial enterprise. Just Google "Harry Potter fan films" and you will find a bunch! Here are some that are gaining a lot of attention:

- Voldemort: Origin of the Heir
  (52 minutes, 15 million views)
- Le Maitre de le Mort/Master of Death
  (45 minutes, 2 million views
- Mischief Managed
  (27 minutes, 750K views)
- Severus Snape and the Marauders
  (25 minutes, 6.7 million views)
- The Founders: The Ravenclaw Ghost
  (27 minutes, 60K views)
- Lily Evans and the Eleventh Hour
  (21 minutes, 54K views)
- Lily Evans and the Stroke of Midnight
  (27 minutes, 161K views)
- Neville Longbottom and the Black Witch
  (17 minutes, 2 million views)
- Dumbledore and Grindelwald: The Greater Good
  (17 minutes, 10 million views)
- Battle of Hogwarts
  (15 minutes, 250K views)
- The Day the Muggles Found Out
  (8 minutes, 250K views)

Flight As A Metaphor for Freedom
in the Harry Potter Films

J.K. Rowling uses a perfect metaphor in her fantasy book series about boy wizard Harry Potter: flying represents freedom in a literal and metaphorical sense. The film adaptations of the books faithfully translate this idea to the screen throughout the series and highlight it as one of the most stunning visual effects.

In the beginning of the story, Harry is a prisoner locked in a cupboard under the stairs and forced to do housework like a boy Cinderella. But his freedom from this suburban hell comes in the form of an acceptance letter to Hogwarts—on the wings of a bird. Harry's hateful guardians destroy the letter before Harry can read it, but soon owls are turning up by the dozen, until the letters themselves come flying through the boarded up mail slot and down the chimney. Eventually Harry does get his letter, delivered by Hagrid on a magical flying motorcycle.

At Hogwarts, Harry has his first lesson in flying along with his classmates, and discovers to his surprise that he is a natural at it. While even the brilliant Hermione Granger is still trying to get her broom up off the ground, Harry's leaps into his hand as if it belongs there. Rowling offers one explanation in her text for why Harry may have inborn flying talent: his father was a top player in the broom-flying game of Quidditch. But the magical systems Rowling creates in her books often hinge upon an individual witch or wizard's personal experiences. For example, Harry is the worst-affected student by the evil dementors in the "Prisoner of Azkaban" because he has the most horrific past.

In the case of flying, I postulate that Harry is the best flier in his class because he has known the greatest need for escape. He is the only one of his classmates to have spent the greater part of his life in a cage. In his very first trip on a broom, Harry thwarts the plans of his nemesis Draco Malfoy and wins the position of seeker on his house Quidditch team.

In his first year at Hogwarts, Harry is the recipient of many wondrous and amazing things, including a cloak which makes him invisible, a snowy owl of his own and his own flying broom. These material things not only move the plot forward but parallel the other things Harry comes to possess, which include his friends, the respect of elders and self-knowledge. The broom in particular is curious as, like the cloak, it comes anonymously as a gift when students of Harry's age are not supposed to have their own brooms. That the gift probably comes from the usually-rule-abiding Professor McGonagall is symbolic of both the respect Harry's elders have for him but also the freedom from mundane rules that he comes to enjoy, as well.

In *Harry Potter and the Chamber of Secrets,* the second installment in the series, the stakes are raised. This time Harry is no longer in the cupboard, but his guardians refuse to let his owl fly out for fear he will pass messages to his "freaky wizard friends." Ultimately they place bars on his window so that neither he, nor Hedwig the owl, can escape. Harry's rescue this time comes again through flight, this time in the form of a flying car driven by his friends. The car comes to the rescue two more times in the story, first when Harry is kept from boarding the train to Hogwarts, and the second when he and his friend Ron are in mortal danger in the dark forest. It is notable that the first time, it is Ron's elder brothers who drive the car, the second time it is Ron himself, and the third time it is Harry who takes the wheel. Harry is becoming more the master of his own destiny and self-determination even as evil forces, not to mention bureaucracy, seek to control him. Ultimately to defeat evil, though, Harry does need one more flying ally, this time a phoenix named Fawkes who not only delivers Harry the weapon he needs for his final battle, but saves Harry from certain death by purifying the poison of the basilisk he defeats.

In the third installment, *Harry Potter and the Prisoner of Azkaban,* Harry's new flying experience comes as the result of a new creature and ally, the dangerous but noble hippogriff Buckbeak. Harry is introduced to Buckbeak during a class and is favored with a thrilling ride on the hippogriff's back. This is indicative of the fact that Harry will soon need to depend on the help of others for his freedom—no longer can he go it alone on pure nerve, as he did when he faced down Voldemort in the first installment or faced the basilisk with a sword in the second. In this case, Harry's greatest ally will turn out to be another person who has been a prisoner: Sirius Black, Harry's godfather who was wrongly accused of betraying the Potters to the Dark Lord Voldemort. Harry spends most of the story believing Black is trying to kill him, even as the evil dementors—who are supposed to be trying to catch Black and return him to the wizarding world's worst prison—seem to be trying to kill Harry at every turn, as well.

In fact, for the first time, Harry's flying in Quidditch goes horribly wrong as the dementors swarm him during a match. He falls from his broom and is only saved from death by headmaster Dumbledore, but meanwhile his broom is destroyed, again indicating that just going it alone like one wizard on a broom will not be enough. Eventually Harry, with much more active assistance from Ron and Hermione, puzzles out the truth and even saves the life of Buckbeak who, like Sirius, was the subject of grave injustice. It is no coincidence then that it is Buckbeak who can save Sirius, flying off with him to parts unknown at the end of the story. And Sirius, once safe, returns the power of flight to Harry as well, gifting him with a new broom that is better than the old one and adorned with a hippogriff feather. The film ends with a joyful shot of Harry trying the new broom for the first time, the fact that his godfather is still wanted wrongly and that Voldemort still wants to kill him completely forgotten during the ecstasy of flight. Freedom from troubles, if only for a short while.

A short while indeed, as the next book opens with an absolute festival of flying (the Quidditch World Cup), the gaiety of which is short-lived as the followers of Voldemort terrorize the event. Here we meet a new character, Viktor Krum, one of the best fliers in the world and the seeker on one of the international Quidditch teams. Ron idolizes Krum and his idol is soon at Hogwarts to compete in the TriWizard Tournament. Harry inevitably finds himself entered into the tournament, even though it is only open to older, more experienced wizards. (I'll give you one guess why: it's a plot of the Dark Lord's.)

Many of the tasks faced in the tournament are potentially fatal and Harry's abilities, particular his flying abilities, will be sorely tested. In the opening round, Harry must out-fly a dragon, which he barely does. The filmmakers in this case took liberties with the scene to create a truly breathtaking action sequence and accentuate the risks in flying a broomstick around (while a six-ton fire-breathing lizard is trying to eat you). Harry survives the dragon, but the symbolism that he is barely ahead in the race (and in the tournament) is borne out by the fact that although he thinks he is one step ahead of evil, in fact Voldemort has been pulling the strings from the beginning in this one.

As Harry enters the final maze, even Krum is not immune to evil and becomes bewitched, aiding the Dark Lord in his plan to get Harry to touch the trophy which will make him the winner, but also transport Harry right into his clutches. The TriWizard Cup has been made into a portkey, a form of transportation superior to the simple broom—faster and more violent, almost like a tornado flinging the witch or wizard who clutches it from one point to another. Harry survives the encounter, but only barely and thanks to a quirk of his wand and Voldemort's being linked. Harry can no longer merely fly from danger. Voldemort has returned.

Voldemort, of course, represents the antithesis of freedom in all forms. He is the ultimate Slytherin, a snake-tongued demon who is as earthbound as the serpent on the Slytherin house banner. If returned to power, he would rule the wizarding world as an evil tyrant. Harry, as the champion of freedom and a Gryffindor (griffins are another mythical flying creature), must try to keep that from happening, this time with the help of some Ravenclaws like Luna Lovegood—the Ravenclaw emblem of course being a large bird (although it's actually an eagle, not a raven).

Let us not forget that the underground fighters Dumbledore gathers to thwart Voldemort's power are called The Order of the Phoenix, another flying creature. But what freedom means and what one must sacrifice to achieve it are questions that only grown more complex as Harry grows older and Voldemort's threat grows as well. The fifth installment introduces a new character to the saga, Dolores Umbridge, who under power of an increasingly bureaucratic Minister of Magic (who refuses to believe Voldemort has returned) slowly takes power at Hogwarts by taking away the students freedoms, one by one. Yes, even Quidditch. There is also a new creature in Rowling's menagerie, the thestrals, bat-winged horses who pull the carriages of students up to Hogwarts from the train every year, but who can only be seen by people who have witnessed someone die. The thestrals become Harry's latest means of transportation when things become desperate, flying to the Ministry when there is no other way for our students to get there.

The theme continues through the final installments. One of the most meaningful comes when Harry leaves Privet Drive for the final time, not to return to Hogwarts, but to join the Order of the Phoenix in their quest to defeat Voldemort once and for all. The Order come to fly him out of there by all possible means: thestral, broom and flying motorcycle. This is literally symbolic of Harry leaving adolescence behind, since once he is of age (17 by wizarding law) he will be able to Apparate (magically teleport) without the Ministry tracking him.

The final scene I'll add here is one of the most spectacular action sequences in the film, in which Harry, Ron and Hermione escape from deep in the depths of Gringotts on the back of an imprisoned guard dragon. In a conversation with screenwriter Steve Kloves, J.K. Rowling said she saw the dragon escape as symbolic of the overthrow of all oppression in the wizarding world. The Gringotts dragon is first mentioned in the very first book, and she always had in the back of her mind that it represented how there are both wonders and injustice in the wizarding world, "just as there are in our world." That the dragon carries our heroes to the next step in their quest to defeat evil is highly fitting as the ultimate symbol of freedom.

Timeline of Book and Movie Releases

July 30, 1997: BOOK Harry Potter and the Sorcerer's Stone
July 2, 1998: BOOK Harry Potter and the Chamber of Secrets
July 8, 1999: BOOK Harry Potter and the Prisoner of Azkaban
July 8, 2000: BOOK Harry Potter and the Goblet of Fire
Nov 4, 2001: MOVIE of Sorcerer's Stone
Nov 15, 2002: MOVIE of Chamber of Secrets
July 21, 2003: BOOK Harry Potter and the Order of the Phoenix
July 4, 2004: MOVIE Prisoner of Azkaban
July 16, 2005 : BOOK Harry Potter and the Half-Blood Prince
Nov 8, 2005: MOVIE Goblet of Fire
July 11, 2007: MOVIE Order of the Phoenix
July 21, 2007: BOOK Harry Potter and the Deathly Hallows
July 15, 2009: MOVIE Half-Blood Prince
June 18, 2010: First Wizarding World theme park/Hogwarts opens at
    Universal Orlando
Nov 19, 2010: MOVIE Deathly Hallows, Part 1
July 15, 2011: MOVIE Deathly Hallows, Part 2

About the Author

Cecilia Tan is the award-winning author of the Magic University series, which puts an adult spin on the "Harry Potter" school trope by sending her hero to college to study sex magick. She is also the author of the *Slow Surrender* erotic romance series, *The Prince's Boy*, *Daron's Guitar Chronicles*, and many other books. The awards amassed in her nearly 30 years in writing and publishing include the *Romantic Times* Lifetime Achievement Award, *Romantic Times* Reviewer's Choice award, and induction into the Saints & Sinners LGBT Writers Hall of Fame.

She can often be found throwing Harry-Potter themed parties at science fiction conventions like Arisia, Wiscon and Worldcon. When she's not traveling the world by Muggle flying device or train, she can be found at either her 1887 Victorian home in the Boston area, where she lives with her partner and two cats, or writing in a tea shop nearby.

If you liked this book,
Please join our mailing list at RiverdaleAveBooks.com

We will be publishing monthly Binge Watcher's Guides
Including 13 volumes of
The Binge Watcher's Guide to Doctor Who

***The Binge Watcher's Guide to Doctor Who:
A History of the Doctor Who and the First Female Doctor***
By Mackenzie Flohr

**You Might Also Enjoy These other
Riverdale Avenue Books Pop Culture Titles**

Magic University: The Complete Series
By Cecilia Tan

How to Throw a True Blood Party: An Unofficial Guide
By Paula Conway

Norman Reedus: True Tales of the Walking Dead's Zombie Hunter
By Marc Shapiro

*Welcome to Shondaland: An Unauthorized Biography of Shonda
Rhimes*
By Marc Shapiro

*You're Gonna Make It After All:
The Life and Times and Influence of Mary Tyler Moore*
By Marc Shapiro

www.ingramcontent.com/pod-product-compliance
Lightning Source LLC
Chambersburg PA
CBHW070019100426
42740CB00013B/2559